WRITING

Power English

explore

poem

Year 5
A Guide to Teaching Writing and Writers

 **Pearson**

Series creators: Ross Young and Felicity Ferguson

Published by Pearson Education Limited, 80 Strand, London, WC2R 0RL.

www.pearsonschools.co.uk

Text © Ross Young and Felicity Ferguson 2019
Edited by Pearson Education Limited and Just Content Limited
Designed and typeset by Pearson Education Limited and PDQ Media
Original illustrations © Pearson Education Limited 2019
Illustrated by Nadine Naude at Beehive Illustration and PDQ Media
Cover design by Pearson Education Limited
Cover photo/illustration © Pearson Education Limited 2019

The rights of Ross Young and Felicity Ferguson to be identified as authors of this work have been asserted by them in accordance with the Copyright, Designs and Patents Act 1988.

First published 2019

22 21 20 19
10 9 8 7 6 5 4 3 2 1

British Library Cataloguing in Publication Data
A catalogue record for this book is available from the British Library

ISBN 978 0 435 19884 8

Copyright notice
All rights reserved. The material in this publication is copyright. Activity sheets may be freely photocopied for classroom use in the purchasing institution. However, this material is copyright and under no circumstances may copies be offered for sale. If you wish to use the material in any way other than that specified you must apply in writing to the publishers.

Printed in the UK by Ashford Press Ltd

Acknowledgements

p11, Informa: Smith, Frank, Writing and the Writer, © 1982, Informa; **p12, Primary English Teaching Association:** Graves, Donald H.; Donald Graves in Australia: "Children Want to Write-- ", © 1981, Primary English Teaching Association; **p13, Penguin Random House:** Macfarlane, Robert, Landmarks, © 2015, Penguin Random House; **p23, The City University of New York:** Trillin, Alice, A Writer's Process: A Conversation with Calvin Trillin, © 1981, The City University of New York; **p24, Heinemann:** Calkins, Lucy, The art of teaching writing, © 1994, Heinemann; **p25, History Ink Books:** Calkins, Lucy, A Teacher's Guide to Standardized Reading Tests: Knowledge is Power, © 1998, History Ink Books; p25, Heinemann: Harwayne, Shelley, Writing Through Childhood: Rethinking Process and Product, © 2001, Heinemann; **p31, Emily Licis:** Licis, Emily, The end of the climb, © Emily Licis. Reproduced with permission; p31, Pearson Education Limited: Calkins, Lucy, Living between the Lines, © 1991, Pearson Education Limited; p32, Heinemann: Atwell, Nancie, Lessons that change writers, Volume I, © 2002, Heinemann; **p43, Frank Smith:** Smith, Frank, Quote by Frank Smith; **p46, The National Council of Teachers of English:** Kaufman, Douglas, Living a Literate Life, © 2002, The National Council of Teachers of English; **p46, Informa UK Limited:** Cremin, Teresa and Oliver, Lucy, Teachers as writers: a systematic review. Research Papers in Education, 32(3) pp. 269–295, © 2016 Informa UK Limited; **p219 (bottom), 220 (top), 238 (bottom), 243 (top), 244 (top), 245 (top, bottom), 248 (bottom), Heinemann:** Serravallo, Jennifer, The Writing Strategies Book, © 2017, Heinemann. Used with permission; **p273 (top), HarperCollins Publishers:** E. B. White, Charlotte's Web, p.4, HarperCollins Publishers 1952; **(bottom) Bloomsbury:** Louis Sachar, Holes, Vol-I, p44, Bloomsbury Publishing, 2010.

Note from the publisher
Pearson has robust editorial processes, including answer and fact checks, to ensure the accuracy of the content in this publication, and every effort is made to ensure this publication is free of errors. We are, however, only human, and occasionally errors do occur. Pearson is not liable for any misunderstandings that arise as a result of errors in this publication, but it is our priority to ensure that the content is accurate. If you spot an error, please do contact us at resourcescorrections@pearson.com so we can make sure it is corrected.

Contents

Mini-lessons: Functional grammar

Welcome to *Power English: Writing*

You are about to begin a hugely rewarding project. You are about to help create a real community of writers in your classroom and become a member of that community yourself!

This year, you and the children will be engaging in lots of different types of writing together. As the teacher, you will also be creating some original and ground-breaking work, giving your apprentice writers more independence to write in their own ways, set their own deadlines and set their own writing goals. This is important because children will be using this independent way of working for the rest of their writing time at school (and beyond!).

About us

We are Felicity (Phil) Ferguson and Ross Young. We are national and writing representatives for the United Kingdom Literacy Association (UKLA). Ross is a teacher at a local primary school and Phil works full-time speaking, reading and writing about teaching literacy in an effective and pleasurable way. We are both committed writer-teachers; teachers who write and writers who teach.

For many years, we have stood on the shoulders of the writing researchers who have brilliantly built such a solid foundation upon which all of us can create writing communities in our schools. This work has culminated in our *Writing for Pleasure* pedagogy, which offers a wholly practical way of encouraging children's motivation to write and improve their writing outcomes. We are proud that the principles of *Writing for Pleasure* are at the heart of *Power English: Writing*, and we are really excited that your school will be creating a whole community of writers who together will write with power, purpose, precision and pleasure.

Phil's biography

I studied French and Russian at Birmingham University, and later gained two MAs, one in Linguistics and the other in Children's Literature. I have worked in both the maintained and the independent sectors as SENCO and Deputy Head.

When I was ten and a new pupil at secondary school, I completed my first set homework assignment for R.E. – a recount of one of the seven plagues of Egypt. I wrote it like a story, with my usual enthusiasm and emotional investment. After a few days my book came back with the comment *Is this all your own work?* To this day I still feel the injury to my early sense of myself as a writer. I was a self-styled Jo March, with a drive to write from a very early age. I wrote out of desire, with engagement, pleasure, absorption and satisfaction, and used writing as escapism too. I wrote a great deal at home: stories, unfinished novels, programmes for shows put on with friends in somebody's back garden, I started a magazine with me as the editor – one issue a month. It is my ambition for every child to gain as much pleasure and empowerment from writing as I did.

Ross' biography

I studied Primary Education with History and Geography as my specialism, at The University of Brighton, and later gained an MA in Education with Linguistics.

I am a serving primary school teacher with ten years' experience. I have worked in both the maintained and independent sectors. When I was young, I didn't realise that literature and the written word were for me to use or enjoy. I was never told I was a writer. This all changed when I began talking, learning and writing alongside the children in my classroom. One day, I tentatively decided to share a rather risky written memoir about the time I accidentally broke a dinner lady's foot to get hold of my favourite dessert – cornflake tart. The children's questions afterwards were so different from the conversations we usually had about writing, and their view of me changed for the better thereafter because they saw me, for the first time, as a fellow writer. I want the children in my class to have a different experience from the one I had at school and instead enter the literacy club as early as possible, so they have control of it and can use it effectively and for pleasure now and in their future lives.

What is *Power English: Writing*?

Power English: Writing is based on four interrelated practices. You'll teach about genre through **genre study lessons.** These lessons bring the class together to take part in a whole class writing project. Together, you and the children learn about and discuss the purpose and audiences for the particular genre, look at how writers have crafted it effectively and generate ideas for how you want to use it for yourselves.

Alongside this focus on genre, **functional grammar lessons** will give your learners explicit instruction in the various linguistic resources they can use to make their writing clear. The lessons show children how and why they use particular grammatical items in the context of their real writing rather than through the completing of exercises.

Writing study provides you with the means of engaging children in critical analysis of all aspects of the writing process. The knowledge and skills developed in these learning opportunities form the basis of **writing workshop**, which is the central part of the curriculum. Writing workshop encompasses: generating ideas, dabbling, planning, drafting, revising, editing, publishing and performing. Children are encouraged to learn valuable writing lessons but also to take the lead in their own writing development. Alongside these class writing projects, they are also given freedom to pursue personal writing projects, using their new understandings of genre and grammar to create their own accomplished pieces and publish them through their own publishing houses for others to enjoy.

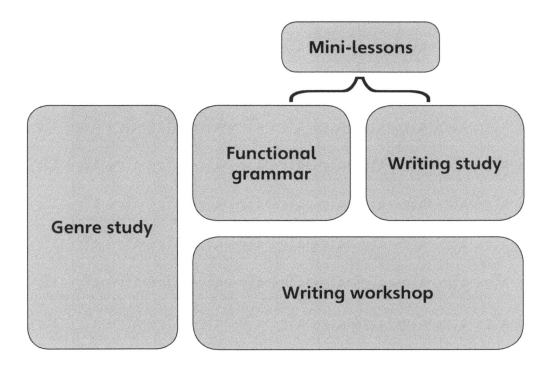

What's coming up in Year 5?

The children in your class will have undertaken both whole-class and personal writing projects as part of *Power English: Writing*, for the past two years. You will notice that children are now fast becoming experienced writers. As such, this year you will be able to afford them a lot more independence, not only in their personal writing but also in their class writing projects. You will be setting publishing deadlines this year and children will need to get used to meeting these deadlines. Therefore, we highly recommend that you teach children the Orientation unit at the beginning of the year. The Orientation unit gives children an opportunity to navigate the writing processes by themselves over the course of the nine writing sessions.

This year, your class will be completing writing tasks in an exciting variety of genres, all of which complement and support each other in different ways and also help children to anticipate the kinds of writing they will be doing in Year 6.

We have summarised the class writing projects for you below to give you an idea of their scope and of the kinds of things you should expect your apprentice writers to be doing in each project, as well as how you can support them in completing each task.

Poetry (two projects)

Besides being a mode of writing in its own right, poetry projects benefit children's future writing in other genres too. In Year 4, children learned about using their senses to inform their poetry writing and that will now be part of their writing repertoire. This year, children will begin to explore how poetry can be hidden within objects and this will aid their other writing.

It may not have occurred to children until now that they can be inspired by certain poets or poems and that they can use these inspirations in their own writing. In this particular writing project, children will learn that other writers' texts can be a rich source of inspiration for their own work, in the same way that it is for professional writers. Children will learn techniques for 'mining' their reading texts for potential new ideas to be used in their own writing.

Explanation

Children will deepen their understanding of information and instructional texts studied in Year 4 and will now begin writing explanation texts. Children will consider the things that they are knowledgeable about and what they can share with others. Children should consider how they can bring themselves to these texts in terms of personal voice, anecdotes and through playing with description in a poetic way.

Memoir

Just as children's story-writing will be developing dramatically this year, so too will their writing for memoir texts. The focus on character and setting in story-writing will have a bigger influence on their memoirs too, allowing children to place more focus on themselves as characters; including their traits, their motivations and what their own memories might represent. Experienced writers are now able to attend to memoir texts in the same way that they do for story writing. They will consider plot, character development and setting description.

Graphic novels

This project is all about narrative writing. Graphic novels are often based on fundamental themes that have been sources for great writing for centuries. Drawing pictures compels children to concentrate on one particular moment in time, within their writing. Everything about a character's motivation, the plot and the setting, has to be described in that particular moment. This project will not only aid children's story and memoir writing this year but it will also prepare them to write flash fiction in Year 6.

Persuasive writing (advocacy journalism)

In Year 4, children learned how to write persuasively for personal gain. Now they will see how persuasion can be used for more communal purposes by writing an article advocating for a charity of their choice. Children's understanding of writing information and explanation texts will be of real use to them here.

Short stories

This year, children will build on their knowledge from Years 3 and 4. The emphasis this year will be on supporting your apprentice writers in bringing together all that they have learned about plot, setting and character, to create wholly memorable stories. Children will continue to require support in enabling them to think more deeply about their character(s): what they represent, their traits and their motivations. As experienced story-writers, children will now begin to fully understand how narrative can be an effective way to express themselves and their own feelings.

Biography

In Year 5, children will build on their People's History writing from Years 3 and 4. They will use what they know to write biographies. Their subjects will be about everyday people who might have otherwise led quite ordinary lives. This project will show children that just like in their memoir writing, the ordinary can also be profoundly memorable and that each and every individual has something extraordinary to say, if only we encourage them to talk or write about it.

Information

This year, children will be moving on to sharing information with others that may well be completely new to them. Instead of sharing their pre-existing knowledge, children could now be investigating and researching information about a subject that is of growing interest to them. Alternatively, they may choose a subject that has roused a sudden curiosity in them. Either way, children will not yet know much about the topic. The more experienced writers in the class may begin to use a formal and informal voice, as well as using figurative language and comparison, when describing phenomena.

A guide to writing for pleasure

Writing for Pleasure has been developed as a research-informed philosophy and a practical pedagogy with the fundamental aim of creating the conditions in which children will write for pleasure and with a sense of purpose, be highly motivated and be academically high achieving.

This pedagogy ensures that children develop as independent writers who:

understand and write in popular genres for their own purposes.

regularly take part in genuine publication to the wider community.

engage in all the writing processes and over time develop their own preferred ways of writing.

know and use linguistic features and grammar for functional and purposeful reasons.

balance both composition and transcription, understanding the importance of organisation, content and precision in meaning-making.

are given agency to choose their own writing topics, genres and genuine audiences.

see themselves, their peers, their teacher and the whole class as a community of writers.

see their own lives and experiences validated as valuable and legitimate subjects for writing.

are helped to understand that writing is more than a school-based task; that it has relevance for them right now in the real world beyond the school gates and that it can be an agent for social, political and personal growth, as well as for change.

engage in personal writing.

get pleasure and satisfaction from writing.

write because they want to, not because they have to.

We are pleased that all of these elements are embedded within *Power English: Writing*.

What is writing for?

Writing touches every part of our lives. **Frank Smith**

1. Writing is a tool for learning and communication within a culture. It gives us the ability to share information over time and space **(explaining, recounting, opinion)**.

2. It can also provide a permanent record or a statement **(history, geography, science)**.

3. Other cultural aspects of writing are artistry, entertainment and playfulness **(narrative, poetry)**.

4. There is also the immensely important personal aspect of writing. Writing allows us to reflect, imagine, express our perceptions of self, socially dream, or be critical **(memoir, poetry)**.

Ultimately, writing is a means for us to express ourselves in the world, make sense of the world and impose ourselves upon it. Unsurprisingly, writing for pleasure leads to high attainment, enjoyment of the craft and satisfaction in finished writing products.

Writing for pleasure pedagogy

All writers, including young apprentice writers, can and do experience pleasure when writing. This is a central consideration for *Power English: Writing*. We believe that there are two types of pleasure to be gained from writing: writing *as* pleasure (enjoyment) and writing *for* pleasure (anticipated satisfaction).

Writing *as* pleasure

Writing *as* pleasure is pleasure gained from practising the craft of writing when engaging in the whole process, or in particular parts of the process, whether it be generating ideas, getting the words down on paper or screen, editing to perfection or publishing with care. Ernest Hemingway recorded that, for him, pleasure was all in the revising. Children, too, can be very explicit about the pleasure they experience from their own processes. Our approach helps them understand and enjoy these processes, and come to use them in their own way.

Writing *for* pleasure

Writing *for* pleasure, however, is different. It is the anticipation of satisfaction after the act of writing, that comes from the expectation of a response from a specific audience to the writing that you have shared (knowledge, feeling, experience). It is also the pleasure of listening back to your own writing voice and fulfilling your purpose, saying what you mean to say and achieving what you want your reader to feel. Our approach, which emphasises agency, purpose and genuine publication, fosters this kind of pleasure.

The *Power English: Writing* approach

Children want to write. **Donald Graves**

The approach we describe here provides you with a strong teaching model, and a rigorous, structured and highly individualised literacy curriculum for all the children in your class and school. It is highly interconnected, linking purpose, audience, creativity and pleasure with content, organisation, precision and genre knowledge. It is this kind of integration that adds tremendous value, breadth and balance to the teaching of writing. A *Power English: Writing* classroom will include a blend of the creativity and openness that you would expect of a writing workshop, as well as the bustle of a professional publishing house.

What is offered to children in school must be culturally relevant and meaningful to them if they are to get the most out of it. The writing classroom should therefore match, as closely as possible, the conditions of real writing communities. Our approach calls attention to the importance of children's lives outside the classroom as valued and legitimate sources of knowledge. We know that, when children's life experiences are acknowledged and celebrated as valuable subjects for writing, children will be motivated to engage with every aspect of the writing process and produce high-quality writing. They will write in their own voice about issues close to their hearts. They will write about the things that concern, interest or inspire them, finding a genre that serves the purpose of their writing and will understanding that attention to grammar and transcription is absolutely essential for the communication of meaning.

The power of a reassuringly consistent approach

We know from research that schools do best when they have a reassuringly consistent approach to teaching writing. Therefore, *Power English: Writing* will help you enact your school improvement plan, drive up standards, save your teachers time so that they can better focus on the things that help children learn as well and ensure that you tick those all-important curriculum boxes. The ultimate goal of course is that, over time, your school will be free to explore and innovate making this approach to the teaching of writing your own.

The big five

Power English: Writing is dedicated to helping children become independent and highly successful writers. It is directed towards helping you create the conditions in which children can write with enjoyment, motivation and to a high standard. The five whole-school principles described below are going to be an essential part of delivering *Power English: Writing*.

I. Creating a community of writers and readers

The psycholinguist Frank Smith (1988) used the metaphor of a 'literacy club' to stress the social nature of literacy learning. We learn from each other when we 'join' this club. Your school will become one large literacy club and everyone is invited to join it! When young writers see their teachers and peers as positive, caring and interested in their lives, they are more likely to engage in writing at a high level of achievement. This is a place where teachers write alongside children and share their own writing practices. Children are helped to talk about and present their writing, as well as their writing processes and enjoy the pleasures of sharing and advising their fellow writers. Everyone, including the teachers, learns to write for and with others in a positive and constructive learning environment.

2. Reading, sharing and talking about writing

Power English: Writing gives children regular opportunities to share and discuss together their own, their peers' and their teacher's writing, to give and receive constructive criticism, and to celebrate achievement. This occurs in daily class sharing time. Writing strategies and individual processes, as well as the content, are taught, discussed, applied and shared in our carefully constructed *mini-lessons*. This happens best when the writing environment is positive and settled in tone. In this way, your writing community begins to build its own ways of talking, thinking and undertaking writing and will use all that they have learned from previous years to help them achieve this.

3. All children as writers

Effective writing schools hold high expectations for all their writers. They see all children, even their earliest writers, as authentic writers. This means that from the outset, they are being taught strategies that lead to greater independence in their writing. Growth mindset research tells us that learning of all kinds is greatly affected by what children perceive they can or cannot do. In *Power English: Writing*, all children have agency and ownership over their choice of writing topic and will be clear about their own writing purposes and audiences for both class and personal writing projects. They begin to see themselves as real writers. Conversations and writerly advice are given and received between teachers and pupils as writer-to-writer through highly effective pupil conferencing strategies (see p26–30).

4. Teachers identifying themselves as writer-teachers

Power English: Writing encourages teachers to become writer-teachers who enjoy writing for and alongside children, as well as for themselves. This is not nearly as daunting as it might seem and you should not feel that you have to be an accomplished, or even a confident writer, to become one. In fact, there are some benefits to be gained from being an *un*confident writer. The idea here is not to 'showcase' your writing, nor to write the perfect piece for children to emulate. Rather, it is to share your own processes, difficulties, failures and successes, as well as to talk, advise and be advised *writer to writer*. The sense of a writing community is strengthened by an environment in which such reciprocal relations are maintained. Children enjoy knowing that their teachers share the same challenges that they do and research shows that their motivation is increased if taught by a writer-teacher.

5. Reading-writing connections

Every hour spent reading is an hour spent learning to write; this continues to be true throughout a writer's life. **Robert Macfarlane**

Power English: Writing recognises the intrinsic connection between reading and writing. Successful teachers of writing know that children who are committed to reading for pleasure are also more likely to write for pleasure and to a higher level of achievement. The personal and individual reading of quality texts provides children with models for writing and suggests ideas and themes for self-chosen projects. By building a class library, crafting your own writing as a writer-teacher and using the excellent exemplars we've included in *Power English: Writing*, you will be able to discuss with children the techniques published writers use to create great writing. Successful teachers of writing also know that reading aloud to the class with regularity and in an engaging way has a significant effect on children's vocabulary and story comprehension. It also increases the range of syntactic structures and linguistic features they can use in their writing. See p298–300 for our recommended texts for your class library, for each genre.

Final words

Power English: Writing offers a fresh approach to the teaching of writing. It keeps central the true purposes of writing as a socially significant act, which is undertaken for the expression and transmission of ideas, for the taking of action, for reflection and for recording experiences.

Through *Power English: Writing*, children make gains from seeing themselves, and being seen by their teachers, as writers. They are given the agency and the skills to write out their thoughts, desires and intentions into their communities, both in and outside school. You, the teacher, are supported by a research-based, integrated and structured pedagogy which is directed towards helping children to write to a high standard about the things that interest and concern them, with motivation, purpose and pleasure. We believe that you will also personally gain from giving more freedom to the children, from being able to provide high-quality teaching based on what published writers do, from establishing communities of writers and a new relationship with the children in your class – and from the pleasure of writing yourself.

Welcome to *Power English: Writing*. Enjoy it!

How to use *Power English: Writing*

Daily writing sessions

Power English: Writing involves teaching writing in a reassuringly consistent and simple way. Each class writing project begins with a week's worth of **genre-study** lessons, which involve investigating why writers use a genre, how they make it work and how genres can be played around with. These lessons are followed by a series of writing sessions.

A typical writing session is split into three parts: a **mini-lesson**, **writing time** and **class sharing**. Writing sessions begin with a mini-lesson – a lesson that is short, wholly practical and will be of long-term use to the apprentice writers in your class. The children will often be able to apply what they have learned in the writing time, as outined below.

Class writing project

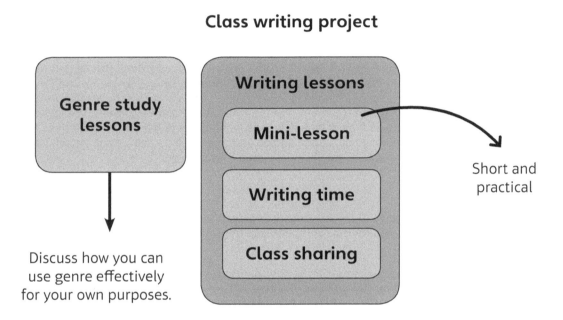

Genre study lessons

Discuss how you can use genre effectively for your own purposes.

Writing lessons

Mini-lesson — Short and practical

Writing time

Class sharing

Teaching mini-lessons

There are two broad types of mini-lesson to choose from: **writing study** and **functional grammar study**. **Writing study** lessons focus on the writer's craft and how children can develop a writing process that works for them. **Functional grammar study** is about children understanding how they already use grammar and punctuation in their writing projects in powerful ways, as well as how they can learn new aspects of grammar, from real examples of writing, to suit the purpose of their own writing. The essential aim of any mini-lesson is always to give children knowledge, strategies and the resources to write with more self-regulation and with a greater understanding of how writers and writing really work.

Class writing projects

Yearly orientation projects

Every year begins with an orientation project. This is a three-week project that settles children into the routine of writing using the writing processes, and sets them up for the year of writing ahead. We know from research that children learn best in reassuringly consistent classrooms and so this project gives you time to teach the routines and structures that will be followed in the writing community for the year. Devoting this big block of time to getting personal writing project books and your routines up and running is beneficial in the long run because once this happens, everything else becomes a lot smoother and more efficient. If children have completed *Power English: Writing* projects in previous years, repeating the orientation project at the beginning of each subsequent year will reacquaint them with the features, techniques and resources related to each part of the writing process.

Class writing projects

Power English: Writing provides resources for up to nine class writing projects per year. Class writing projects centre around a genre. Some of these genres will be known to your class from previous years while others may well be a new experience for them. In the **genre study lessons** at the beginning of each class writing project, you and the class will unpick the following: why the genre exists in a social context; why writers use it; what effect it has on a reader and how you might personally want to use it.

You will then establish the **distant writing goal** for the class writing project, which is the purpose and potential audience(s) for the writing. Once this is established, you and your class will then discuss the **product goals**. You will define these by reading examples written by you, as the writer-teacher, or by previous year groups, by looking at ineffective examples or by looking at the exemplars within the *Power English: Writing* genre booklets.

	Definition	Example of how to introduce to children
Distant writing goal	Distant goals are often the end goal of a writing project – the final writing 'product'. The purpose and audience for the writing is revealed, considered and discussed at this point.	*As you know, our next writing project is to produce new poetry for an exhibition. You now have six writing sessions in which to publish a series of poems about objects that are special to you. Make sure you keep to this deadline!*
Product writing goal	Often writers will talk about their finished writing being their 'product' – the thing they have created. Product writing goals are the intentions we have for the writing. *'What will we have to do to make this an effective … ?,'* This is very different from the less effective idea of 'success criteria' which often fail to attend to the *intentions* for the writing; nor are success criteria always authentically generated with the whole writing community.	*You have had a look at a few really good instructional texts from last year's class and you have also looked at mine. So, what might you need to think about to be successful at writing an excellent instructional text? Let's write some product goals on this flip-chart paper.*
Writing process goal	These are goals that need to be achieved over a certain period of time.	*Reminder! You have only three more writing sessions in which to make sure that your poems are ready for the exhibition.*

Once you know the goals for your project, *Power English: Writing* helps you make explicit to children the processes of writing. Children learn how to: **generate ideas, dabble, plan, draft, revise, edit** and **publish**. They then use this knowledge and the appropriate resources to support their negotiation of these writing processes to complete accomplished, varied and personally significant pieces of writing.

Unlike Years 3 and 4, the **writing sessions** in Year 5 will not include setting a process goal. Instead, children complete their writing at their own pace, using their own preferred writing style, over a number of sessions. This gives all children, regardless of ability or experience, ample time in which to publish their finished product. Importantly, there will also be enough time for you, as their teacher, to provide verbal feedback on how children are getting on with their writing. As every class writing project follows this reassuringly consistent routine, children begin to use what they have learned year on year and will also use the same strategies when undertaking their personal writing projects (see p17–18).

Each class project involves lessons teaching children real writer techniques on how to **generate an original idea** from their personal interests, knowledge, passions, thoughts and from texts they have read. Children then learn, through these projects, how writers take an original idea and see it through to **publication**. At the end of each writing session, children are given the opportunity to talk with their partners, in groups or with the whole class, about how their writing pieces are coming along. They share advice and strategies when difficulties arise. They also learn from good examples of writing from around the classroom, from other year groups, from previous years' writing and from having a rich class library.

For most of the genres covered in *Power English: Writing*, you will have the opportunity to revisit them later in the same year or in subsequent years. This gives children the opportunity to build on what they already know about the genre, by learning how they can play around with it, hybridise it with different genres and look at the genre from different perspectives.

Class sharing

Time is made before the end of a writing session, for children to talk with their partners, in groups and as a whole class, about how their writing has been developing that day. It is an opportunity for children to talk about their process, their ideas, where they are taking their writing and to get feedback from a potential audience. After children have had a discussion among themselves, there should be time made for 'author's chair'. This is where children can come to the front and share their work. It works best when you follow this kind of routine:

1. Have the children consider what they might like to share at their table, or pick children to come to the front of the class and ask them to 'warm up the text' by explaining a little bit about background behind it.

2. Then ask the child whether there is anything in particular they would like the class to listen out for or any advice they would like to receive.

3. Then, allow the writer to read their whole piece or a particular extract of the writing.

4. Once the piece has been read put, invite children in the class to explain what it was about. Ask what struck them as being interesting about the piece, whether it reminded them of anything from their life or anything they have seen or read, and whether they have any questions for the writer.

5. Your last question should be whether anyone in the class feels they would like to give some advice. This is also an opportunity for you, as the writer-teacher, to give some advice on the writing piece too. This is a powerful part of the sharing because all children can listen and apply the advice you have given to their future writing projects too. To keep things fresh, it is also beneficial to have the occasional draft book ceremony, where children display on their tables their favourite example of dabbling, planning, drafting, revising, editing or published work. This has hugely positive results on children's writing and shouldn't be underestimated.

6. Instead of a whole-class sharing experience, you can have children share with their partners or across tables. Children can still follow the typical class sharing routine once they have internalised the process.

7. Finally, there is also the concept of 'process shares'. This differs from sharing the writing itself. Instead, children describe or show an aspect of their writing process and how they go about writing in a certain way. For example, you might have a child explain how they go about writing a character description.

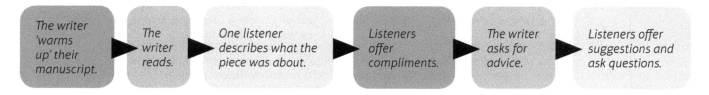

The writer 'warms up' their manuscript. → The writer reads. → One listener describes what the piece was about. → Listeners offer compliments. → The writer asks for advice. → Listeners offer suggestions and ask questions.

Personal writing projects

The rationale for personal writing project time

Personal writing is central to the success of *Power English: Writing*. It should never be made peripheral. This is because writing daily, and having agency and opportunity to pursue personal writing projects, is a huge motivation for children and creates a sense of volition, rather than duty, in developing themselves as authentic writers. Effective writing teachers understand that writing is not easily or quickly mastered. Children need opportunities for repeated practice. Of course, this does not mean mechanical drills and empty exercises. It means daily and sustained engagement with writing that is enjoyable but also purposeful.

There are clear and profound links between writing for pleasure and the opportunity for personal writing projects. Personal writing projects allow ideas and themes to travel around the class, with groups of writers beginning to buzz around common interests. This results in some collaborative writing, much conversation and enrichment for the community of writers in your class. The experience of receiving a genuine response from an interested reader makes a significant difference to reluctant writers, as does the satisfaction of having their work read out loud, shared and enjoyed. Unsurprisingly, research shows that if children enjoy and care about their writing, they will work harder at it. This means that they will take personal writing time incredibly seriously and hold it in the highest possible regard. Whilst children are afforded a lot of autonomy during this time, you should expect the routines, expectations and behaviours of class writing project sessions to be well-maintained when undertaking personal projects too.

Personal projects give children freedom, time and space to write and publish strange, experimental, purposeful, informative and memorable pieces of writing that mean something to them and to the community of writers to which they belong.

How personal writing projects work

- At the beginning of the year, the orientation project will show you and your class how personal writing time works.
- During personal writing time, children can use the genre booklets to help them, as they did for class writing projects. They will often choose to use these booklets because it gives them access to clear guidelines on how to generate ideas, plan, draft, revise and edit their pieces in a largely independent manner.
- When a child has completed the class writing goal for a particular lesson, they can continue pursuing their personal writing, by writing about whatever they wish, including anything arising from curriculum topics or foundation subjects, in any genre of their own choosing. This writing should also be done in their own way and at their own pace, using the genre booklets to help them.
- Invite children to take their personal writing project books home or onto the playground so they can continue their writing there, if they so wish.
- Finally, you should provide 'blocked time' throughout the year for children to simply pursue their personal writing. For example, you should schedule regular 'personal writing weeks'.

Choosing a personal writing project

The writing wheel and genre booklets are good places for children to start to think about their personal writing project. Looking at the writing wheel helps children to establish the purpose, audience and potential genres for their writing idea. The genre booklets offer many ways children can generate ideas for their personal writing projects:

- They explain which genre children might want to use in their writing and what is typically included in each genre.
- They give examples of how to play around with a genre.
- They give advice on ways children can plan their writing and remind them of the drafting rules.
- They suggest ways in which children can revise written pieces.
- Children are also provided with checklists for editing and publishing their pieces.

Publishing personal writing

When children have completed a number of personal writing projects, they can choose one piece for formal publication. This should be a piece of writing that fits the class publishing house criteria, or alternatively can be written for a child-run independent publishing house (see p19). Children should meet with the designated editors of that publishing house, to get their opinion and advice before publishing into the class library on their imprint. Depending on the type of writing, the child might have a different audience in mind and may want to take the writing home or send it to someone.

It is important for children to understand that not everything they write down deserves to be drafted, revised, edited and published. Sometimes they will never get around to turning their little bit of dabbling into anything, nor should they feel like they need to. Not everything that is written in a notebook turns into something significant. Any personal projects that a child decides to abandon should simply have the word 'dropped' written in the margin. If a child wishes to reopen a piece, it can be photocopied or simply restarted on a fresh page. You will be amazed to see how much the children are applying what they have learned during class, into their writing projects.

Top tips for personal writing time

- Write your own piece while sitting with your class of children, at least at the start of personal writing time. Share your writing notebook with the class regularly.
- Conduct pupil conferencing as you would for class writing projects.
- Share an idea-generating technique at the beginning of some of the personal writing sessions. Alternatively, generate a host of ideas together as a class, on flip-chart paper.
- Encourage children to share with others what they are writing about.
- Encourage children to write *Inspired by …* or *Retold by …* pieces if they are suffering from writer's block.
- Encourage children to use the class library as a source for writing ideas and techniques.
- Give children time to collect from their reading 'lines I wish I had written' and 'memorable passages.' These can often be sources for future or current writing.
- Allow children to work with one another or even in groups, on particular projects.
- Let the children talk and share ideas with one another, just as they do during class project times.
- Make children aware that not everything they write down has to be published or even fully drafted. They can abandon pieces or simply 'dabble' on an idea without following it through.

Setting up classroom publishing houses

It is not enough for children to simply publish their work into the class library. As part of the orientation project at the beginning of each year, *Power English: Writing* encourages classes to consider what their class library stands for. What sort of texts do you want to publish for each other? What is your mission as a class? What type of writing is important to you all? This will need to be discussed at the beginning of the year but also throughout the year, as new ideas for writing develop. Early in the year, you will need to establish your own whole-class publishing house, with its own mission statement. You will also need a name, slogan and a logo for the class publishing house. The logo will have to be something that everyone feels they will be able to draw so it can be added to published pieces easily.

It is important to let children know that not everyone within their community of writers might feel represented by the whole-class publishing house. Therefore, there should also be an opportunity for smaller, independent publishing houses to be established, which are run by groups of children in the class. These independent publishing houses will also need mission statements, names, slogans and logos. It should be agreed that these independents need to be varied enough so as not to encroach on the whole-class publishing house. A poster of the different publishing houses, their mission statements and who the Commissioning Editors of those houses are, should be made available to the class.

If children wish to be published by a particular publishing house, they will have to meet with the Commissioning Editor of that house, to seek advice and revision ideas for their manuscript, before having permission to publish. Children will come to realise that a Commissioning Editor is a critical friend. They will support and champion individual writers within the class but they also tell you when things need untangling. You may feel that your class needs a lesson on how to be a good Commissioning Editor. Obviously, their best role model is you as the teacher, and how you conduct yourself during pupil conferencing sessions.

Feedback and assessment

A major benefit of teaching through *Power English: Writing* is that it affords you time to conduct high-quality **pupil conferencing**. This is where you can carry out real-time verbal feedback and set writing goals with the children in your class whilst they are undertaking their writing. Through *Power English: Writing*, assessment becomes a reliable and enjoyable experience. Over the course of the year, children will produce **a rich and varied portfolio of writing** that is written largely independently. This means you can feel confident when making **summative assessment decisions** about a child's progress. These writing products are also a valuable resource in themselves. You should always be on the lookout for any rich writing that you will be able to use with your new class the following year.

A practical guide to writing workshop

The rationale behind the writing workshop approach

Research has consistently shown that explicit instruction in writing processes is one of the best ways of teaching apprentice writers. Therefore, the **writing workshop** approach, with its focus on what writers really do, helps children develop 'self-regulating' strategies, by setting them up with the resources and techniques to undertake the different writing processes largely independently. Independently does not, however, mean working in isolation. The collaborative element of the writing workshop can and should invigorate, enliven and promote a sense of socialising about writing and create a community of writers working and learning from each other as they write.

The writing processes

There is not a single agreed-upon whole-writing process and, because of individual differences, children will come to develop their own personalised way of working when it comes to their writing. *Power English: Writing* also acknowledges that many children are unaware of the typical processes involved in writing and as such may not, at first, be able to control them all at once. Therefore, each process has been explicitly taught and frequently referred to in Years 3 and 4 and now that children are in Years 5 and 6, they can shape their own preferred way of working and writing. Mini-lessons are also provided for additional support, should you feel that your class still requires some additional instruction in one or more areas of the various writing processes.

The writing process typically includes:

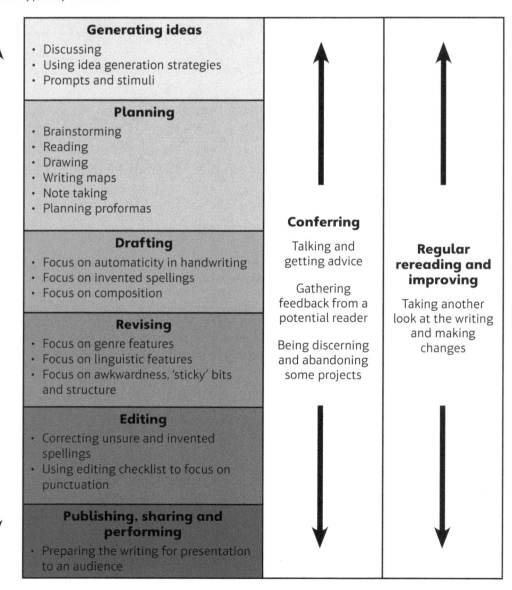

Generating ideas
- Discussing
- Using idea generation strategies
- Prompts and stimuli

Planning
- Brainstorming
- Reading
- Drawing
- Writing maps
- Note taking
- Planning proformas

Drafting
- Focus on automaticity in handwriting
- Focus on invented spellings
- Focus on composition

Revising
- Focus on genre features
- Focus on linguistic features
- Focus on awkwardness, 'sticky' bits and structure

Editing
- Correcting unsure and invented spellings
- Using editing checklist to focus on punctuation

Publishing, sharing and performing
- Preparing the writing for presentation to an audience

Conferring

Talking and getting advice

Gathering feedback from a potential reader

Being discerning and abandoning some projects

Regular rereading and improving

Taking another look at the writing and making changes

Children and teachers alike need to know that writers move between these processes all the time. It is vital that your school has a consistent writing-process poster, such as the one on the previous page, placed in every classroom. It is also important that when the children move into different year groups, they know that these processes remain largely the same.

Power English: Writing teachers in Lower Key Stage 2 will have taught the writing processes and the vocabulary associated with them. These processes include: generating ideas, dabbling, planning, drafting, revising, editing, publishing, as well as sharing and performing, with a view to increasing children's flexible and independent use of these processes. Particular focus will still need to be applied to the recursive nature of these processes in Upper Key Stage 2.

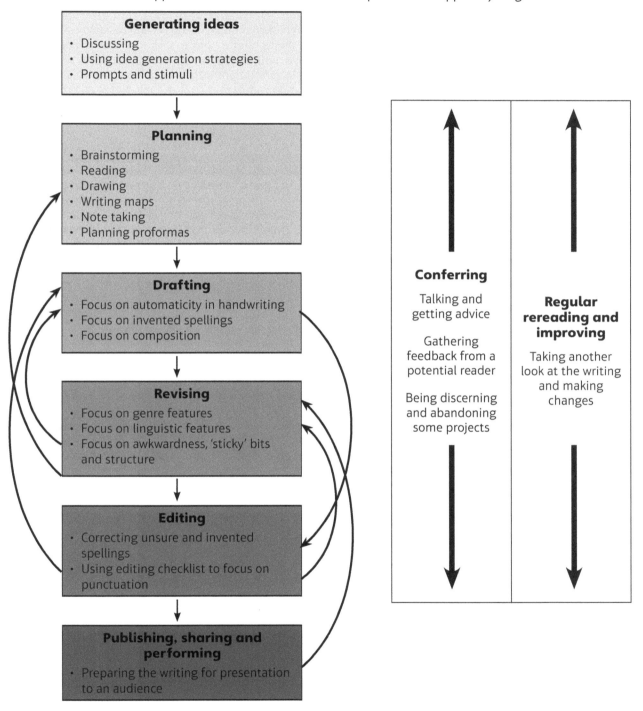

A writing classroom that does not acknowledge the recursive nature of these processes, and insists that children undertake them in a linear way without socialising with other writers, will ultimately run into difficulties. It may be that your class needs more time to complete a particular writing process goal. Our approach means this can be taken into consideration when planning your next day writing session. For example, you may feel that some children in your class need extra drafting time. You may also find, over time, that some more experienced writers are able to move ahead of the class and onto the next writing process goal. Because of the reassuringly consistent approach *Power English: Writing* takes and because of the quality of our genre booklets, you can feel confident in letting these children continue their writing at their own pace. *Power English: Writing* ensures that your writing environment, writing study mini-lessons, resources and displays are always promoting this kind of self-regulation.

Through the writing workshop approach, the apprentice writers in your school will learn to regularly reread their work as they compose, to make changes to their plans as they write them, to revise *as* they draft and perhaps edit a sentence they have just written. All of this, over time, will happen automatically and unconsciously. Additionally, children will learn to be discerning about their personal writing and be able to decide whether a project is worth pursuing through to publication, or not.

Personalising the writing process

Many children in your class will now be fluent or experienced writers and will therefore be ready to start developing their own writing processes. There are many benefits to this. There is no single way of undertaking writing tasks so children will benefit from being given freedom to attend to their writing using their preferred process. This will mean that they can write more naturally and to their greatest strengths. Below, we have outlined just some of the approaches that might define you and the children as working writers. You can allow children to experiment with these different processes in the orientation unit at first, and eventually, when they are experienced enough, allow them to use their preferred process in class writing projects too.

Approaches to the writing processes

Discoverer	Planner	Drafter	Paragraph piler	Sentence stacker
Likes to write a draft first before looking at it and using it as a plan for a second draft.	Likes to plan in great detail, working out exactly what will be written and where it will go before they begin their draft.	Likes to write their piece out from a plan, before attending to revision and editing.	Likes to write a paragraph, reread it, revise it and edit it before moving on to drafting their next paragraph.	Likes to write a sentence and ensure it is revised and edited just how they want it before moving on to the next sentence.

Generating ideas

When you write, ideas crazily spill from your head, tumble down your arm, into your pen and out along the crisp, white page. They are colourful, squirming, squiggly things that slide and slip through the nooks and crannies of your brain. Some of them crash against the walls of your head in roaring waves. Others come more slowly – each droplet of water a letter. Once you gain control of the sea – the droplets make out your idea.

Year 5 child

Research clearly shows that if children choose their own topics, their enjoyment of writing, and therefore the progress they make, is increased. Children may initially need to generate a whole raft of topics and ideas that they feel they *could* write about. Throughout *Power English: Writing*, we provide techniques to children for generating their own writing ideas. This concept works well because, when children write about what they already know and care about, they have the information at their fingertips. This means they can focus on the writing! It allows them to think about *how to write it* instead of having to concentrate principally on *what* it is they are being asked to write about. Use of these techniques facilitates children's choice of writing topic and you won't have to spend time worrying about some of the children not having anything to write about.

Top tips for generating ideas

There are three ways of approaching idea generation:

1. You can do it as a whole-class activity – taking ideas from the whole class and writing them up on flip-chart paper.

2. You can put children into groups or pairs and they can generate ideas together.

3. Children can generate ideas independently, in their books.

Finding the diamond moment

One of the most important lessons we can teach children in our class is the idea of finding a diamond moment. Often apprentice writers have too much to say in one piece of writing. Some young writers struggle to focus a piece of writing, resulting in a loss of impact on their reader. To combat this issue, we use the analogy of a writing topic and a mountain of rocks. The writer's job is to find the one important writing *idea* – **the diamond** – within this huge heap of 'rocky' topics, and then develop it into a piece of writing. This process is vitally important across all the genres, so this lesson is one that is repeatedly referred back to in our class writing projects. Over time, when asked what their diamond moment is, children can almost always identify it. The children who cannot are often the ones you will want to work with first.

Here are a couple of examples. In a piece about a day by the sea, a young writer writes vividly about her sudden discovery of a crystal. She tells of her excitement at finding something so beautiful and so special. This is the diamond moment she has picked out, and it makes her piece entirely memorable. Another example is a writer who has written a memoir about a trip a safari park. She has written brief, conventional descriptions of some of the animals and has then picked her diamond moment – the unforgettable experience, with the line '… with my heart beating faster and faster', as well as the line relating to holding a snake and feeling it ' … slithering round my neck, rough and adorable. For a moment, though, I thought it was going to bite me.'

Planning

Children's writing usually benefits from time spent planning. There are many ways to plan and over time children should be given choice about how they go about it. Class writing projects will, however, always provide you with a *'planning grid'* frame. Dabbling is an especially enjoyable way to plan. It is a process of playing around with drawings, words, phrases, thoughts and ideas on paper to develop an early writing idea. A great dabbler is the children's writer David Almond. Remember, many writers begin tentatively when thinking about what they want to write about and in what direction they want it to go. To aid this process, children should be given plenty of time to discuss their plans for their writing with their peers and with you. Planning is often an underdeveloped and underappreciated part of the writing process. Your role as the teacher is to make sure that the drafting stage will go as smoothly and as quickly for the children as possible. Ultimately, you will want children to have plenty of time for revision because this is where many writing gains and developments are made. When planning, children are considering purpose, audience and genre. Writing study lessons are of course a good opportunity to share a teacher's or child's planning notes, to show good practice.

Drafting

I do a kind of pre-draft – what I call a 'vomit-out' . **Calvin Trillin**

A first draft is where children discover the content and use it to form their writing. Transcription is often attended to later but children are encouraged during drafting to circle their 'unsure spellings', mark with boxes where they are unsure of punctuation and underline places where their writing does not 'sound right'. These are what we call 'sticky' bits, where the writing doesn't run smoothly. Children are also encouraged to underline 'yawny' bits. These are moments in the children's writing where they feel they are mentioning things that are unnecessary. These writing strategies, used by the children, assist the focus on composition extremely well.

It is very important that, early on in the writing development, children separate composition from transcription during the drafting stage. Once they are more experienced writers, they can begin to combine the elements of drafting with revision and editing. It is important, as a writer-teacher, that you share examples of your *own* drafts, so children can get an understanding of what crossings-out, false starts and invented spellings can look like on the page and that this is what published writers do.

We recommend that children always use double pages when writing in their books. The left-hand side is used for drafting and the right-hand side is for any revision and editing.

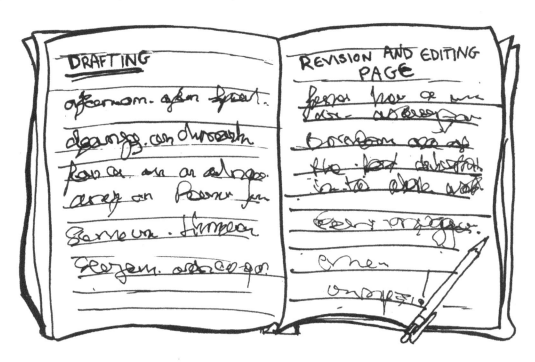

Drafting rules

Got a sticky or yawny bit?	Don't know how to spell a word?
- Put a line under the bit you are unsure about. - Carry on.	- Invent the spelling. - Put a circle around it. - Carry on.
Don't know what to write next? - Read it to a partner. - Get your partner to ask you questions.	**Not sure of punctuation?** - Put a box where the punctuation might need to go. - Carry on.

Think you have finished?
Start or continue with a personal writing project!

Revising

Revision does not mean repairing a draft; it means using the writing I have already done to help me see more, feel more, think more, learn more. **Lucy Calkins**

Revising is, in many ways, the most important part of the writing process. Often, apprentice writers terminate the writing process as soon as they complete a draft, believing that once their ideas are on paper, the writing task is complete and they announce 'I'm finished'. In fact, they often regard the encouragement to revise as a consequence of not having got it 'right' in the first place. Worse still, they may depend on you to revise and edit their work for them through written feedback, thereby learning very little.

When revising a draft, children act on the suggestions and conversations that have taken place with their peers, as well as during pupil conferencing sessions with you, as the teacher. In their genre booklets and as part of the writing study mini-lessons, children will learn about the different types of rereading and improving revisions writers usually make on their drafts. Our revision tips are based on what adult writers have said they often employ in their work. They include searching for 'sticky' and 'yawny' bits, reconsidering openings and endings, and trying out certain linguistic features or poetic language. The Writing Tips and Tricks cards can help children here.

Having a revision and edit page gives children a place to showcase their understanding of certain linguistic features, required by the National Curriculum. Using this page means they can be discerning about which features they wish to include. This is important because sometimes inclusion of certain features for the sake of it can make the writing worse. By revising in this way, children are thinking more like mature independent writers. We suggest that writing revision in the earlier year groups is done on the opposite page to the draft, using symbols such as asterisks or numbers, to show where larger amounts of content have been changed. However, more experienced writers or children in the older years often outgrow these techniques and prefer to undertake a full second draft. Finally, we recommend that all writing revision should be done in a different coloured pen.

Editing

The most important thing we can do for our students is to help them write freely and unselfconsciously. No one learns well while feeling afraid and ashamed. Our students need to realise that it's okay to make editorial errors as they write; all of us do, but we always correct them when we edit. **Lucy Calkins**

Editing is an important and explicit stage in the writing workshop. Without it, all the children's hard work can be in vain as their readers will find it hard to follow what it is they wanted to say. Regular use of the editing checklist (see p273) helps children to become excellent proofreaders. The CUPS (**C**apitalisation, **U**se of vocabulary, **P**unctuation and **S**pellings) strategy ensures children don't over-burden themselves when editing and instead focus on one thing at a time. It is also important that, as a writer-teacher, you model how editing is done. All editing should be done by the child in their book using a different coloured pen so that the changes are visible, just as professional writers or copy-editors do. In writing study mini-lessons, children are taught how proofreading is a specific activity in which you read carefully word-by-word and hunt for errors, focusing on one or two types of error in each reading. You will also notice that our class writing projects recommend a number of resources for checking and correcting unsure spellings. These include spelling dictionaries, the 1000 common spelling words (see p295–297), electronic spell checkers, search engines and of course the children's reading books.

Publishing

When young writers publish their work, when they send their work out in to the real-world, and receive real-world feedback, they begin to value punctuation, grammar, handwriting, and spelling. Children need to write every day, to publish frequently, and to learn the skills of editing as they go along … the more children publish, the more they want to keep on writing and writing well. **Shelley Harwayne**

Publishing is where children concentrate on their writing product and how the final piece will look and read. Children also make all the necessary revision and editorial changes to the piece. This is when we can say the piece is 'reader-ready'. Children must ensure that their handwriting and presentation of the work is of a high standard and that any spelling, grammar or punctuation errors have been corrected. Children whose spelling is particularly poor and who cannot identify their own 'unsure' spellings very well, should only be given around five common words to look up and change at any given time. Other errors can be corrected according to your judgement, as the teacher. Once these pieces are published, they need to 'get to work'. They should be published by the whole-class or independent publishing houses, within the classroom. They could also be performed out loud, shared with peers, other classes, friends and family to the enjoyment of all. Perhaps they could also be sent out to other recipients or could be entered in local and national competitions.

Books for writing projects

We recommend that children have at least two writing project books: one for class writing projects, one for personal writing projects and, if you are not allowing personal writing project books to go home, a third book for personal writing projects that can be brought to and from school.

A practical guide to conferencing

Rich verbal responses, by both teacher and peers, are crucially important. Reading, sharing and talking about writing is an essential part of writing for pleasure and being part of a community of writers. Conferencing is one way of talking about writing and is one of the most important aspects of the *Power English: Writing* approach. Children need to feel secure in their teacher's presence and assume that the teacher will be interested in their writing. Therefore, it is important for you, as the teacher, to respond in the first instance to *what* has been written and not to *how* it has been written.

So, what is a conference?

Conferences can be among the best, most purposeful and productive interactions you can have with the young writers in your class. The benefit of giving verbal feedback over written feedback is that it is immediate, relevant and allows children to attend to learning points while they are really engaging in their writing. In addition, the exchanges you have in the conference can be used to make assessments of and for learning.

However, conferencing has a more important purpose than that of simply improving the written product. The huge significance of giving children strategies and techniques for instant application in their written piece is that you will be helping them become *better writers*. During the conference, you will be giving them a little more 'real writer' knowledge, for children to take forward into their new writing projects, as well as into their present and future lives outside the school gates.

Conferring with pupils is one of the main principles of a writing for pleasure pedagogy because it allows children to have agency, become self-directing and feel greater motivation in the act of writing. Think of each conference as a conversation in which you are the trusted and sympathetic adult who will help and advise children about their writing, without being judgemental. In instances where teachers are only operating as judges, children's writing is limited to focusing only on what the teacher wants. As a result, the writing is almost always tentative and children learn far less. Your aim should be to build up children's pride in their own work, and their motivation to improve on it through self-regulation.

You will draw on your own experience and insights as a writer-teacher, writing alongside the class and will therefore be able to communicate with children as writer-to-writer. We cannot stress enough the importance of sharing the difficulties *you* have encountered in writing and the solutions *you* have found. This puts you, as the teacher, in a position of an empathetic responder and you should always draw on your personal experiences, when conferring with children.

We suggest that you don't concentrate on transcription issues at this stage unless the conference is taking place at the editing stage of the child's writing process. You should not seek to 'fix' the child's writing by imposing your own ideas relating to what direction the piece should go in. Instead, you should make suggestions and guide the child towards making their own reflective and informed writing decisions. Most of all, you will know that you are giving children some responsive, high-quality and focused tuition in a very short space of time (a conference can sometimes take less than a minute).

How to conduct a conference

A good conference has a definite shape. To begin the conference, simply ask children 'How's it going?' In response, the child might discuss their writing piece and this often sets the agenda for the conference, as you help them identify an area of difficulty or an uncertainty that they are having.

You then take in the information that the child is giving you and tease out more ideas through questioning. On the basis of what you have been told by the child, you can make a decision to teach one or two things, as outlined in the example transcription below.

Conference conducted between a teacher (T) and a pupil in an Upper KS2 class (P) at the start of one of his personal writing projects.

T: How's it going?

P: Well, I want to write a piece about my grandma, and so to start with I've been trying to make a whole list of things about her that I could put in. **[Talking about the writing]**

T: (Scans list) There are lots of ideas here, aren't there? I can tell she's quite an unusual person, isn't she? And I sense that you're really proud of her, and you'll probably want to get that across to your reader. **[Responding briefly with interest to content; getting a line on the pupil's intention as a writer; thinking about making a teaching decision]**

P: Yeah. I'd like people to know she's great and she's done some brave things, but I'm having trouble with getting it into a plan, I don't know where to start and what order to put stuff in, or what sort of ending to write. **[Reflecting; stating problem and setting agenda for the conference]**

T: Mmmm, so you've got lots of information and it's hard to organise it all. Well, I can tell you something published writers often do when they have this problem. They focus on the most interesting thing about that person and they just write about that. You just said you wanted people to know about her courage, right? Well, how about picking the thing that shows that most clearly about her? **[Summing up the problem, referring to mentors, giving a writerly suggestion]**

P: (Thinks for a while) Mmmm. I suppose that would be when she ran in the marathon, and she never gave up even when she got so tired she nearly couldn't breathe!

T: Great! I'd certainly like to hear more about that and so will all your other readers. So what will you do next? **[Encouraging self-regulation]**

P: Well, I could plan it – like a story, maybe? Beginning at the start of the race and then the middle could be what it was like when she was running, did she talk to anyone and things like that. Then I can write about the ending when she nearly didn't make it, or something? **[Pupil becoming self-directing]**

T: Sounds good to me! So I'll leave you now to get on with your plan. **[Supporting pupil's self-direction]**

Practicalities

- Conferencing takes place throughout any and all stages of the writing process. The reason for this is not to 'fix' children's writing but to help them become better writers throughout the process.
- Each conference should be short and no more than a few minutes in length.
- Aim to conference with all children at least once during the week, but also give priority to those who request a conference or those who are in most need of one.
- Look to train any support staff or parent volunteers in pupil conferencing.
- Children will often 'listen in' to a conference being held with another child and children can and will often conference with each other. This is fine too!
- Set high expectations for the behaviour and noise-level in the class while you are conferencing. Avoid being interrupted.
- Conferencing is a skill to be learned and developed through regular practice but you will, in time, become more adept at asking the sorts of questions that will draw out the information you need, and will enable you to give your pupils the kinds of advice that will help them as writers.
- Give children real advice based on your own experience of what you do when you have found yourself in similar writing situations to the ones your children are expressing in the conference.

Questions

Invite pupils to set the agenda by asking them open-ended questions. Use these as predictable openings:

- *How's it going?*
- *What are you doing in your writing today?*
- *What do you need help with today? (Children will often be very explicit about this, such as stating 'I don't know how to start', ' I need to know how to suggest time is passing.')*
- *Tell me about your writing piece. What is it about?*
- *Is there anything you want to run by me?*
- *Are there any sticky bits you can't untangle?*

Now take the lead: **ask open-ended 'research questions'** to encourage children to say more about their work and make it possible for you to lead them towards a more effective piece of writing. For example:

- *What did you have in mind?*
- *Can you tell me more about …?*
- *What did you mean when you said …?*
- *What's the diamond moment of your writing piece?*
- *Why did you repeat this line several times?*
- *Why did you decide to add on this bit of writing here?*
- *Do you think you have any 'yawny' bits in your piece? Could you show me where?*
- *Where do you think I might be hungry for more information or detail? Where do you think my 'reading tummy' is rumbling?*

A good technique, particularly when helping struggling writers, is to play the naïve reader or listener and parrot back what you have learned from listening to an extract of their text. You won't need to read the whole piece. You can do this for two reasons:

1. It often makes reluctant or sparse writers in your class reveal more information verbally, in response to your summing up of the content of their piece, particularly if you sum them up in a questioning tone, such as: 'So the pirate decided to throw the treasure overboard?'

2. It exposes young writers to the fact that their writing may be confusing to their reader and encourages them to clarify areas in their writing.

Common conferencing topics

Planning

- Children will often ask if they have to stick to a plan rigidly and whether they have to include everything that is in their plan. Reassure them that it is up to them to decide the merits of including the items that they planned for or to move away from their planning once they have started drafting.
- Encourage children to 'story tell' their plan to their peers. This can often be enough to save you a conference.
- Sometimes, children will be concerned that their initial plan has ended up being their first draft. Reassure them that this happens sometimes when they are in the flow of writing and that it is perfectly fine to use it as their first draft.
- Children may sometimes be concerned that their plans are sparser than their peers' plans. Explain that as long as they have talked through their plan with their partner and neither of them can see any gaps in their ideas for the writing, then they shouldn't worry.
- Children may ask whether they can take their plans home to work on. This can happen particularly with non-fiction texts and can be of huge benefit to children.
- Children may decide they want to change their writing idea or plan, depending on their enthusiasm and commitment to their idea. Allow children time to plan again, particularly if they are willing to put some extra effort in at home or use their free time.

Drafting

- When a child says that they don't know what to write, it is often the case that they just need to 'story-tell' their writing piece first. Simply asking children how they would like it to start the piece verbally is enough to get them started. Try asking children to turn over their book and simply tell you verbally how their piece might start. To get children going with their writing, you may need to offer your own suggestions, but give them the option of changing the ideas later if they want to. If children are writing a narrative or memoir, draw their attention to the types of openings writers typically use, perhaps using an example in a reading book, and suggest that they experiment with ideas on their revision and editing page (see p253 for a mini-lesson about openings).
- If a child says that they don't know what to write next, simply ask them: *'Might this mean your writing is finished? Maybe you haven't got anything else to say?'* This will often prompt children to reveal any additional information that they want to add. It is often the case (in narratives) that children don't always know how to move between space and time. Remember to advise children how to use paragraphing or how to use a time adverbial, to change the direction of their writing piece.

- Children might ask: *'How much do I need to write?'* Giving children a limit to the amount they can write (particularly for class writing projects) is advantageous. It is unnecessary for children to write more than a couple of pages maximum, even in Year 6. Usually, one page will be sufficient. In reply to the question, you could just say: *' Keeping writing until you have written everything that you want to say'*. This will usually put children at ease. It is also a good idea to address the misconception that more writing is better writing. Children can often feel that their teacher wants to see quantity, including lots of detail. This can sometimes result in children writing far more than is necessary and ending up including too many 'yawny' bits, which can ruin the impact of their piece.
- Children might ask you whether their 'sticky' bits make sense. Read the 'sticky' bit back to the child and ask them if it is saying exactly what they want it to say. Children can also ask a partner to give their opinion about the 'sticky' bit, for additional peer support.
- Early on, children might ask you to help them with spellings. Explain to children that they will need to write down the syllables that they can hear and then put a circle around the spelling, ready to look it up at a later stage when they come to edit their piece.
- Sometimes children might simply ask your opinion on how you think their piece is coming along. You should feel able to give the child an honest assessment of their writing.
- If children struggle with ideas for the ending of their piece, you can suggest to them the types of endings that published writers typically use (see p254 for a mini-lesson about endings). Children can also experiment with different endings on their revision and edit page.
- Never feel that you need to hesitate in telling a child that you don't understand sections of their piece or that you are confused by their subject choice. Give children an opportunity to clarify those points.
- Always explain to children what a professional writer (including yourself) might do, throughout the drafting stage.

Revising

- When conferencing with pupils during the revision stage, encourage children to experiment with revising their writing on their revision and edit page first. If they are happy with what they have created, they can add it into their piece.
- Children might ask where they should add their revisions. If they are revising a lot of the writing, explain to children that it is helpful to use numbers or asterisks for each point and then add their revisions to their revision and editing page.
- Revision checklists will often suggest certain linguistic or grammatical features that usually support the genre. If they cannot see a good place to use them in their piece, this is quite acceptable. The Writing Tips and Tricks cards can help children see how these features might improve their writing. Encourage children to try out the features on their revision and edit page, just to experiment. Children often find this helpful and will sometimes revise their piece accordingly.
- Encourage children to do a complete rewrite if their revisions are extensive.

Editing

- When children first begin to learn about proofreading and editing, they can find it hard to understand that they have to read their writing piece in a completely different way. Explain to children that they will need to read it like a robot and not be so concerned about reading for meaning. Advise children that their job now is to read their piece carefully, in order to find errors. Explain that this should be done one word at a time. You may need to model the technique with them (see editing mini-lessons, p261–262).
- It is always helpful for children to proofread each other's pieces. Explain to children that when other people read their writing, they can see it with 'a fresh pair of eyes' and may be able to spot errors that they may have missed.
- Giving children a few days away from their writing project before proofreading it for publication, can often be helpful. In these instances, you might choose to allocate a few personal project writing sessions dedicated to this process.

Finally, you may find our conferencing cards are helpful when you first begin to participate in pupil conferences. The conferencing cards can also be used as an aid for classroom assistants or parent-helpers participating in the process.

Pupil conferencing

Things to remember!

- You want to know about the writing and the ideas behind it.
- Parrot back to the child what they have told you in their piece, for clarity.
- You want the child to teach you or for you to learn something.
- Ask questions. Don't tell.
- Don't talk more than the child.
- Don't try to redirect the child onto something you find more interesting.
- Don't try to redirect the child to a different course or subject.
- Don't ignore the child's original intention for the piece.
- Don't supply words and phrases that *you* like.

Conferencing questions:

Opening questions:

- *What do you think about your writing?*
- *How is it going?*
- *How can I help you?*
- *What do you need from me?*
- *What surprised you?*
- *What is working?*
- *What needs work?*

- *What are you writing about now?*
- *Where are you now in your draft?*
- *So, tell me about your piece.*
- *How is your piece coming along?*
- *How is your writing going today?*
- *Where are you in the piece now?*
- *How did you happen to get into this piece?*

If the child doesn't know what to do or write next, ask them to turn their paper over and talk about the original intentions of the piece. The child must lead the conversation, while the teacher responds in kind.

Following questions:

These are questions that follow or reflect what the child has already written in their piece. The questions deal with the obvious areas to focus on.

- *Are there any places where you think your writing needs some work?*
- *What isn't going so well?*
- *What are you going to do with your piece now?*
- *How are you going to start?*
- *What did you have in mind?*

- *What did you hope to happen here?*
- *Can you tell me more about ...?*
- *What made you choose this topic?*
- *Which part do you like best?*
- *I don't understand this part. What do you mean?*

Process questions:

These are questions that help children organise the ongoing direction of their writing.

- *What do you think you will write about next?*
- *What are you going to do with the piece now?*
- *Where do you think you will add this new information in? Can you see where it should go?*

- *What will you do with this piece when it is all finished?*
- *Convince me that this piece is ready for publishing.*
- *Why do you think this piece is good?*

Keeping writing portfolios

A child's portfolio should include:

- children's formally assessed and published class writing projects
- any published personal writing projects that children have chosen as their most pleasing and successful texts.

Personal writing projects used as additional evidence of progress

These texts can be useful if you require additional evidence of progress. They are often just as high in quality as class writing projects. Indeed, in some cases children's personal projects can show exceptional quality when compared to their class project writing. This is often the case because the children have gone through all the stages of the writing process, at their own pace, without strict deadlines, and because they care about these pieces a great deal and so take great care over them. It can also be useful to skim through children's other personal writing projects (ones that didn't reach publication) to see if they have applied certain grammatical items, punctuation, or linguistic features related to the National Curriculum objectives.

We do not advocate the formal assessment of personal writing projects. However, as a teacher, you will find it comforting to know that you now have a whole portfolio of varied and interesting writing from children, which provides evidence of good independent writing being undertaken.

Writing development scales

What is laid out below, including age ranges, **is only a guide to progression** in the common genres encountered throughout *Power English: Writing*. As you know, many children and lots of examples of writing can be the exception to what is said here. Therefore, we encourage you to examine children's progress in writing for yourself and see what patterns you notice over time. Let these points inform your teaching, as they have done for us.

Story writing

Beginning and inexperienced writers

Writers who are beginning to write with some ease and clarity

It is useful to see the stories written by beginning and inexperienced writers in a similar way to their drawings. Their drawings are usually dominated by people or objects. Once these items are drawn, children will often verbally describe some action associated with the object or character in the drawing. The same process is often evident in children's early fiction writing too.

When asking beginning and inexperienced writers about their planning, you are likely to be given a general statement of what is going to happen. This will soon develop into drawing and 'telling the drawing' with a trusted adult or peer. Planning won't necessarily come naturally to beginning and inexperienced writers, though they might like to talk at length before they write.

Beginning and inexperienced writers will often write retellings of the TV, films, internet media or games they have been exposed to. Alternatively, they will write about things from their own recent past. The chosen characters will often be borrowed from popular culture or may be their friends and family members. This familiarity with the characters means they don't feel any need to develop the character in question. It may be that they are yet to experience the pleasure of placing themselves in a story of complete fiction. Their stories are usually limited in scope and are often quite literal retellings, possibly including some basic description. They may sometimes lack a clear dilemma or conclusion. Their stories may be written simply to amuse themselves or for the pleasure of sharing what they know about their favourite narratives from popular culture. They may often write for the immediate and not consider potential wider audiences or publication.

In conferences, these beginning and inexperienced writers will typically provide more information about the story verbally than is shown in their writing or in their drawings. Older children at this stage will often need the chance to retell or 'play out' their stories with a trusted adult. These retellings will often exceed their writing ability and they may find putting these ideas on paper challenging, but will nonetheless be motivated to do so. They will require regular reassurance and praise, perhaps even after writing every sentence.

Beginning and inexperienced writers of narrative often need help with ensuring that their story has a clear beginning, middle and end; or at the very least, some kind of structure. They can find it hard to manage a whole writing project. In this instance, children should talk a lot, draw a lot and break their story down into manageable chunks. Helping children formulate a potential ending before they begin writing can be really helpful here.

At this stage of their development, you can expect to read many 'chain of event' stories, including what happened and who was there, rather than why. Any focus on character will often be related to their physical traits. Children will also find it difficult to move between place and time and so will tend to include everything that happens in between events, even if it is irrelevant or tiresome for their reader.

There is likely to be little rereading of the text for setting description as well as a lack of character motive for any action taking place. If children do revise their work, it will be to add in more action since this can be seen by the child as making a story more exciting or interesting. Their stories will typically have a beginning, middle and end.

Fluent and well-organised writers

Fluent writers' main concern is that their stories are exciting, humorous, exaggerated and interesting to their friends and likely to get an instant reaction. They will set up questions in their narratives that readers will want to know the answers to and will have understood the need to develop a plotline.

Fluent writers can use exemplars and planning grids to plan and write cohesive paragraphs but their ideas often lead the structure of their writing and so it can soon lose cohesiveness. They may also like using story maps, drawing their ideas with connected arrows, indicating a logical story arc. Once they have completed the planning process, they will appreciate being able to discuss it with their peers. Fluent writers will use relatively simple story arcs. They will be able to use transitional phrases and move between periods of time – though it is often clunky.

Fluent writers will sometimes choose plot lines that are too large for them to control, resulting in their narratives being rushed in a clichéd way. This is probably a reflection of their reading habits since they will be beginning to take on longer chapter books and will want to replicate the style for themselves. Fluent writers begin to consider their readership beyond their teacher and are now far more interested in their peers' opinions of their writing. Writers at the earlier stage tend to see their writing as an extension of themselves, but by this stage children have a greater need to make their writing work for others.

These fluent writers will begin trying out things that they are picking up on from their reading, but not always successfully. They can and will focus on creating a strong opening. They will often give a basic description of settings but this isn't usually sustained throughout the narrative. Their character descriptions will continue to rely largely on 'cartooning' physical features and may well lack dimensionality. They may continue to use generic characters from popular culture but may now be venturing into first person narratives. Description will be separate from the plot and won't be integrated into the story. Their main concern still resides with action and event and these children will need to be pushed during conferencing to start considering the motives of their characters. Longer pieces may finish abruptly, due to a lack of stamina or not knowing how to formulate the ending.

Writers who show a high degree of fluency and clarity in their writing

These more experienced writers begin to see that narrative writing can be a form of escapism – a way of placing themselves 'through a character or otherwise' in fictional situations and perhaps to 'socially dream'. They begin to weave together what is true to their life, or what they wish were true, into their fictional characters and fictional worlds. With this stage of writing development, children's obsession with plot begins to move towards character-driven narratives. They tend to move beyond simple physical description towards how individual characters might behave, what they think, how they feel and how they converse with others.

At this stage, children will plan using planning grids and appreciate the importance of having an ending in mind, even if this is not yet set in stone. As always, they will appreciate being able to discuss the plan with their peers.

Experienced writers are able to attend to plot, character development and setting description, as they construct their narratives. For example, they can weave plot, character description and dialogue together. They are now beginning to understand how narrative can be an effective way in which to express yourself and your own feelings. They are able to write cohesively, use transitional phrases and move between periods of time with ease.

Experienced writers are beginning to view their role as writer in similar ways to that of a film director or camera-man, panning their words across the screen to reveal to their reader what is occurring. Their settings are beginning to be written in such a way that they become additional characters in their own stories. They begin to pay particular attention to their openings and endings and will revise these repeatedly, until they appear just how they want them.

Children's writing at this stage really begins to be informed heavily by their reading choices, and their writer's voice and personality is beginning to show. Children may consciously or subconsciously begin to place themselves or the people they know in their characters. They will also begin to experiment with creating original characters and providing them with original names, using dialogue appropriately to push the story forward or to reveal important messages about their character.

Experienced writers can use 'showing' or descriptive detail effectively. They will even begin using rhythm, rhyme, alliteration and other sound effects appropriately and perhaps unconsciously. They have stamina for writing but at times write pieces which are too long and rambling. However, they are often reluctant to cut these pieces down during the revision and editing stages of the writing process.

Writers who show a high degree of self-reliance, confidence and assurance in their writing

Advanced writers who show a marked degree of maturity and independence in their writing

Your independent and advanced writers begin to complain that the planning grids are quite limiting and consequently want to devise their own way of planning that gives them more freedom. They are likely to use their personal writing project book to collect notes from their reading about potential characters, settings and plots. They may collect favourite lines, poetic moments, effective dialogue – anything they think one day might be useful to them.

Children at this stage will have their own stance as a writer; they write and then read their own writing with a sense of purpose and audience. They have started to develop their own writing process and ways of working.

These writers will write strong leads / openings as well as genuinely interesting and unexpected endings to narrative pieces. They will choose topics that are honest, have strong feelings and show their personality. They are now casting a wider net and allowing a range of fictional genres to enter into their writing. You will begin to see more examples of realistic, political and historical fiction. They may write on social issues that matter to them either implicitly or explicitly. You may also find they are more subversive and want to push the boundaries of what is conventional within literary traditions.

Independent and advanced writers will readily manipulate fantastic sentence constructions, poetic and figurative language, ideas and words from the books they are reading and use them for their own purposes. There is a real variety in sentence use, structure and type and this is beginning to develop quite naturally. They have embedded the concepts of character development and setting description into their writing habits. This includes creating and sustaining empathy with their characters, using internal reflection and making links between their growing understanding of people and their wider knowledge of the world.

You may well find at this stage of the writing development, that children are writing about children who are older than they are. Their strong characters will produce the most believable plots which will often result in the best fiction in your class. Their stories will usually offer a message or something to think about. They will imitate their favourite writers almost unconsciously. Finally, they are able to use flashbacks, tension, atmosphere, deception, character flaws, symbolism, hint at wider meaning and give clues as to what might happen next. They can also tell more than one related story within a single narrative piece.

Information

Beginning and inexperienced writers

Writers who are beginning to write with some ease and clarity

Beginning and inexperienced writers will often write about the books, TV, films, internet media or games they have been exposed to. Alternatively, they will write about things from their recent past. They may run the risk of choosing an attractive topic but one they know too little about. Alternatively, they will know a great deal about their subject but will assume too much knowledge in their reader, resulting in an unclear text. Their information pieces may sometimes turn out to be more in keeping with personal narrative and vignette.

When conferenced, these beginning and inexperienced writers will typically provide more information about their topic verbally than is shown in their writing. Older children at this stage will often require lots of talk with a trusted adult. These verbal explanations will often exceed their writing ability and they may find putting their knowledge to paper challenging but will be motivated to do so. They will require regular reassurance and praise, maybe after the writing of each sentence. They will use technical vocabulary relating to their chosen topic. They may not always use these in the correct context or assume that their reader will understand these terms without giving explanation.

These writers of non-fiction will find 'chunking' their information into sections difficult. They are likely to throw their information at their reader in a long list of facts, without any kind of orientation for their reader. They will often fail to adequately finish these types of texts.

Fluent and well-organised writers

Fluent writers will know what makes a good topic for non-fiction. They will know that it takes more than simply having an interest in the subject but that you also need to have some depth of knowledge to share with the writing community of the classroom. These children will often write at length about their subject but fail to keep their reader in mind. This will result in a lack of clarity or cohesion. That being said, their opening paragraphs will typically orientate their reader and introduce the subject that is going to be written about.

Fluent writers may begin to play more with modality, picking up on how non-fictions texts are designed in the texts they read in the class library. They may begin to add captioned pictures, diagrams, tables and other non-fiction devices, including bubble writing, 'key facts' and 'did you knows'. They are now able to divide their topic into subtopics and use headings for cohesion. They may also begin to merge non-fiction genres together and so you may see aspects of persuasion, instruction and explanation, as well as information. Their endings will draw conclusions, suggest ways forward or ask questions of their readers.

Writers who show a high degree of fluency and clarity in their writing

These experienced writers are now motivated to ensure that their readers understand their information clearly. They will classify their subject of choice before moving on to discussing its nuances. They are also beginning to include descriptions as well as definitions for technical vocabulary that their readers may not know. Experienced writers may also include quotes or signalling to other information sources. This means that they have collected information from a variety of sources, including personal experience.

Experienced writers may begin to use formal and informal voice as well as figurative language and comparison when describing phenomena. They will take part in writing 'faction' and will begin to naturally mix non-fiction genres together, through hybridisation. They can maintain their focus on their topic, give weight to significant moments and develop their own and others' thoughts on a particular subject. They will also begin to reveal their personal response to their subject, providing personal anecdotes and feelings towards their subject that really bring an extra dimension to their writing. They conclude their pieces well, leaving their reader with a final insight to meditate over.

Writers who show a high degree of self-reliance, confidence and assurance in their writing

Advanced writers who show a marked degree of maturity and independence in their writing

Your independent and advanced writers begin to complain that planning grids are quite limiting and want to devise their own ways of planning that give them more freedom. They are willing to delete the parts of their writing that impede the cohesiveness of their piece and will add content to the writing at the request of their peers or teacher. Independent writers seek the opportunity to play around with non-fiction genres, deliberately turning them on their head in new and creative ways.

Independent writers' non-fiction writing is usually able to lead their audience the whole way, keeping them on track and ensuring that their thoughts and ideas are easy to follow. They can write formally or informally with ease, even within the same piece. They will use examples to imply relationships between different phenomena or to clarify their point. They will also use other sources to back up the points they want to make. They may quote sources and provide a list of references for their reader. They may also show signs that they can analyse and pick apart sources.

Independent writers will reorganise material to improve sequencing. They have complete control over their writing and use subtleties and nuances of language that evoke all the senses and leave their reader genuinely in awe, entertained, thrilled, emotional, persuaded and / or informed, often all within the same piece. Their conclusions will ensure that final insight, potential actions, challenges or implications are all considered by their reader.

Independent writers are able to have their own style and voice within non-fiction writing. They can explain with clarity and imply hidden depths of meaning. This can include using figurative language or personal narrative. They assert their individuality, which is valued by the writing community of the classroom. They constructively resist dominant writing values if they are inconsistent with their personal values.

Memoir

Beginning and inexperienced writers

Writers who are beginning to write with some ease and clarity

Beginning and inexperienced writers will often find memoir the most comfortable genre to write in and they will thoroughly enjoy sharing anecdotes and vignettes from their lives. With this said, their oral retellings will often be far more entertaining than their written pieces. This is because they will still see personal narrative, such as memoir, as recounting, rather than as a type of story-telling. This will often result in 'and then' retellings that which focus solely on who was there and what actions took place when.

When conferenced, these beginning and inexperienced writers will typically provide more information about the story verbally than is shown in their writing or indeed their drawings. Older children at this stage will often require regular oral retelling with a trusted adult. These retellings will often exceed their writing ability and they may find putting these ideas to paper challenging but will still be motivated to do so. They will require regular reassurance and praise, perhaps after the writing of every sentence.

Beginning and inexperienced writers of memoir will feel they have to mention every part of the experience they have decided to write about. This can include mentioning or listing things which are largely unimportant to the story. They find moving between place and time difficult.

Fluent and well-organised writers

Fluent writers can use exemplars and planning grids to plan and write cohesive paragraphs. However, their ideas seem to lead the structure of their writing and as a result, can soon lose cohesiveness. Fluent writers will sometimes choose subjects for their memoirs that are too large for them to control and lack a focus on a diamond moment. For example, children will write about their 'holiday to North Wales' as opposed to a particular significant moment on the trip.

These writers can begin to get tangled in long, complicated pieces that are difficult to manage. This usually reflects their reading habits since they will be beginning to read longer chapter books and so will want to replicate these sorts of stories for themselves. Fluent writers begin to consider their readership beyond their teacher and are now far more interested in their peers' opinions of their writing. Where writers in the earlier stage tend to see their writing as an extension of themselves, by this stage they have a greater need to make their writing work for others. They will often want to write down episodes that will get a response from their peers. They will often 'bounce' onto any writing 'fads' sweeping through the writing community of the classroom. Other children's pieces will spark in them a desire to express an anecdote of their own, on the same subject.

These fluent writers will begin trying out things that they are picking up on from their reading but not always successfully. They will give basic description of settings, particularly in the opening scene, but this may not be sustained throughout a piece of memoir. Their character descriptions will continue to largely rely on physical features. Longer pieces may run out of steam or finish abruptly, due to a lack of stamina or not knowing how to end.

Writers who show a high degree of fluency and clarity in their writing

These more experienced writers can now attend to memoir as story writing. They will consider plot, character development and setting description.

They see their role as a writer in a similar way to that of a film director or camera man, panning their words across the screen to reveal to their reader what is occurring. Their settings start to be written in such a way that they, too, become additional characters in their memoirs. Experienced writers are able to understand that story and memoir blur and that writers will often use artistic licence, bending the truth or using hyperbole to tell a better 'story'.

Their writing really is starting to be informed heavily by their reading choices and their writer's voice and personality is also beginning to show. They may consciously or subconsciously begin to reveal parts of themselves in their memoirs: their hopes, fears and thoughts about their life so far, or even into the future.

Experienced writers can use 'showing' or descriptive detail effectively. They will even begin using rhythm, rhyme, alliteration and other sound effects appropriately and perhaps unconsciously. They will have stamina for writing but at times write pieces that are too long and rambling. Children at this stage are often reluctant to cut these pieces down during the revision and editing stages of the writing process. With their experience, writers will begin focusing on a topic, give weight to significant moments and develop characters and settings. They will readily revise their titles, openers and endings. Their memoirs may begin to reveal deeper significance about the events they are recounting and their thoughts about them.

Writers who show a high degree of self-reliance, confidence and assurance in their writing

Advanced writers who show a marked degree of maturity and independence in their writing

Your independent and advanced writers begin to complain that planning grids are limiting and that they want to devise their own ways of planning which give more freedom. They will have their own stance as a writer; they write and also read their own writing with a sense of purpose and audience. They have started to develop their own writing process and ways of working.

These writers will write strong leads / openings, as well as genuinely interesting and unexpected endings to memoir pieces. They choose topics that are honest, have strong feelings and display their personality. They may well use memoir as the driver for non-fiction writing, including persuasion, explanation, discussion, information and instructional writing.

Independent writers will readily manipulate fantastic sentence constructions, poetic and figurative language, ideas and words from the books they are reading and use them for their own purposes. There is real variety in their sentence use, structure and type, which is beginning to develop quite naturally. They have embedded the concepts of character development and setting description into their writing habits. This includes creating and sustaining empathy with their characters and making links between their growing understanding of people and their wider knowledge of the world. Their memoirs will usually offer a message or something to think about. They will imitate their favourite writers almost unconsciously. Finally, they will be able to use flashbacks and tell more than one related story in a single memoir.

Assessment

You might recognise the children in your class from the descriptions detailed. These descriptions include the *typical* behaviours of both **beginning and inexperienced writers** and of **writers who show a high degree of self-reliance, confidence and assurance in their writing**. You will probably have some of both types of writers in your class, as well as a few who don't quite fit these descriptions. We have grouped these Year 5 writing topics into fiction, information and memoir and have also given some thought as to what you might expect to see in the children's work during the year, as they undertake different kinds of writing. It is particularly difficult to judge children's progress in poetry writing, so we have not included that particular genre here.

Fiction: story writing

The emphasis this year will be on encouraging your young writers to think beyond plot and to move towards character-driven narratives. Children will move beyond simple physical description and begin to think about how characters behave, what and how they think, how they feel and how they talk to others. Children are able, at this stage, to attend to plot, character development and setting description, as they construct their narratives. They can weave their plot, character descriptions and dialogues together cohesively and their settings begin to be written in such a way that they too become additional characters in the children's stories. Children pay particular attention to their openings and endings and will revise these until they appear just how they want them to. Experienced writers can also use 'showing' or descriptive detail effectively.

Information

Children are now motivated to ensure that their readers understand the information in their writing clearly and effectively. They will first classify their subject of choice before moving on to discuss its nuances. They are also beginning to include descriptions as well as definitions for technical vocabulary that their readers may not be aware of. They are also able to use a formal and informal voice, as well as using figurative language and comparison, when describing phenomena. Children will take part in writing 'faction' and will begin to naturally mix non-fiction genres together through hybridisation. They can maintain their focus on their topic, give weight to significant moments and develop their own and others' thoughts and ideas on a particular subject. Children will also begin to reveal their personal responses to their chosen subject; providing personal anecdotes and feelings towards their subject that really brings an extra dimension to their writing. Children begin to conclude their pieces in a well thought out manner, leaving their reader with a final insight on the subject matter upon which to meditate.

Memoir: personal narrative

Children are now able to attend to memoir as story writing. They will consider plot, character development and setting description, just as they do with their fictional pieces. Settings also begin to be written in such a way that they become additional characters in the children's memoirs. Children are able to understand that story and memoir can blur together and that writers will often use artistic licence, bending the truth or using hyperbole to tell an even more enticing 'story'. They will consciously or subconsciously reveal parts of themselves in their memoirs: their hopes, fears and thoughts about their life so far, or the future. As a result, children's memoirs may begin to reveal deeper significance about the events that the children are recounting, as well as their thoughts about them.

The *Power English* characters

The *Power English: Writing* characters model the traits of growth mindset learners and encourage resilience by prompting and questioning children as they work. Appearing frequently in the genre booklets, they are your allies in teaching and discussion, helping to model processes, alternatives and mistakes, and to pose questions. They encourage and support your children, too: they are all hardworking, enthusiastic and unafraid of making and talking about mistakes.

Meet the team!

Determined Dexter is resolute, resilient and systematic. He concentrates hard, always tries his best and he will never give up.

Flexible Flo is open-minded and sometimes indecisive. She likes to think differently and come up with a variety of writing ideas.

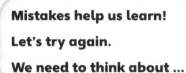

Mistakes help us learn!

Let's try again.

We need to think about ...

Let's try it this way ...

Can we do it differently?

I've got another way of doing this!

I'm going to try this.

I will start by ...

I will share my ideas!

Curious Ash is eager, interested and inquisitive and he loves finding out new things. Ash asks lots of questions but sometimes gets distracted.

What if we tried this ...?

What will my audience think of this?

I wonder if ...

Sparks the cat

Miaow!

Brave Astrid is confident, willing to take risks and unafraid of failure. She's never scared to jump straight into writing and although she often makes simple mistakes, she's happy to talk them through with others.

Supporting beginning and inexperienced writers

Never assume the world is divided into people who know how to write (writers, grown-ups) and those who don't (children).

Power English: Writing is inclusive. All children, regardless of their needs, have something to write about, in terms of memory, feeling, interest or experience. Every child can write, even if it is only mark making. If children can say it, they can also write it. Most young writers do this happily and when asked what their marks mean can often explain with complete clarity. What stops children from writing is a preoccupation with correct spelling and being required to write about something they do not know much about or are not engaged with.

We acknowledge from the outset that all children deemed as having SEND have their own unique needs and that no two children are the same. However, adjustments can be made to support beginning and inexperienced writers with a range of additional needs. To clarify, 'beginning and inexperienced writers' can be of any age; what we mean is that they are *early on* in their experience of writing. See p35–40 for more details on progression descriptions.

For these early writers, we suggest that the writing process be simplified to the following three stages:

You can expect children's writing process to progress over time as follows:

1. Storytelling -> Drawing and Talking -> Writing
2. Talking -> Writing
3. Moving toward conventional planning, dabbling and revision
4. Planning, revising and basic editing

How to set up a writing workshop for children with SEND

Working alongside an adult

It is important for *all* children to see adults writing for real purposes. By watching and working alongside an adult, children can see that writing is worth doing. It is particularly beneficial for these early writers to work alongside a sympathetic adult co-writer. This also includes taking some time to read aloud and taking part in oral storytelling with these children before they begin writing. Alternatively, an adult can co-write on a computer with the child or allow the child to write at the computer and slowly wean them off these strategies, once they are motivated and ready to write independently. It is important that these children have a reader in mind at the earliest moment in the writing process. This could be their best friend, the class, another class, their teacher or a family member. What is important is that they have to be writing for someone.

Generating ideas

Storytelling

Storytelling can be used either alongside or instead of a drawing activity.

The stories you tell and encourage the children to tell should be about true personal experiences. You can create a really strong bond with all the children in your class by doing this, but particularly in relation to the sorts of writers that you will be working with intensively. These children will soon notice that they also have stories to tell.

When telling stories, particularly with beginning and inexperienced writers, the following ordering will help them learn about the linguistic and genre patterns and features of narrative and memoir.

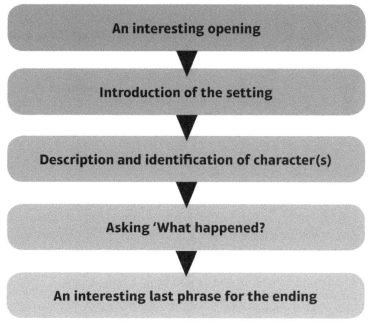

An interesting opening

↓

Introduction of the setting

↓

Description and identification of character(s)

↓

Asking 'What happened?

↓

An interesting last phrase for the ending

Planning

Drawing

All children can tell stories by the time they are at school and most can draw. Children can therefore plan or rehearse for writing by drawing. In our eagerness to see writing on the child's page, it is easy to dismiss these picture stories; but do so at your peril! Drawing a topic immediately allows the teacher and the child to discuss what the drawing is about, teasing out lots of information and then dabbling with key words, phrases or ideas. Writing captions over the picture and labelling the *who, what, where, when* and *why* onto a photocopy of a picture can certainly be seen as an early version of planning and helps set many children up for drafting. Another big advantage to drawing is that it focuses the child's attention on a single moment in time, that 'diamond moment', rather than creating a long repetitive *'and then …'* story or memoir.

Talking

Children will gradually become less reliant on drawing, as time progresses. This is a significant developmental shift. Talking about their ideas will eventually replace drawing them and precedes conventional planning. Encourage children to write down any spoken 'dabbles' onto paper before they 'lose' them. This is a sign of early planning.

Drafting

Something to be tolerant of is the extent of a child's writing stamina.

Spelling

There is little point in learning to spell if you have little intention of writing. **Frank Smith**

Spelling is one of the biggest obstacles for early writers. To limit the impact of this, all children, but particularly those with additional needs, should be encouraged to invent spellings if they need to, whilst drafting their pieces, using whatever knowledge they have of letter-sound correspondences. The important thing for children to realise is that once they know even a small number of letter-sound correspondences, they can invent any spelling they like!

If you can, make available a letter-sound board. Children can then see the letter-sounds displayed, often with a matching picture. Children should also have access to the 1000 common spelling words (see p295–297). Over time, you will want to move the children away from using letter-sound correspondence to counting and writing down the syllables they can hear in the word that they want to spell.

Revising

The earliest sign of a child being ready to revise their work is when they begin to alter their drawings to reflect what they are about to write. Encourage children to alternate between their writing and drawing, making changes to both. Children then further develop their revision skills by attaching extra information, often to the end of their pieces, usually as a result of talking with a peer or an adult. Often this information will not make sense structurally but should be seen as an important developmental step.

Eventually, you can begin to discuss with early writers where their writing is leaving you 'reader hungry'. This is where you can feel your belly rumbling whilst they are reading – because it wants more detail from them to leave you satisfied.

Mini-conferencing

Early writers often require more than most to hear the sentence they say or read repeated back to them. Children have a natural instinct to reply with more information. This is where the revision 'gold' is to be found. After a child says something extra to you, they will often return to their piece of writing and add that information in, for future readers.

Editing

This stage should come last and should not be too overwhelming for the child. Work on tentatively introducing the basics to children, such as capital letters and full stops, using a personalised editing checklist. The aim is to encourage the child to apply these conventions little by little. Notice and celebrate the conventions any early writer can use independently. These conventions are added to a list glued to the inside front cover of the child's writing book. For example:

Things Anna can do:

1. Write her name on her book.

2. Write the title in her book.

3. Write the date in her book.

4. Begin each sentence with a capital letter.

5. Use speech marks.

6. Use a question mark at the end of a sentence.

7. Use a full stop at the end of a sentence.

Publishing

Publishing does not make an appearance in our early writers' process, as early writers often do not like the idea of having to copy out what they consider to be a finished piece. Instead, the chosen final draft can be taken straight to publication after drafting by an adult. When publishing, it is wise to correct the child's invented spellings so that the piece can be read by them and others easily. You should also support a child's writing by asking them to sit in the author's chair and read their published story out loud to the class. To help you, consider enlisting the aid of parent-helpers who are often very happy to help type up and publish children's manuscripts for them. Knowing that one of these helpers will need to understand their transcript gives children extra focus when editing their writing too.

The importance of personal writing project books

Early writers need to be writing more than anyone in the school. Therefore, encouraging a child to write in their personal writing project book is vital. They should be carrying it around with them everywhere and filling it up; often with drawings but sometimes with writing as well . Personal writing project books should be going back and forth between school and home, as home can be a rich resource for facilitating topic choice and potentially allows care-givers at home an opportunity to provide further support with the writing being done at school.

Treasures from home

Personal writing project books can be accompanied by artefacts and pictures from home, including play things. Children can then use dramatic play as a source for writing.

Paragraph piling and sentence stacking

Some children find negotiating the writing process quite challenging. With these children you can make the process more manageable by encouraging them to negotiate their pieces one paragraph at a time. This is where they will draft, revise and edit paragraphs one at a time. This can usually be performed in groups.

This is the same with the process of sentence stacking but instead of composing, revising and editing a whole paragraph, the child goes through this process for each sentence.

Supporting advanced writers

While it is uncommon to have advanced writers within KS2, you do occasionally come across children who have huge experience and skill in the craft of writing. These children need to be developed and supported too. Below are some suggestions you might want to pass on to such writers to experiment with.

I. Create a community of authentic writers

- Create a small peer workshop environment in which you as the teacher can write with other mature, experienced writers.
- Consider ways both home and school writing can merge and influence one another.
- Allow children the freedom to use their own writing processes and ways of producing a final writing product.
- They will need to feel they are living a literate life.

2. Genre experts

Encourage these writers to move away from simply taking part in the class writing project as normal and instead ask them how they could actively hybridise or subversively manipulate it.

3. Connecting their reading with their writing

Collecting: Collecting words, collecting sentences / poetic moments, collecting themes, trying out types of openings, types of endings, collecting metaphors, collecting characters as metaphors, collecting / discussing psychological / philosophical ideas as plots / characters / settings for narrative writing.

Acting like a film director: In narratives, use flashbacks, multiple perspectives / changing perspectives, consider 'camera angles,' using delay, try out different chronology and use of tenses and consider pace.

Reading for pleasure and 'with rigour': Build a reading for pleasure culture in the classroom and home. Provide children with particular books and exemplars that could showcase with particular teaching points and provide 'rigour'.

Developing narrative:

- Help children understand what psychological or philosophical points they want to make through their narrative first, then build or disguise this idea within their characters, settings, objects and events, such as a plot, character and setting that deals with *fear*. Or the philosophical idea that *the ends always justify the means* or *people and the environment must be able to live peacefully together.*
- Give children time to dig deep into the consciousness of their characters. Encourage some of the writing to be character-led rather than plot-led. Children should be doing more than simply making up a character and then trying to explain and authenticate them. They should interrogate their character until they know everything about them and why they do the things they do.
- Know about and use a variety of story arcs.
- Help children appreciate that the narrative is made up of the structural units of 'description', 'dialogue' and 'action'. Children need to be able to develop these units in both an individual way (almost as pieces of poetry or art in themselves) and as part of the collective whole.
- Encourage children to see the descriptions they use as always being affected by the mood of their characters and their present feelings.
- Children can check the variety and length of sentences by actively looking at pace and flow. They don't fall into the trap of 'subject-verb-object', 'subject-verb-object', for example.
- Children's writing could deal with the concrete as opposed to the abstract. It's the difference between *That autumn day* as opposed to *autumn* or *happiness* or someone's *specific* happiness.
- They should be encouraged, at times, to revise their piece multiple times. No aspects should be left untouched or underappreciated.
- Suggest to children that they could write their piece (or part of their piece) from another character's perspective. Remember, character can include settings too. Alternatively, children could try and write it from the point of view of different narrator (1st, 2nd, 3rd).
- Encourage children to move the chronology of their story around. The stories could be photocopied and paragraphs cut and moved around. For example, placing their ending at the beginning of their narrative. Children can also experiment by writing different types of openings and endings (see genre booklets and mini-lessons p253–254).
- Show, don't tell. You could encourage children to cut out words such as *is, was, are* and *were* as these are *telling* words and replace them by *showing* your readers what is happening instead (see mini-lesson p230).
- Be playful and silly with words. Use puns, alliteration and repetition.

A quick note on non-fiction

- Children should seek the opportunity to play around with non-fiction genres, deliberately turning them on their head in new and creative ways. They will take part in writing 'faction' and will also begin to naturally mix different non-fiction genres together through hybridisation.
- Children should classify their subject of choice before moving onto discussing its nuances. They could include rich poetic descriptions as well as definitions for technical vocabulary that their readers may not know.
- Children can begin to use the formal and informal voice as well as figurative language, when describing phenomena.
- Children shouldn't be afraid to reveal their personal response to the non-fiction subjects they write about, providing personal anecdotes and feelings about their subject, which really brings an extra dimension to their non-fiction.
- Encourage children to develop their own style and voice within non-fiction writing. This can include using figurative language, poetry or personal narrative to enhance their piece and the information they want to get across.

Unconfident high achievers

There are children who are mature, experienced writers yet struggle to settle on a piece. These children should be a high priority for daily conferencing. If they have a particularly strong draft, you can encourage them to share it during class sharing time. Encourage the rest of the class to ask questions to give these children the chance to reveal information they know but have failed to include in their piece.

Being a writer-teacher

Teachers who perceived themselves as writers offer richer classroom writing experiences and generate increased enjoyment, motivation and tenacity among their students than non-writers. **Teresa Cremin and Lucy Oliver**

As you may have noticed when reading this guide, developing yourself over time as a writer-teacher will be beneficial to the success of your classroom practice. By becoming a writer-teacher, you will be motivated to feed back to the children in your class. You will be able to use your knowledge of writing strategies and the writing process to help guide children in producing highly accomplished texts. You will be doing this largely through pupil conferencing. Being a writer-teacher does not mean that you only share the product and processes of your own writing but actually join your children (on occasion) whilst they are engaged in the processes of writing. You will feed back to them by suggesting strategies for the children to try, setting process-learning goals and by advising them on their compositions – all in real time. You will partake in this kind of writing and feedback because you will know that it not only helps children write better but also facilitates writing for pleasure.

Why be a writer-teacher?

- Writer-teachers write in the hope of better understanding how to build writing communities.
- In a more traditional way, writer-teachers model and make visible the normally invisible processes writing goes through. This includes showcasing the inner dialogue that writers often undertake whilst composing.
- Writer-teachers write to ensure they can talk with children about writing authentically and from a position of empathy
- Writer-teachers write to gain a better understanding of the writing processes.
- Writer-teachers write to share their own writing learning goals with their class.
- Writer-teachers write to build up a repertoire of useful strategies from which the children can learn too.
- Writer-teachers write to help generate agency and showcase the power of personal writing projects with their class.
- Writer-teachers write in order to give effective pupil conferences whilst children are in the act of writing.
- Writer-teachers write in order to model how writers can use their reading material as inspiration.
- Beyond this, and probably most importantly, writer-teachers write because of the pleasure it affords them.

How to be a writer-teacher

I immersed myself in writing for pleasure, and brought my pleasure into the classroom. The effect was palpable. I saw my lived life become an educative experience. **Doug Kaufman**

- Don't ever assume you can't write.
- Get yourself a notebook. The more notebooks you have, the better, and in a variety of sizes.
- Use a note-taking app on your phone. This is particularly helpful when a moment of inspiration strikes.
- Write down lines or phrases you like from your reading or from the things you hear people say.
- Dabble in your notebook. This means draw, make little notes, write words and phrases.
- Have a moment in the day where you sit down and write something.
- Consider starting a journal. You don't have to write in it every day; only when something significant comes to mind.
- Write up funny anecdotes or episodes that you talk to your friends about.
- Purchase books about writing.
- Join or create a writer-teacher group.

The following tips for writing memoir, stories and poems are useful for setting out on your writer-teacher journey.

Tips for writing your own memoir, stories and poems

Focus on a diamond moment:

a small detail, a brief moment in time which holds significance, the message, the philosophy

Introducing settings:

location, weather, time of day, historical period, treat your setting as an additional character

- **Set up basic philosophical oppositions:** Disguise them, translating ideas into appropriate characters and events.
- **Why do you care about this idea?:** Nothing can be of interest to your reader that is not of vital concern to you, the writer.
- **Be the film camera:** Imagine the moment is caught on camera and is playing in your mind like a film. Use wide view and close-ups.
- **Be omniscient:** Listen in to your characters. Keep a cool distance away as the narrator.
- **Provide proof:** Closely observe details.
- **Use drama as explanation:** Show through action not through narrator telling.
- **The climax should be there to prove something.**
- **You must create a dream:** Create a cinematic film in your reader's mind. Nothing is more important than continuous and vivid detail.
- **Check sentence variety:** Not always subject-verb-object. Use both short and long.
- **Expand one or two 'slots' with modifiers.**
- **Are you being writer-based or reader-based?:** Amateurs are 'writer-based' (thinking of themselves) accomplished writers are 'reader-based'.
- **Read the story at least a hundred times.**

Types of strong opening and ending:

shock, dialogue, action, monologue, question or description

Sensory details:

sight, sound, taste, touch, smell, thoughts

Focuses for poetry:
- imitate / innovate (read and dabble; ask questions)
- suggest things
- give an impression
- express a belief
- personal reflection
- found poems
- borrow voices (pretend your someone else)
- impossible writing

- common made uncommon
- being specific (capture a moment)
- combine sound and senses
- passion and wonder
- metaphor
- playfulness

Planning and dabbling sequence:

1. Gather some general plot ideas.
2. characters:
   - What are you disguising your character as?
   - What would you compare them to?
   - Sight: What do they look like?
   - Smell: What might they smell like?
   - Touch: What is their mood like and what would they feel like to touch?
   - Sound: What do they sound like and what might they say?
   - Action: What might they do and how they might do it?
   - Taste: If your character had a taste, what would they taste like?
   - What do they spend their time thinking about?
   - What is their reputation? What do other people think of them?
   - How do they live their life?
3. setting
4. strong opening
5. potential ending

Ask: what, why, how questions about your character.

Introducing characters based on a psychological / philosophical idea:

physical appearance, speech, emotions, monologue and motive for actions

opportunity to upgrade **nouns** and **verbs**

Painting with words:
- making comparisons
- using personification
- symbolism
- hyperbole
- show don't tell (delete the noun)
- show don't tell (remove is, are, were, was and replace)

- strong verbs
- imagism (you can't say what you think or feel – you have to describe)

Working with sounds:
- alliteration
- repetition

Writing sequence:

1. strong opening
2. opening paragraph (grab – set up questions)
3. character / settings – described when introduced
4. descriptions based on character mood
5. use chunks: action, dialogue / monologue, description, work your way back from your story's climax or moving forward from an initial situation

Power English: Writing resources

Teacher guide

This teacher guide is a handbook to guide, support and inspire your day-to-day teaching. Clear and concise, your teacher guide will help you make the best possible use of every individual lesson. It also provides wrap-around professional development, enhancing your own subject knowledge and helping you to develop your own confidence as a writer-teacher.

There is a teacher guide for every year group, with project- and lesson-level guidance and support.

There are ideas about things you might see in children's writing, such as where children might start to hybridise two genres.

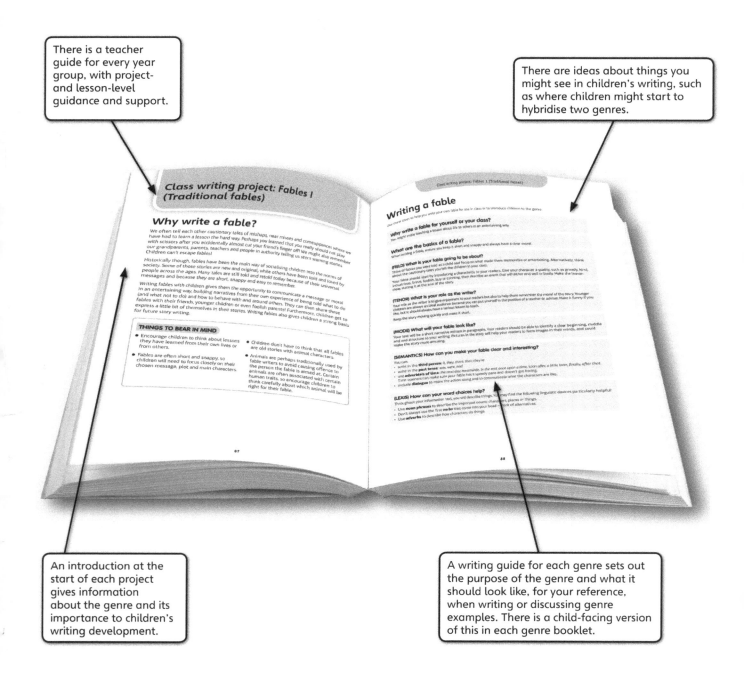

An introduction at the start of each project gives information about the genre and its importance to children's writing development.

A writing guide for each genre sets out the purpose of the genre and what it should look like, for your reference, when writing or discussing genre examples. There is a child-facing version of this in each genre booklet.

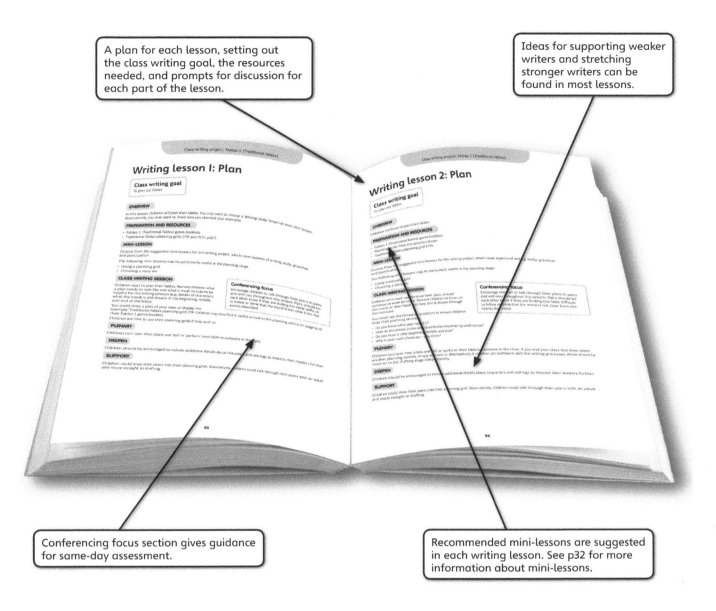

A plan for each lesson, setting out the class writing goal, the resources needed, and prompts for discussion for each part of the lesson.

Ideas for supporting weaker writers and stretching stronger writers can be found in most lessons.

Conferencing focus section gives guidance for same-day assessment.

Recommended mini-lessons are suggested in each writing lesson. See p32 for more information about mini-lessons.

Writing Tips and Tricks cards

The Writing Tips and Tricks cards are designed to be a quick reference tool to give children usable techniques and strategies when they are writing. There are tips for spelling, punctuation and grammar.

Each card is double-sided. The first side gives a definition of the relevant spelling pattern, punctuation mark or grammatical term. The second side explains, with examples, the function of the item and why you might want to use it in your writing.

Online subscription

The online subscription will give you access to essential pupil-facing resources and the online interactive planner.

Genre booklets

Genre booklets provide children with the tools they need to produce successful writing in each genre.

- The opening page sets out the essentials for writing in each genre.
- There are examples to inspire children's own writing, with prompt questions for discussion.
- There are genre-specific ideas for each step of the writing process, from generating ideas to revision checklists.
- The reassuringly consistent format means they can be used independently by children for personal writing projects, as well as during class writing time.
- The online resource can be printed or allocated for children to access in their own time.

Online interactive planner

Every lesson and mini-lesson plan can be found in the online subscription, organised using the online interactive planner. The online interactive planner allows you to create your own editable yearly, medium-term and daily plans.

- You can reorder or remove projects to fit in with your yearly timetable.
- Within each project, you can reorder or remove lessons according to the needs of your class.
- Within each writing session, you can decide whether the recommended mini-lesson will suit the needs of your writers or choose from nearly 100 alternatives covering all stages of the writing process.
- All plans can be downloaded and edited.

Interactive teaching resources (ITRs)

The online lesson plans also link to the interactive teaching resources you will need for that lesson or mini-lesson.

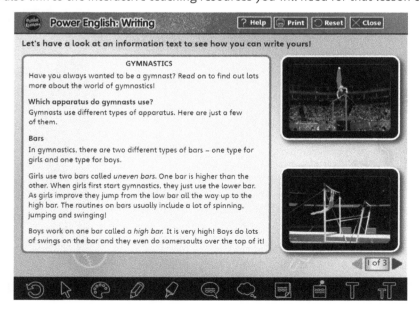

Videos

To encourage children to make links between the writing they do in the class writing project and published writers, each class writing project starts with a video of a writer talking about why they write in that particular genre, who they are writing for, what they enjoy about it and how they overcome challenges.

Getting started with *Power English: Writing*

As you prepare to put *Power English: Writing* into action, you might find the tips and advice below helpful.

STEP 1: Train up!

A practical, up-front professional development course will give you and your team a brilliant head-start as you begin your *Power English: Writing* journey. You will learn more about the pedagogy, how it works and why.

STEP 2: Check out the online interactive planner

Take a look at the yearly and medium-term plans, adapting them if necessary to match the pace of your class.

STEP 3: Read through the orientation unit

Take some time to look at the first class writing project you will embark upon – usually the orientation unit. Think about gathering ideas for your own pieces of writing to share with the class as a writer-teacher.

STEP 4: Prepare for your first lesson

Familiarise yourself with the class writing goal, discussion questions and the resources you will need. The lesson plans in the teacher guide and online offer tips and ideas for individual lessons to help you guide discussion and support and stretch where needed.

STEP 5: Teach and reflect

Deliver your lesson – and enjoy!

Afterwards, reflect on how the lesson went. Which children might benefit from a pupil conference the next day? What mini-lessons might be helpful to teach later in the week?

Useful books

To find out more about being a **writer-teacher**, read these:

- Elbow, P., (1998) *Writing Without Teachers,* London: Oxford University Press
- Fletcher, R., (2011) *Mentor Author, mentor texts: short texts, craft notes and practical classroom uses,* USA: Heinemann
- Locke, T., (2015) *Developing Writing Teachers,* London: Routledge
- Provost, G., (1985) *100 ways to improve your writing,* USA: Mentor Texts
- Wrigley, S., Smith, J., (2015) *Introducing teachers' writing groups,* London: Routledge

To find out more about the **writing process and self-regulation**, read these:

- DeMile, T., (2008) *Making Believe On Paper: Fiction Writing With Young Children,* USA: Heinemann
- Fletcher, R., (2000) *How Writers Work: Finding a process that works for you,* USA: Harper Collins
- Harris, K. R., and Graham, S., (1996) *Making the Writing Process Work: Strategies for Composition and Self-Regulation,* Brookline, Massachusetts: Brookline Books
- Horn, M., (2007) *Talking, Drawing, Writing: Lessons For Our Youngest Writers,* USA: Stenhouse Publishers
- Jacobson, J., (2010) *No More 'I'm Done!',* USA: Stenhouse Publishers

To find out more about **personal writing project books**, read this:

- Dyson, A.H., (1997) *Writing Superheroes: Contemporary Childhood, Popular Culture and Classroom Literacy,* New York: Teachers College Press
- Graham, L., Johnson, A., (2003) *Children's Writing Journals,* Royston: United Kingdom Literacy Association

To find out more about the **writing workshop** approach, read these:

- Atwell, N., (2014), *In the middle,* USA: Heinemann
- Calkins, L., (1998) *The art of teaching writing,* Portsmouth, NH: Heinemann
- Graves, D., (1983) *Writing: Teachers & Children At Work,* USA: Heinemann
- Fletcher, R., (2001) *Writing Workshop: The Essential Guide,* USA: Heinemann
- Harwayne, S., (2001) *Writing Through Childhood: Rethinking Process and Product,* Portsmouth: Heinemann
- Loane, G., (2016) *Developing young writers in the classroom: I've got something to say,* London: Routledge

To find out more about **pupil conferencing**, read these:

- Anderson, C., (2000) *How's It Going?,* USA: Heinemann
- Fisher, R., Myhill, D., Jones, S., Larkin, S., (2010) *Using Talk To Support Writing,* London: SAGE
- Kaufman, D., (2000*) Conferences and conversations: Listening to the literate classroom,* USA: Heinemann
- Rosen, M., (1998) *Did I hear you write?,* UK: Five Leaves Publications

To find out more about **building a community of writers**, read these:

- Cremin, T., Myhill, D., (2012) *Creating Communities Of Writers,* London: Routledge
- Graves, D., (1991) *Build A Literate Classroom,* USA: Heinemann
- Wray, D., Beard, R., Raban, B., Hall, N., Bloom, W., Robinson, A., Potter, F., Sands, H., Yates, I., (1988) *Developing Children's Writing,* Leamington Spa: Scholastic

To find out more about **how reading and writing can connect**, read these:

- Cremin, T., (2014) *Building Communities Of Engaged Readers: Reading For Pleasure,* London: Routledge
- Harwayne, S., (1992) *Lasting Impressions: Weaving Literature In The Writing Workshop,* USA: Heinemann
- Heller, M., (1999) *Reading-Writing Connections: From Theory To Practice,* London: Routledge
- Rosen, M., (2018) *Writing For Pleasure,* London: Michael Rosen

To find out more about **the teaching of writing**, read these:

- Chamberlain, L., (2018)(2nd Ed) *Inspiring Writing in Primary School,* London: SAGE
- Cremin, T., Myhill, D., (2012) *Creating Communities Of Writers,* London: Routledge
- DfE (2012) *What is the research evidence on writing?* Education Standards Research Team, London: Department for Education
- Dombey, H., (2013) *Teaching Writing: What the evidence says UKLA argues for an evidence-informed approach to teaching and testing young children's writing,* Leicester: UKLA
- Ings, R., (2009) *Writing Is Primary: Final research report,* London: Esmee Fairbairn Foundation

To find out more about the teaching of **genre**, read these:

- Martin, J., Rose, D., (2008) *Genre relations: Mapping culture,* Sheffield: Equinox Publishing
- Tompkins, G. E., (2011) *Teaching writing: Balancing process and product,* Upper Saddle River, NJ: Merrill

To find out more about **writing-study**, read these:

- Atwell, N., (2002) *Lessons That Change Writers,* USA: Heinemann
- Anderson, J., Dean, D., (2014) *Revision Decisions,* USA: Stenhouse Publishers
- Anderson, J., (2007) *Everyday editing,* USA: Stenhouse Publishers

- Fletcher, R., Portalupi, J., (2007)(2nd Ed) *Craft Lessons*, USA: Stenhouse Publishers
- Graves, D., (1989) *Investigate Nonfiction*, USA: Heinemann
- Harris, K.R., Graham, S., Mason, L., Friedlander, B., (2008) *Powerful Writing Strategies For All Students*, USA: Brookes Publishing
- Heard, G., (2014) *The revision toolbook: teaching techniques that work*, USA: Heinemann
- Serravallo, J., (2017) *The Writing Strategies Book: your everything guide to developing skilled writers*, USA: Heinemann

To find out more about the teaching of **grammar**, read these:

- Anderson, J., (2005) *Mechanically Inclined*, USA: Stenhouse Publishers
- Bearne, E., Reedy, D., (2013) *Teaching Grammar Effectively in Primary Schools*, London: UKLA
- Coffin, C., Donohue, J., North, S., (2009) Exploring English Grammar, London: Routledge
- Crystal, D., (2004) *Making Sense Of Grammar*, UK: Longman

To find out more about **teaching poetry**, read these:

- Graves, D., *Explore Poetry*, USA: Heinemann
- Heard, G., (1998) *Awakening the* heart, USA: Heinemann
- Rosen, M.,(2016) *What Is Poetry? The essential guide to reading and writing poems*, London: Walker Books
- Brownjohn, S., (1980) *Does it have to rhyme? Teaching children to write poetry*, UK: Hodder Education

To find out more about **memoir writing**, read these:

- Bennett, A., (2014) *Writing Home*, London: Faber & Faber
- Fletcher, R., (2007) *How to write your life story*, USA: Collins
- Moses, B., (2016) *Keeping Clear Of Paradise Street*, UK: Candy Jar Books

To find out more about **creating publishing houses**, read this:

- Heffernan, L., (2017) *Back And Forth: Using An Editor's Mindset To Improve Student Writing*, USA: Heinemann

Introducing *Power English: Writing*

The *Power English: Writing* orientation unit is intended to ensure that children are conversant with every stage of the writing process and prepares them to undertake their first personal writing project of the year. This unit looks to build on the good work undertaken in Lower Key Stage 2 where there was tighter control and instruction over children's implementation of the writing processes. Children at this time were carefully directed through the techniques and routines of planning, dabbling, drafting, revising, editing and publishing. The aim of this unit, and for Upper Key Stage 2 more generally, is to give children greater freedom, flexibility and opportunity in their writing, so that they can gain a deeper understanding of their *own* writing processes, as well as allowing them to write in a way that best suits them.

In Years 5 and 6, the majority of the children you will be working with would be classed as fluent or experienced writers. As such, they will have naturally started to develop their own writing style and processes and, over the past two years, will have been writing in a more fluid and recursive way; particularly in their personal writing projects. For example, children may skip the planning stage and instead go straight into writing a draft; spending more time revising it once an early sketch is written out. Other children, however, may prefer to construct their pieces slowly, attending to revision and editing as they work through each piece of writing. Different writing styles will suit different writers in your class. We know from research that once children are experienced enough with the writing processes, having freedom over how they write and complete their writing projects is of huge personal and developmental benefit to them and should be encouraged throughout Upper Key Stage 2. This orientation unit also reacquaints children with the features, techniques and resources related to *Power English: Writing* more generally. Additionally, it gives you time to set up your class publishing houses and to choose your class cause or charity for focus this year.

Week 1: Experimenting with writing styles

Lesson 1 focuses on generating new ideas for writing. Children will continue to generate and use their own ideas for writing throughout the year. It is useful and important for them to collate a bank of ideas that they can draw on and add to at any time.

In **Lesson 2**, children learn about the importance of clarity in their writing from the outset, as well as the importance of considering the purpose and audience for any piece of writing. The children will not be expected to focus on any specific features of genre at this stage. Deciding on the form that the writing will take usually follows on from establishing the purpose and the audience for the piece of writing. Children will learn how to use the writing wheel (p272) which explains the main purposes for writing and the different genres that are available to them when generating ideas.

In **Lesson 3**, you and the class will discuss which you think your preferred writing styles are. You can talk about the perceived advantages and disadvantages of the different writing styles, such as *discoverer, planner, drafter, paragraph piler* and *sentence stacker.* Children then choose a style that they ordinarily don't use but would like to try out for their next personal writing project.

In **Lesson 4**, children reacquaint themselves with the technique of locating the diamond moment within a piece of writing. Using this metaphor early on in the writing process really helps children to understand the importance of refining their ideas and the significant impact that this has on the planning and composition of all the writing that they do, regardless of genre. To expand upon this metaphor for Upper Key Stage 2, you can also begin to discuss with children the idea that writers should ask themselves *'who cares* and *so what?'* in relation to each piece of writing.

Lesson 5 focuses on setting children's distant goals. You will explain that the children now have nine writing sessions in which to publish at least one of their personal writing projects. This will be useful early practice of the way class writing projects will run this year and next. In Year 5, once class writing projects have been introduced, discussed and product goals have been set in the traditional way, it will now be up to the children to ensure that they have their writing published by the deadline or publication day!

Week 2: Readying your writing for publication day!

The second week of the orientation unit focuses on children navigating themselves through their writing process, in time for publication day. Children will have the opportunity to make their writing publicly available, to be enjoyed by others which can be very motivating for them. If you feel that your children need to revisit any of stages in the writing process, there are a number of mini-lessons available which cover all aspects of the process and can be found on pages 214–271.

This week also includes a lesson on what makes a good pupil conference with a teacher, as well as how children can support and teach each other, as peers. This lesson also gives you as a teacher, the opportunity to set out your expectations for behaviour when peers are conferencing with the teacher.

Week 3: Creating a community of writers

During the third week of the orientation unit, children will be encouraged to think more deeply about the publishing process. They will have the opportunity to set up a class publishing house that will provide them with the sense that they are part of a community of writers from the beginning of the school year. This sense of community can be built on as time progresses. Children will think about particular causes that they might want to champion and how that might impact on the type of writing that they publish this year.

Writing lesson I: Generating ideas for personal writing projects

> ## Class writing goal
> To generate our own ideas for writing

OVERVIEW

In this lesson, children will learn about one particular way of generating their own writing ideas, using an ideas heart.

PREPARATION AND RESOURCES

- Use an ideas heart (ITR)
- Ideas heart template (ITR and PCM, p275)
- Ask yourself … (PCM, p280)
- Flip-chart paper

You may find the following books particularly helpful and you should consider making them available in your class library:

- *My Map Book* by Sara Fanelli
- *You Have To Write* by Janet S. Wong
- *Nothing Ever Happens On 90th Street* by Roni Schotter
- *Ralph Tells A Story* by Abby Hanlon
- *You Wouldn't Want to Live Without Books* by Alex Wool

STUDY

Explain to children that much of the writing they will be doing this year will be generated from their own ideas and experiences. Clarify that there are two main types of writing projects they will encounter in class:

- class writing projects: during which children will learn about a particular genre and begin to write in that same genre
- personal writing projects: during which children can write about whatever they like in any genre they choose.

Display the 'Use an ideas heart' ITR on the whiteboard. Explain to children that creating a collection of all of the things that are important to them in and around an outline of a love heart is one technique they can use to generate ideas for their own writing projects. Tell them that they will be making their own ideas hearts that they can add to during the course of the year, so that they always have a place to refer to for ideas.

Display the blank 'Ideas heart template' ITR on the whiteboard or draw a heart on a flip-chart. Begin to write your own ideas in and around the heart, verbalising the following kinds of questions as you do so.

- *What do I like? What is important to me in my life? People? Places? Animals? Objects? Things I do? Interests? Hobbies?*

Model moving from the general to the specific: *Which particular place, person, animal, book?* and write them in your heart. Tell children that asking these questions will help their ideas to flow.

Hand out copies of 'Ask yourself …' (PCM, p280). Children can use these questions as prompts for their ideas hearts.

DISCUSS

Using a new blank heart on the whiteboard or flip-chart, create a whole-class ideas heart, asking the class to contribute ideas, considering the same questions modelled in the first part of the lesson.

CREATE

Once children are confident in the concept of an ideas heart, they can then create their own ideas hearts by using the 'Ideas heart template' (PCM, p275) or by drawing their own heart. Encourage children to think more deeply about the ideas that they have already placed in their hearts, by adding more specific details to them.

> ### Conferencing focus
> Encourage children to request a conference with you if they struggle to generate ideas. Prompt children further by asking:
> - *Can you remember something you have done or someone you have seen recently that has stayed in your mind?*
> - *Why have you remembered this event or those people?*

PLENARY

Children share some of their ideas hearts with the class and describe where the ideas came from.

SUPPORT

If children have difficulty writing down their ideas, encourage them to draw their ideas instead, or have someone write down their ideas for them.

Writing lesson 2: Thinking about audience, purpose and genre

Class writing goal

To discover different writing genres and the importance of audience and purpose when writing

OVERVIEW

In this lesson, children will learn about different writing genres as well as the importance of audience and purpose in all the writing that they do.

PREPARATION AND RESOURCES

- Children's completed ideas hearts from the previous lesson
- Class ideas heart from the previous lesson
- Audience, purpose, genre (ITR)
- Writing wheel (ITR and PCM, p272)

STUDY

Display the 'Writing wheel' ITR. Explain to children that it will help them to make important decisions about their personal writing projects, such as:

- **Audience:** explain to children that all writing needs an audience, even if they are only writing for themselves. Knowing who their readers are going to be can really help them to write in a particular way.
- **Purpose:** explain that there are many reasons for writing. Encourage children to read the list of purposes on the writing wheel and talk about them as a class.
- **Genre:** explain to children that on the outside of the wheel are listed all the different types of genres that children could use in their own writing. Some of the genres will be completely new and others will be familiar to them. Explain that sometimes they can mix up the genres to create a hybrid (a mix of genres) such as a persuasive poem or a fictional story to help inform your readers about something.

Model how children can decide on a purpose, an audience and a genre for their own personal writing project, using one of the ideas from your example ideas heart or the example detailed on the 'Audience, purpose, genre' ITR.

DISCUSS

Ask children to discuss in pairs how they could develop one of the ideas on the class heart using the 'Writing wheel' ITR. Record the discussions on a flip-chart to remind children how writing is shaped by audience, purpose and genre.

CREATE

Explain to the class that they will now use their own ideas heart and the 'Writing wheel' ITR to make a list of ideas for their future personal projects, detailing the purpose, audience and potential genre. When they have finished, they can share ideas in pairs or in small groups.

PLENARY

Children share with the class how they developed one of their ideas using the writing wheel.

DEEPEN

Encourage children to think about how they might use a hybrid (a mix) of different genres to communicate their ideas more effectively in their writing projects.

SUPPORT

Some children may benefit from receiving additional encouragement to share their ideas.

Conferencing focus

Encourage children to talk through their ideas with you and ask specific questions of them, to ensure that they are generating a range of ideas for writing projects, such as:

- *Which idea appeals to you the most? Why?*
- *Do you have a specific reader in mind?*
- *What would you like your reader to get from your piece of writing?*

Writing lesson 3: Choosing a writing style

Class writing goal
To try out a writing style we don't normally use

OVERVIEW

Children will look at different approaches to the writing process and choose a style they don't normally use.

PREPARATION AND RESOURCES

- Children's ideas lists from the previous lesson
- Different ways to plan (ITR)
- Writing wheel (ITR and PCM, p272)
- Planning grids (ITR and PCMs, p288)
- Upper KS2 editing checklist (ITR and PCM, p273)

STUDY

Explain to children that this year they are going to have more choice and control over how they write both their class and personal writing projects.

Show children the 'Different ways to plan' ITR. Children should be able to recognise their preferred way of writing when they have written their personal writing projects in the previous two years. Explain to children that, for this particular personal writing project, they are going to choose a writing style that they haven't tried before because they may find that they like it and want to use it in the future or that it offers them something to think about in their writing tasks for this year.

Explain to children that they are going to be given a 'distant goal'. This means they will be told how many writing sessions they have to complete and hand in a published piece of writing. They will be given these distant goals throughout Years 5 and 6 for all class writing projects. Explain to children that, including today's lesson, they will have nine writing sessions in total, in which to publish at least one personal writing project. Children should consider this a practice run for how class writing projects will run throughout Year 5.

Top tip
This year, you might want to consider having pots somewhere in the class labelled 'generating ideas and dabbling', 'planning', 'drafting', 'paragraph pilers and sentence stackers', 'revising', 'editing', and 'publishing'. Children can move their named lolly stick from pot to pot depending on where they are in the writing process. This allows you to see who is on track to reach the writing deadline.

DISCUSS

In pairs, children discuss what their usual or preferred writing style is and what writing style they are going to try out for this personal writing project.

- *Who is going to be a discoverer?*
- *Who is going to be a planner?*
- *Who is going to be a drafter?*
- *Who is going to be a paragraph piler? What resources will you need?*
- *Who is going to be a sentence stacker? What resources will you need?*

CREATE

Using one of the ideas that they developed in the previous session, children begin to work on their piece of writing. Make sure planners have access to planning grids for their chosen genre.

Ensure paragraph pilers and sentence stackers have access to revision and editing checklists.

Conferencing focus
As children are writing, conference with individuals who need support and also with those who request a conference.

PLENARY

Children share with you and the rest of the class how their writing tasks have progressed today and how they have found trying out a new writing style.

Writing lesson 4: Finding the diamond moment

> ## Class writing goal
> To learn how to identify our diamond moments

OVERVIEW

Children will learn how to refine their ideas to ensure that their piece of writing is focused.

PREPARATION AND RESOURCES

- Children's plans from previous lesson
- Diamond moment (ITR)
- Writing wheel (ITR and PCM, p272)

STUDY

Explain to children that they might have lots of ideas for one topic but that it is important to focus on just one area of the topic, to avoid confusing your reader.

Encourage children to imagine themselves finding a diamond within a pile of rocks. Explain that this is a bit like finding one idea from all their ideas that shines out the most. They will need to observe this one idea (or diamond moment) carefully, then really focus on and develop it within their writing. Invite children to try to find the diamond moment in the plan that you modelled for them in the previous lesson. Encourage them to find the most important part of that idea so that it can be given the most amount of attention.

DISCUSS

Display the 'Diamond moments' ITR on the whiteboard. Children look at some examples of writing and in pairs or small groups discuss where they think the diamond moment is in each piece of writing.

CREATE

Children continue to plan their piece of writing keeping their diamond moment in mind. If children complete the plan before the end of the lesson, encourage them to develop even more ideas for their writing, using the 'Writing wheel' ITR.

PLENARY

Invite children to talk briefly about their planning process. Did they have any problems? How did they solve those problems?

DEEPEN

Children who complete their plan before the end of the lesson can begin developing more writing ideas using the writing wheel.

SUPPORT

Work alongside children to help them identify the diamond moment in their writing if they are struggling locate it on their own.

> ## Conferencing focus
> You could ask children the following questions to help them locate the diamond moment in their writing:
> - *Have you decided what your diamond moment is going to be?*
> - *So your plan so far is … . Do you want to add or take anything away?*
> - *What is the one event, thing or topic that you are going to write about?*
> - *What is the most important part of the writing that you are going to focus your attention on?*

Writing lesson 5: Drafting our writing projects

Class writing goal
To draft our writing projects

OVERVIEW

Children will learn about the rules for drafting their writing, the different kinds of drafters they might be, and how to create their own drafts.

PREPARATION AND RESOURCES

- Teacher and children's writing ideas from previous lesson
- Drafting rules (ITR and PCM, p276)
- 1000 common spelling words (PCM, p295–297)

STUDY

Explain to children that they are going to begin drafting their pieces of writing. Display the 'Drafting rules' ITR on the whiteboard and ensure that children have access to a copy of the 'Drafting rules' (PCM, p276).

Emphasise that the main focus when drafting is for children to write down the things that they want to say as quickly and as easily as possible. Model drafting your own writing, observing the drafting rules and talking through the process as you write.

Explain that there are a few different ways that people like to draft, and that children will gradually find out which type of drafter they are.

- **Continuous drafters:** write continuously, rereading and checking their writing frequently as they write. These types of drafters only properly revise and edit their writing when the piece is nearing completion.
- **Paragraph pilers:** like to make sure every paragraph is perfect before they move on to the next.
- **Sentence stackers:** like to make sure that every sentence is perfect before they write the next.

DISCUSS

In pairs, ask children to talk about what kind of drafter they think they might be. Do they like to write everything down on paper quickly or do they prefer to make sure their writing is perfect before they move on to the next section?

CREATE

Children begin drafting. Remind them of the drafting rules and take this opportunity to draft something of your own alongside the children. By doing this, you will be actively participating in the writing process along with the rest of the class. Ensure that children draft their writing on the left page of their English books and leave the right page for dabbling with ideas, revising and editing.

PLENARY

Invite children to read out a section of their draft to the class. Encourage the rest of the class to give feedback and advice.

SUPPORT

Encourage children to refer back to their plans and talk briefly about each section. If spelling is a significant problem and is interrupting the flow, encourage children to say the syllables of the word out loud and write down how they think it should be spelt. For some children, having the list of 1000 common spelling words (PCM, p295–297) to hand is particularly useful.

Conferencing focus

As children are drafting, conference with individuals who need support and those who request a conference. You could ask:

- *What can I help you with?*
- *Can you tell me more about …?*
- *Are there any 'sticky' bits in your writing? Talk me through them.*

Encourage children to use additional support strategies such as sharing their ideas in pairs or small groups, or consulting a mentor text (taken from your class library).

Top tip

You are likely to have many children asking you for spellings. Encourage these children to write down the sounds in the syllables they hear, put a circle around the word to let them know they need to look it up later, and then can carry on drafting.

Writing lesson 6: Drafting our writing projects

Class writing goal
To draft our personal writing projects for deadline day

OVERVIEW

There are six writing sessions before deadline day. Children will learn more about the drafting process and the importance of their audience. They will then continue to work on their personal writing projects.

PREPARATION AND RESOURCES

- Yawny bit (ITR)
- Drafting rules (ITR and PCM, p276)
- 1000 common spelling words (PCM, p295–297)

STUDY

Display the text in the 'Yawny bit' ITR and read out the example piece of writing to the class. Make it clear that the example is a short story with the purpose of entertaining the reader. Explain that a writer sometimes adds unnecessary detail to their writing because they have not always kept the reader in mind. This can make the writing seem boring and a bit 'yawny'.

Look again at the example text and ask children to find the 'yawny' parts of the story. Then ask children to look out for the diamond moment and consider its location within the story. Is it too far into the piece of writing? Why is this a problem? (Because the reader may lose interest if they have waited too long to find it).

DISCUSS

In pairs, children discuss the example story, focusing on any 'yawny' bits they find as well as the location of the diamond moment. Children discuss how this piece of writing could be made more interesting and enjoyable for the audience.

CREATE

Remind the children that they have six writing sessions left to complete their project. Ask them to regularly read though their writing today to see whether they have fallen into the trap of adding a 'yawny' bit.

Conferencing focus
As children are writing, conference with individuals who need support, as well as with those who request a conference.

PLENARY

Children read their drafts out loud to the class and then take questions or ask for advice from their peers. At a later point, read through children's drafts and note any suggestions that you may have for a revision mini-lesson.

SUPPORT

Guide children through the drafting process, referring them back to their plans, focusing on one section at a time. Remind them of the drafting rules and encourage them to guess spellings based on the sound of each syllable.

Writing lesson 7: Pupil-to-pupil conferencing

> ## Class writing goal
> To learn about conferencing so that we can do it for each other

OVERVIEW

In this lesson, children will discuss why pupil conferencing has been so helpful to them in previous years, how it works and why they should start conferencing for each other.

PREPARATION AND RESOURCES

In preparation for this lesson, please read the guidance on pupil conferencing (p26–30).

STUDY

Explain to children that a conference is like a short conversation or a chat. Anyone can have a conference and they can take place between peers as well as between teachers and children. Encourage children to think of any examples of when they have been part of a conference.

DISCUSS

Ask children how their teachers have conferenced them over the past two years. You could use the following questions as prompts for discussion.

- *How do teachers usually start a conference?*
- *Who does most of the talking?*
- *What's the best conferencing advice you have had from a teacher?*
- *What makes a conference a good one?*
- *What sort of questions do teachers ask?*
- *Do you think you could start conferencing each other when you have finished your writing for the day?*

CREATE

Model an effective conference with one of the children, using their current writing project. Ask the class what they notice about the way the conference went. Ask the children what they think constitutes a good conference.

Remind the children that they have five writing sessions left to complete their project. Children can then continue their writing. Any children who feel they are ahead of schedule for the publishing deadline could practise giving conferences around the classroom for others.

> ### Conferencing focus
> As children are writing, conference with individuals who need support and with those who request a conference. For children who are conferencing you might want to give them our child-friendly guide.

PLENARY

If time, encourage children to read their pieces out loud to the class and then allow them to take questions or ask for advice from their peers.

DEEPEN

Start by allowing the more experienced writers in your class to give writing conferences with their peers during this session.

SUPPORT

Give your early or moderately fluent writers a conference today.

Writing lesson 8: Revising our writing

Class writing goal
To revise our personal writing projects for deadline day

OVERVIEW

There are now four writing sessions before deadline day. In this lesson, children will learn about the different types of revision checklists, as well as how to revise their drafts.

PREPARATION AND RESOURCES

You will have read the children's writing before the lesson and prepared some comments about their compositions, to be shared during conferencing sessions:

- Writing drafts from the previous sessions
- Upper KS2 narrative revision checklist (ITR and PCM, p277)
- Upper KS2 non-fiction revision checklist (ITR and PCM, p278)
- Upper KS2 poetry revision checklist (ITR and PCM, p279)
- Tips and Tricks cards

STUDY

Explain to the class that revising is an important part of the process of writing. Children will need to choose the most appropriate revision checklists for their individual piece of writing. If children are writing non-narrative texts, they should refer to the non-fiction and / or poetry revision checklists.

Explain that revising is a normal part of the writing process that most writers go through, and that some writers will reread and improve their drafts over one hundred times. Display the 'Upper KS2 narrative revision checklist' ITR on the whiteboard and explain that all of the checklists have been split up into different sections to make revision easier. Children should do one type of revision at a time:

- 1st reread and improve: what do I want my reader to think? Look at 'sticky' and 'yawny' bits.
- 2nd reread and improve: pay attention to outstanding openings, and powerful and thoughtful endings.
- 3rd reread and improve: can I experiment with some language features?
- 4th reread and improve: can I experiment with some poetic moments?

Emphasise to children that they should be looking at their composition to check that it makes sense, is interesting for their reader and that its purpose has been achieved. Explain that attention to spelling and punctuation comes at a later stage, when editing.

DISCUSS

Using your own draft, model revising your piece for composition and sense, using the revision checklist.

Ask children to contribute ideas for possible revisions to your piece of writing. Use the revision checklist and talk about any changes as you make them.

CREATE

Remind the children that they have four writing sessions left to complete their project. Children can then continue their writing. Any children who feel they are ahead of schedule for the publishing deadline could practise giving conferences around the classroom for others.

PLENARY

Children share their writing by reading it out loud to the class. Invite the rest of the class to say what they liked about the piece. The writer can then either ask for advice, or you can invite children to offer suggestions for improvement.

Conferencing focus

As children are writing, conference with individuals who need support and with those who request a conference. For those children who are conferencing, you might want to give them our child-friendly guide.

Writing lesson 9: Editing our writing

Class writing goal
To edit our personal writing projects for deadline day

OVERVIEW

There are three writing sessions before deadline day. In this lesson, children will learn how to edit their writing using the editing checklist and CUPS system.

PREPARATION AND RESOURCES

- Children's revised drafts from the previous lesson
- Upper KS2 editing checklist (ITR and PCM, p273)
- Editing a piece of writing (ITR)
- 1000 common spelling words (PCM, p295–297)

STUDY

Explain to children that they are now going to edit their revised drafts using the CUPS system. That is: **C**apitals, **U**se of vocabulary, **P**unctuation and **S**pelling.

Explain that editing is a very different process to revising, because editing focuses specifically on correcting spelling, grammar and punctuation. Explain that after all of the hard work that they have put into their writing, they don't want their readers to be put off because of a few spelling or punctuation errors.

Show children the 'Upper KS2 editing checklist' (ITR and PCM, p273). Explain that they will use this checklist to find and correct any transcription errors in their text.

DISCUSS

Display the 'Editing a piece of writing' ITR on the whiteboard or alternatively use your own draft. Use the editing checklist to model the process of proofreading and correcting the text using the CUPS system, reminding children to check each of the CUPS items separately. Make it clear that this means children will edit their work at least four times.

CREATE

Remind the children that they have three writing sessions left to complete their project. Children can then continue their writing. Any children who feel they are ahead of schedule for the publishing deadline could practise giving conferences around the classroom for others.

PLENARY

Children share their writing with the class. Ask the other children in the class to say what they like about each piece of writing.

Top tip

Explain to children that their main focus at this stage is to check for errors and that proofreading for errors and reading for pleasure are two very different processes. Model proofreading for errors in your own writing so that children become familiar with the process. Read each word slowly and carefully. Explain that a useful technique is to read your writing from the end to the beginning. Alternatively, encourage children to leave their writing for a few days and edit it then, so that they are seeing it afresh.

Conferencing focus

As children are writing, conference with individuals who need support and with those who request a conference. For children who are conferencing you might want to give them our child-friendly guide.

Writing lesson 10: Getting our writing 'reader ready' and publishing

Class writing goal
To publish our personal writing projects

OVERVIEW

There are two writing sessions before deadline day. In this lesson, children will learn how to publish their writing and will revisit the writing wheel.

PREPARATION AND RESOURCES

- Children's writing projects
- Writing wheel (ITR and PCM, p272)
- Upper KS2 editing checklist (ITR and PCM, p273)

- Presentation tips (ITR and PCM, p274)
- Tips and Tricks cards

STUDY

Explain that the final part of the writing process is for children to publish their finished pieces and, if they wish, place them into the class library for the whole class to enjoy. This is an exciting time in the writing process as this is when children will see their writing in action, being consumed by their eager readers. It's often a writers' favourite moment.

Remind children that is it important that their handwriting is sufficiently neat and that their writing is accurate so that others can read it. This means including all of their revisions and edits in the published text. Remind children that neat handwriting is important as it allows the reader to read the piece easily and enjoy it even more.

Revisit the 'Writing wheel' ITR and ask children to think again about their intended audience. Who is the writing for? Will they enjoy it?

DISCUSS

In pairs or small groups, children discuss the reasons why they wrote their pieces, as well as discussing the motivation for writers and publishers to publish books and articles more generally.

Write a list of potential places where readers of their work might be found. Where could they leave their published work to be read? Start with places in the school and then consider places they could give their writing to outside of school. Places where people need to wait are always good. Places where books or writers can be found; places where people read magazines or are sat for long periods of time are also good. Write a list together and consider ways in which to encourage these places to showcase their work on their behalf. Who in the community could help?

Display the 'Presentation tips' ITR and hand out copies of the 'Presentation tips' (PCM, p274) as part of the discussion.

CREATE

Remind the children that they have only today and tomorrow to complete their project. Children can then continue their writing. Any children who feel they are ahead of schedule for the publishing deadline could practise giving conferences around the classroom for others.

Conferencing focus
As children are writing, conference with individuals who need support and with those who request a conference. For children who are conferencing you might want to give them our child-friendly guide.

PLENARY

Children share their writing with the class by reading their pieces out loud. Encourage the rest of the class to say something they like about each piece and ask any questions they have.

SUPPORT

Some children may require additional support when publishing their pieces. In this instance, you or another adult could publish the text on the child's behalf.

Writing lesson 11: Publishing our writing

Class writing goal
To publish, perform and share our writing

OVERVIEW

Today is deadline day! In this lesson, children publish, perform and share their writing in a celebration of what they have achieved.

PREPARATION AND RESOURCES

- Presentation tips (ITR and PCM, p274)
- Tips and Tricks cards

CREATE

You may want to have a publishing party and invite friends and family in to celebrate with you. Children should be invited to perform their pieces, read each other's work and celebrate their achievements. You could think about how to make this session feel like a readers' / writers' café, such as by having an 'author's chair' to perform from or playing music. Use the 'Presentation tips' (ITR and PCM, p274) for support.

Conferencing focus

Take this opportunity to discuss your assessment of children's writing and set writing goals for their future class and personal writing projects.

PLENARY

Talk to the children about what it was like to keep to a deadline. What might the benefits be of returning to a piece of writing after a couple of days before revising or editing it?

SUPPORT

Some children may find it difficult to write out their composition again once they have fully drafted, revised and edited it. If those children are still keen to publish their work, you or another adult have the option of publishing it on their behalf.

Writing lesson 12: Setting up our class publishing house

> ## Class writing goal
> To create a class publishing house

OVERVIEW

In this lesson, children will set up your class's publishing house for the academic year.

PREPARATION AND RESOURCES

- Banger Books (ITR)
- Flip-chart paper and marker pen

The following books may be helpful: *How A Book Is Made* by Aliki, *Back and Forth: Using an Editor's Mindset to Improve Student Writing* by Lee Heffernan and *The Best Story* by Eileen Spinelli.

STUDY

Explain to children that when publishing their writing and putting it on display in the class library, it is important to think about who uses the library and who will be reading their published material.

Encourage your class to think about what a library stands for and who will be using it. What sort of texts do they want to publish for each other?

Talk through the processes a writer goes through before publishing, and explain the role of a 'commissioning editor':

- A writer creates a piece of writing and sends their revised and edited text to a commissioning editor.
- The commissioning editor reviews the piece of writing and provides comments on how the text could be improved.
- Once the text is finalised, it is designed with covers and pictures added if required.
- The writer's work (their book) is then printed and sent to book shops or published online as an eBook.

Explain that you are the children's commissioning editor and that your role is to be a critical friend who will give support and sort out problems with their writing. You will be looking to push their ideas and writing to its maximum potential.

Ask children to find out which publishing houses published the class library books. Do particular publishing houses publish particular types of book? If necessary, guide children to where they can find this information inside the books. Display 'Banger Books' ITR on the whiteboard. Read the *Banger Books* slogan and mission statement, and look at the logo. Ask children for their comments, opinions and observations.

DISCUSS

Now explain that, as a class, we are going to create our own publishing house which will publish children's writing.

Ask the following questions.

- *What is our mission as a class?*
- *What type of writing is important to us?*
- *What are your favourite kinds of writing and things to read?*
- *What sort of writing do we want to write for each other?*

On flip-chart paper, write the words 'Mission statement'. Ensure children understand that a mission statement is a formal summary of the aims and values of a company, organisation, or individual. Ask children:

- *What should our mission statement include?*
- *What should be some of the criteria for publishing with us?*

CREATE

Children work in pairs or in small groups to put forward suggestions for a name, slogan and logo. Remind children to make sure the logo is something that everyone feels they will be able to draw easily so that it can be added to published pieces of writing.

Cast a vote on the name and the logo of your class publishing house and create a poster advertising it so that it can be displayed in your library.

> ### Conferencing focus
> Throughout this lesson, remind children of your role as their commissioning editor. Ask them what you should be looking for when publishing children's writing using the class publishing house?

PLENARY

Read the class publishing house final mission statement together.

Writing lesson 13: Setting up independent publishing houses

Class writing goal
To set up independent publishing houses

OVERVIEW

In this lesson, children will create independent publishing houses that they will run throughout the academic year.

PREPARATION AND RESOURCES

- Independent publishing houses (ITR)
- Writing folders (one per independent publishing house)
- Flip-chart paper
- Art and stationery materials

STUDY

Children are likely to be very pleased with their earlier work to create a class publishing house. However, explain to them that individual preferences within your writing community might mean that some children do not feel represented by the writing that has been produced for the whole-class publishing house. To tackle this, children now have the opportunity to create smaller, independent publishing houses, established and run by smaller groups of children within the class.

Explain that these independent publishing houses will also need mission statements, names, slogans and logos. Children could use ideas generated for names, slogans and logos in the previous lesson, if they wish. Make it clear that these independent publishing houses need to be unique, so as to avoid encroaching on the publishing ideas and works created by the whole-class publishing house.

Children who don't want to create a publishing house on their own or with some of their writing colleagues can begin work on a new personal writing project.

DISCUSS

Display the 'Independent publishing houses' ITR on the whiteboard. As a class, discuss the examples provided and consider which themes children's individual publishing houses could champion. Ask children to put forward their ideas.

CREATE

Group together children who have expressed similar ideas and allow them time to create their independent publishing houses. Children will each be given the title of joint editor-in-chief for that particular publishing house. Some children may begin the year running a publishing house on their own and this is also fine to do.

PLENARY

Allow children to present their independent publishing houses to the rest of the class, explaining how they came up with the idea, who their readers are likely to be and what sorts of writing they will be expecting to publish this year. Once the children have created their independent publishing house, give each group a writing folder to store published pieces. The cover of the folder is then given the independent publishing house name, slogan and logo.

Conferencing focus

Encourage children to think of any individuals or ideas that they think their whole-class publishing house doesn't represent. Then invite them to use this information to generate ideas for writing that they might publish within their independent publishing houses. If you notice that two or more groups have very similar ideas, join them together. Discuss the mission statements with the groups in your class. Give your opinion on each of their ideas and offer recommendations. Remember to also offer advice for slogans and logos.

Writing lesson 14: Setting up independent publishing houses

Class writing goal

To set up independent publishing houses

OVERVIEW

Children continue to develop their own independent publishing houses in small groups or individually.

PREPARATION AND RESOURCES

- Writing folders
- Art and stationery materials

CREATE

Children can build on their independent publishing houses, working in small groups, in pairs or on their own. Remember, these publishing houses don't necessarily need to centre around a specific genre. Rather they could be about certain themes, interests or hobbies. They will need time to create covers (including the publishing house logo) for their independent publishing house. If children have finished setting up their publishing house, they can continue with their personal projects.

PLENARY

Allow any new or remaining independent publishing houses to present their publishing house ideas to the rest of the class, explaining why they came up with the idea for the publishing house and what sorts of writing they will be expecting to publish this year.

Conferencing focus

Continue to discuss the mission statements of the independent publishing houses. Give your opinion and recommendations. Offer advice for slogans and logos.

Top tip

Children's independent publishing houses will be subject to change throughout the year. Some publishing houses may be disbanded while others may be introduced. You may find that some are suitable for children's personal writing projects but you may also find that they help support class writing projects too. Whatever happens, use them flexibly and creatively.

Writing lesson 15: Finding our class charity or cause to champion

> ## Class writing goal
> To find a focus of interest for the class publishing house

OVERVIEW

In this lesson, children will work together to choose a local charity or cause that you are going to champion as a class for the year. Children might consider the damage plastic is having on the environment, or perhaps they could focus on helping children whose countries are at war.

PREPARATION AND RESOURCES

- Writing folders
- Paper and writing materials to record ideas

STUDY

Children consider the cause that they are most interested in or would like to support during the school year. They may want to support a local or national charity, a local campaign to save a building, an amenity or a landmark. Alternatively, they may want to support a national campaign to improve the quality of life for everyone.

Consider things that the children are passionate about in terms of looking after people, looking after animals or looking after the environment.

DISCUSS

Having generated some ideas and recorded them on paper, children work in small groups and discuss their chosen causes. Use the following questions as prompts for discussion.

- *What are the best ways to give our support to these causes?*
- *What do charities, causes or campaigns need the most? Publicity? Volunteers? Money?*
- *What different kinds of charities are there?*
- *How can we keep ourselves up to date on our cause? Are there any ways that you can look out for news features or events that are related to the cause?*
- *Can we write about our cause in lots of different ways?*

Once several specific ideas have been selected, children can vote for their favourite idea to support.

CREATE

Children decide on a number of activities they might carry out as a class to support their cause. They might consider collecting and writing articles relating to the cause or completing other types of writing about it over the course of the year. Children can then continue with their personal writing projects.

> ## Top tip
> Once the area of focus has been established, allow children to use the class charity in whichever way they wish. This could be through their personal writing projects, but you might want to consider how it could influence their class writing projects too. You may even consider giving the class charity its own publishing house or section in the class library.

Class writing project: Poetry I (Poetry that hides in things)

Why write poetry that hides in things?

This unit focuses on poetry that hides in things. This provides children with an opportunity to showcase sensory detail as 'things' that can often be touched, smelled, observed, tasted, heard and thought about. The things children own, find interesting, or are disconcerted by will also tell them a lot about themselves. This personal connection makes for a great writing project.

Writing about things can lead children to share and suggest something they might have in common with their reader. They might notice the same things or show something in a new light. The familiar can suddenly become unfamiliar.

Children will learn about symbolism. They will understand that the things we hold at a distance or the things we love can be a symbol for something else – once we dig a little deeper for those diamond moments.

Objects often carry within them memories that can be shared through poetry. This project could culminate in an exhibition for families and the local community to visit. The exhibition could be a great opportunity for others to reflect on and reminisce about things from their pasts.

This project also has strong connections to memoir. Children will be able to bring what they have learned about writing effective memoirs into their poems.

THINGS TO BEAR IN MIND

- This writing project should open up a whole new way of writing poetry. Once children have understood the concept that poetry can hide and be found in *anything*, they can bring this idea to all their future writing, including narrative writing. They should describe objects of significance in a deeper way. They should also be able to see that the objects they choose to include in their narratives are often symbols to mean something else. Children can describe people or objects in tune with their character's mood.

- Remember that children may want to write multiple poems during the writing week and build up a collection to choose from when it comes to publishing.

- You may also see that they begin to understand and use figurative language to describe phenomena within their non-fiction pieces too.

- Children will learn that objects can carry revealing things about us and our lives and that these can be shared and perhaps understood by others.

- Children will see that objects are used by writers to carry symbolism, of a much larger psychological or philosophical meaning.

- You may find that you and your class become so immersed in thinking about your objects that you may want to also write memoirs to accompany your poems.

Writing a poem

Use these ideas to help you write your own 'where poetry hides' poem for use in class or to introduce children to the genre.

Why write a poem for yourself or your class?

Poems help you share thoughts, feelings, experiences and dreams, and say things in new ways. Poetry is writing that comes from the heart.

What are the basics of a poem?

Free-verse poems are the best to start with. You don't have to have regular rhythm, line length or rhyme. Best of all, you can play around with words and put them together in any way you like. You can also play around with punctuation if you like. There are no rules, but below are some tips for writing a strong poem.

(FIELD) What is your poem going to be about?

Poems can be about something ordinary, or extraordinary. Try the following:

- Whilst dabbling with your poem idea, write lots of lists of words and phrases.
- When dabbling, write down the feelings you want to express in your poem.
- Try to compare what you are writing about to something else to help you better understand it.

(TENOR) What is your role as the writer?

When writing poems, your aim is to express something or show something to your readers in a new and interesting way. You can write from your own point of view, or imagine things from another point of view – perhaps even the point of view of an object. You role is to express what you have noticed, felt or imagined, and share that feeling with your readers.

(MODE) What should your poem look like?

- Use line breaks or stanzas (groups of lines) to show where you want pauses in your poem. Try out lots of possibilities.
- You can be multi-modal. Combine your poem with a picture; accompany it with music or drama in a presentation.

(SEMANTICS) How can you make your poem clear and interesting?

- Once you've written your first attempt, identify your diamond moment and zoom in on it intensely.
- Explore the most passionate part of your poem – where you reveal the most emotion.
- Explore your use of **strong verbs** because this is where your poem is really hiding.
- **Repeat** some of your favourite words or phrases. Maybe repeat the first and last lines.
- Notice your use of **metaphor** and add detail to it.
- Notice where you are playing around with **sounds, rhythm, rhyme** and **repeated lines**.
- Try out **sound effects** such as **alliteration** or **onomatopoeia**.
- Use **line breaks** or **stanzas** to show where you want your reader to pause. Try out lots of possibilities.
- Move lines around until you get the best effect.
- Let your last line leave your readers with something to think about.
- Give a lot of thought to the title.

(LEXIS) How can your word choices help?

- Use **sensory images** – hearing, touch, smell, sight and taste.
- If it works, use **figurative language**, such as **similes** and **metaphors**. If you like, choose a subject and make it a **symbol** for something else: *the sun – kindness; the wind – loneliness; a sword – courage; an eagle – power.*
- Notice where you've made something not human become human through **personification**.

Genre study I: Introducing the idea that poetry hides in things

> ## Class writing goal
> To learn what our class writing project will be

OVERVIEW

In this lesson children will be introduced to the idea that poetry can be found in anything. They will consider how poetry can make ordinary things seem extraordinary and how objects can tell us more about ourselves or another person.

PREPARATION AND RESOURCES

- Ask your class librarians to display a variety of poetry books.
- Video: 'Why I write poetry about everyday things'
- Writing wheel (ITR and PCM, p272)

STUDY

Show children the video 'Why I write poetry about everyday things'.

The video shows the poet Adisa the Verbaliser, speaking about how he tries to find a unique angle when writing poems about ordinary things. He also talks about one of his favourite poems about ordinary things and how he uses symbolism in his poetry.

Explain to the class that their class project will be to write their own collection of poems based on the idea that poetry is 'hidden' in things and can be found anywhere. Their poems will be about ordinary things with hidden meanings.

DISCUSS

Ask children what they think it means when we say poetry can be 'hidden' in anything and 'found' anywhere?

Discuss the children's thoughts on the video they have watched.

Ask questions such as:

- *Why do you think poets write about ordinary, everyday things?*
- *Who do they write it for?*
- *Where / how do you think poetry can be found?*
- *Can you think of an item / thing / object that has a special meaning to you or tells us something about you?*
- *Do you think you could use symbolism in your poetry?*

Display the 'Writing wheel' ITR on the whiteboard, and hand out printed copies.

PLENARY

Children share writing from personal projects, following the established class sharing routine.

DEEPEN

Read a selection of poems and discuss how symbolism is used. Encourage children to share their own ideas for poems.

SUPPORT

Share your own ideas for finding poetry hidden in things. Explain how something ordinary can be made extraordinary using poetic language. Consider and demonstrate how the same object can be described or viewed in different ways.

PERSONAL WRITING PROJECTS

Throughout the class writing project, once the class writing goal for each session is complete, children carry on with their personal writing projects at their own pace and using their preferred writing processes. See pages 17–19 for more information on personal writing projects and pages 26–30 for more information on pupil conferencing.

Genre study 2: What makes an effective 'where poetry hides' poem?

Class writing goal

To discover what makes an effective 'where poetry hides' poem

OVERVIEW

In this lesson, children will read and discuss a range of poetry that demonstrates poetry is hidden in things.

PREPARATION AND RESOURCES

- Poetry 1 (Poetry that hides in things) genre booklets
- Pre-written exemplar poetry texts (genre booklet and ITRs)
- Exemplar poems created by children from previous years
- Flip-chart paper

> As you develop your confidence as a writer-teacher, you should aim to create your own poem exemplar using the writing project's opening guidance. This should be about something that is significant to you.

STUDY

Children look at and read the poems in your class library, and discuss the following questions in pairs or groups:

- *What did you like about the poems you read?*
- *What ideas did they give you for writing your own poem?*

Children then read and discuss exemplar poetry texts. Ask them to refer to the questions again.

DISCUSS

Explain to the children that the poems are looking at ordinary, everyday objects and giving them new meaning.

In pairs, children discuss the following questions:

- How do you think the poet feels about the 'thing'?
- What do you think the poet might want us to think about?
- How does the poet make an ordinary thing seem extraordinary?
- Do you think symbolism is used and how?
- Which is your favourite poem? What do you like about it?

CREATE

As a class, using the information on page 1 of the Poetry 1 genre booklet, start creating your poster of product goals. These goals should indicate what is needed to publish a great 'where poetry hides' poem.

PLENARY

Children share writing from their personal projects, following the established class sharing routine. Alternatively they could be invited to read aloud poem exemplars they like.

SUPPORT

Share your own thoughts on the poems. Identify poetic language used to make ordinary things seem extraordinary.

PERSONAL WRITING PROJECTS

Throughout the class writing project, once the class writing goal for each session is complete, children carry on with their personal writing projects at their own pace and using their preferred writing processes. See pages 17–19 for more information on personal writing projects and pages 26–30 for more information on pupil conferencing.

Genre study 3: Where can poems go wrong?

Class writing goal
To understand how 'where poetry hides' poems can go wrong

OVERVIEW

In this lesson, children will consider how 'where poetry hides' poems can go wrong and what makes an effective poem. They will look at how 'where poetry hides' poems are about more than simply describing the thing.

PREPARATION AND RESOURCES

- Poetry 1 genre booklets
- Pre-written ineffective poem exemplar (ITR)

STUDY

Display on the whiteboard and read together the exemplar ineffective poem and your own ineffective poem.

DISCUSS

Use the poems to show the difference between simply describing your object and revealing your connection to it.

Write your own ineffective poem using the following as a guide:

- Focus on one 'thing' but just describe it without evoking feeling.
- Don't use strong verbs.
- Don't use poetic language such as metaphors, similes and personification.
- Make it difficult to follow and understand.
- Don't write about why the 'thing' is important to you.
- Don't give the 'thing' any hidden meaning.

In pairs, using your class product goals poster from the previous lesson and the information on page 1 of their Poetry 1 (Poetry that hides in things) genre booklets, children discuss and explain for themselves why the examples are ineffective.

Encourage the children to consider what makes a 'where poetry hides' poem successful or unsuccessful. The poem should evoke feeling / meaning, tell us something about the poet or use symbolism and comparison rather than be a straightforward description.

You could ask questions such as:

- *How do the examples compare? What do you notice about the poems?*
- *How does the poet show feeling or use symbolism?*
- *What lines did you particularly like? Why do you think this is?*

PLENARY

Children share writing from personal projects, following the established class sharing routine.

SUPPORT

Children may want to bring in their own objects of significance – or at least a photo or a drawing.

PERSONAL WRITING PROJECTS

Throughout the class writing project, once the class writing goal for each session is complete, children carry on with their personal writing projects at their own pace and using their preferred writing processes. See pages 17–19 for more information on personal writing projects and pages 26–30 for more information on pupil conferencing.

Genre study 4: Generating ideas

Class writing goal
To generate ideas for our 'where poetry hides' poems

OVERVIEW

In this lesson, children will learn about and experiment with a number of techniques for generating ideas for writing their own poems. They will then choose one idea to use for their class writing project.

PREPARATION AND RESOURCES

• Poetry 1 genre booklets

• Ask your class librarians to display a variety of poetry books.

STUDY

Children turn to page 8 of their Poetry 1 (Poetry that hides in things) genre booklets. Read and discuss some of the techniques used by writers to generate ideas for writing poems.

DISCUSS

In this lesson, you might want to explain that you are going to put on an exhibition of poetry and artwork relating to the theme of 'poetry hides in things' and if possible display some artefacts. You can then invite the local community in to view and discuss their own favourite objects or memories too.

As a class, discuss the following questions:

• Have any poems in the class library given you ideas for your own poem?

• What 'things' give you a strong sense of feeling?

• What 'thing' would you like to write about?

CREATE

Encourage the children to work in pairs or groups to generate their own ideas for 'where poetry hides' poems. You could suggest they try some of the following ideas:

• Close their eyes and write down the first things that come into their head.

• Tell a partner about things that are really special to them and why.

• Make a list of things / items / objects that are important to them and why.

• Make a list of their hobbies and the equipment they use.

• Think about objects they loved when they were younger and simply haven't been able to throw away.

• Think of an object that might be special to their family.

• Create a mindmap of things that are important to them or their family and the emotions they evoke.

• Draw a picture of an object that holds a special meaning.

• Write a list of things they or their family have lost which were special to them.

PLENARY

Children share their chosen idea for a poem using the established class sharing routine.

DEEPEN

Encourage children to discuss with a partner what their chosen object reveals about them as a person or what they might like to compare it to.

SUPPORT

Share your own ideas as a teacher with children. Explain where your ideas came from for your own exemplar poem. Look at and discuss exemplar poems from the Poetry 1 (Poetry that hides in things) genre booklet to give ideas.

PERSONAL WRITING PROJECTS

Throughout the class writing project, once the class writing goal for each session is complete, children carry on with their personal writing projects at their own pace and using their preferred writing processes. See pages 17–19 for more information on personal writing projects and pages 26–30 for more information on pupil conferencing.

Writing lesson I: Plan and dabble

Class writing goal
To dabble with our own ideas for a 'where poetry hides' poem

OVERVIEW

Children dabble, plan or draft their poem.

PREPARATION AND RESOURCES

- Poetry 1 (Poetry that hides in things) genre booklets
- Your own dabblings to share with the class
- Children may wish to bring in the objects that are the inspiration for their poem. Alternatively, they could bring in a photograph or a drawing.

MINI-LESSON

Choose from the suggested mini-lessons for this writing project, which cover aspects of writing study, grammar and punctuation.

The following mini-lessons may be particularly useful at the planning stage:

- Favourite objects
- Seeing things differently 1

CLASS WRITING SESSION

Before you begin your writing week, tell children that they have six writing sessions in which to publish their favourite poems. Remind them of the different writing styles writers often use. These include being a discoverer, planner, drafter, paragraph piler and sentence stacker. Explain that, depending on their preferred writing style, they are likely to be dabbling or drafting today.

Explain to the class that they are going to begin dabbling, expanding on and exploring their ideas for a poem about 'where poetry hides' ready for drafting. Ask children to look at the dabbling information on pages 10–12 of their Poetry 1 (Poetry that hides in things) genre booklets. Encourage children to use mind maps, write lists of words and phrases and draw and annotate pictures of their ideas. Model dabbling your own ideas for a poem.

Conferencing focus

Encourage children to talk through their dabbling or drafts in pairs and with you throughout this session.

You could ask the following questions:

- *What feelings might you want to express in your poem? How could you express these feelings by painting with words?*
- *Could you compare what you are writing about to something else (similes/metaphors/symbolism)? What does 'the thing' remind you of? What is 'the thing' similar to? What could it be representing?*
- *What do you want the poem to say about you as a person?*
- *If the 'thing' was a person, what might they be like?*
- *Can you write a list or draw and annotate a picture?*

If children choose to plan their pieces, they can now do so. Other children may leap straight into drafting their poem. Encourage these children to refer to the drafting rules on page 13 of their Poetry 1 (Poetry that hides in things) genre booklets.

PLENARY

Children who have planned their poem turn over their plans and 'tell' their poem to someone in the class. If you and your class feel they need another planning session, please add one in. Alternatively, if children are confident with the writing processes, you can let them move on to the next stage independently.

DEEPEN

Encourage children to think about how painting with words can best elicit the emotions they are trying to create.

SUPPORT

Show children your own dabblings and discuss them. Encourage children to draw and annotate a picture of their object.

Writing lesson 2: Draft

Class writing goal
To draft our poems

OVERVIEW

Children use the plans they created in the previous session to start or continue drafting their poem. Some children may have finished their drafts at this point and can move on to revising their pieces.

PREPARATION AND RESOURCES

- Poetry 1 (Poetry that hides in things) genre booklets
- Children's dabblings from the previous session
- Drafting rules (ITR)
- Children may wish to bring in the object they are writing about. Alternatively, they could bring in a photograph or a drawing.

MINI-LESSON

Choose from the suggested mini-lessons for this writing project, which cover aspects of writing study, grammar and punctuation.

The following mini-lessons may be particularly useful at the drafting stage:

- A picture speaks 1000 words
- Use the senses

CLASS WRITING SESSION

Explain to children that they are going to begin to draft their 'where poetry hides' poem using the dabblings they created in the previous session. Remind children to use the drafting rules and to look at the drafting advice on page 13 of their Poetry 1 (Poetry that hides in things) genre booklet. Encourage them to discuss their work with a partner as their poem develops.

Some children may have finished drafting their poem at this point and can move on to revising their pieces using the revision information and checklist on pages 14–15 of their Poetry 1 (Poetry that hides in things) genre booklets if necessary.

Top tip
Sometimes it's helpful to suggest that children leave it a couple of days before they decide to revise or edit their pieces. This means they can look at their writing with fresh and objective eyes.

Conferencing focus
Help children to identify and expand on the sensory images in their poems. Can they explore the senses of touch, sight, sound, taste, smell?

Ask children to consider 'painting with words' by using similes, metaphors and symbolism. What can they compare their object too? What effect does this have on their poem?

Suggest that children find their favourite words / phrases / lines. What do they like about them? Why do they get a reaction from their reader?

Ask children to look at the verbs they have used in their poem. Can they strengthen these?

Encourage children to make their poems specific rather than general. Can they identify the diamond moment and focus in on it?

PLENARY

Invite children to share their favourite line / phrase with the class, following the established class sharing routine. Ask:

- *What impact did this line / phrase have on you?*
- *What emotion do you think it evokes?*

DEEPEN

Encourage children to explore the rhythm of their poem. Ask them to practise reading their poem aloud.

SUPPORT

Model and share your own draft with children. Support children to use specific verbs and nouns. Encourage children to write down any words, sentences and phrases as they can revise them into their poems later.

Writing lesson 3: Draft

Class writing goal
To draft our poems

OVERVIEW

Children continue drafting their poems. Some children may have finished their drafts at this point and can move on to revising their pieces.

PREPARATION AND RESOURCES

- Poetry 1 (Poetry that hides in things) genre booklets
- Children's dabblings from the previous session
- Children may wish to bring in the object they are writing about. Alternatively, they could bring in a photograph or a drawing.
- Drafting rules (ITR)

MINI-LESSON

Choose from the suggested mini-lessons for this writing project, which cover aspects of writing study, grammar and punctuation.

The following mini-lessons may be particularly useful at the drafting stage:

- Where poetry hides
- The best line

Top tip

Sometimes it's helpful to suggest that children leave it a couple of days before they decide to revise or edit their pieces. This means they can look at their writing with fresh and objective eyes.

CLASS WRITING SESSION

Explain that children will continue drafting their 'where poetry hides' poem using the dabblings they have already created in the planning session. Remind children to use the drafting rules and to look at the drafting advice on page 13 of their Poetry 1 (Poetry that hides in things) genre booklet. Encourage them to discuss their work with a partner as their poem develops. Also suggest that children read the poems aloud to themselves.

Some children may have finished drafting their poem at this point and can move on to revising their pieces using the revision information and checklist on pages 14–15 of their Poetry 1 (Poetry that hides in things) genre booklets if necessary.

Conferencing focus

Help children to identify and expand on the sensory images in their poems. Can they explore the senses of touch, sight, sound, taste, smell?

Ask children to consider 'painting with words' by using similes, metaphors and symbolism. What can they compare their object to? What effect does this have on their poem?

Suggest that children find their favourite words / phrases / lines. What do they like about them? Why do they get a reaction from their reader?

Ask children to look at the verbs they have used in their poem. Can they strengthen these?

Encourage children to make their poems specific rather than general. Can they identify the diamond moment and focus in on it?

PLENARY

Invite children to share their draft poem, following the established class sharing routine. Ask the rest of the class:

- *Did the poem remind you of anything from your life?*
- *Did the poem remind you of anything else you've read or seen?*
- *What lines or phrases stuck in your mind? Why?*

If you and your class feel they need another drafting session, please add one in. Alternatively, if children are confident with the writing processes, you can let them move on to the next stage independently.

DEEPEN

If children complete their draft, encourage them to begin another poem and explore another idea. They could write about the same object from a different perspective.

Writing lesson 4: Revise

Class writing goal
To revise our poems

OVERVIEW

Children begin the important process of rereading and revising their writing. Focus should be on ensuring that the text makes sense and children have included everything in their plans. Some children may have finished revising their poem at this point and can move on to editing their pieces.

PREPARATION AND RESOURCES

- Poetry 1 (Poetry that hides in things) genre booklets
- Children's draft poems from the previous lesson
- Upper KS2 poetry revision checklist (ITR and PCM, p279)
- Upper KS2 editing checklist (ITR and PCM, p273)
- Tips and Tricks cards
- Reading books

MINI-LESSON

Choose from the suggested mini-lessons for this writing project, which cover aspects of writing study, grammar and punctuation.

The following mini-lessons may be particularly useful at the revision stage:

- First reread and improve
- Second reread and improve
- Third reread and improve

CLASS WRITING SESSION

Conferencing focus

Read children's poems aloud to them so they have the opportunity to hear their own poem, discuss what it sounds like and what they would like to revise.

Ask the following questions:

- *What emotions are you trying to evoke?*
- *What sounds are evident in your poem?*
- *Have you used sensory details? Do you want to share the part you like?*
- *Why not try 'painting with words' on your revision and editing page by using metaphors, similes and symbolism in your writing?*
- *Which is your favourite line / phrase / word? Why do you like it?*
- *Are you happy with the line breaks?*

Suggest looking at word choices. Identify strong word choices together and highlight any words that could be revised.

Explain to children that many of them are now going to start revising their piece of writing, whilst others will be ready to move on to editing their pieces. Remind them that if they have many changes to make they can create a new version opposite their draft in their English book. This is particularly the case for children whose preferred writing process is that of 'discoverer'.

Support children to choose the poem they would like to revise and publish from their collection of drafts. Encourage them to read and reread their poems. Direct children to the revision checklist on page 15 of their Poetry 1 (Poetry that hides in things) genre booklet or display this on the whiteboard. Help them to identify features in their work.

Ask children to use the relevant Tips and Tricks cards to help them with spelling, grammar and punctuation. They can also use their reading books to check the spellings of common words.

Some children may have finished revising their poem at this point and can move on to editing their pieces using the 'Upper KS2 editing checklist' (PCM, p273).

PLENARY

Invite children to share their revised poem, using the established class sharing routine. Ask the rest of the class:

- *Did the poem remind you of anything from your life?*
- *Did the poem remind you of anything else you've read or seen?*
- *What lines or phrases stuck in your mind? Why?*

DEEPEN

Encourage children to strengthen their word choices by being specific with their nouns and verbs.

Writing lesson 5: Edit

Class writing goal
To edit our poems

OVERVIEW

Once children are happy with their revised poems, they move on to editing the text and developing their transcription skills by checking spelling, punctuation and grammar. Some children may have finished editing their poems at this point and can move on to publishing their pieces.

PREPARATION AND RESOURCES

- Poetry 1 (Poetry that hides in things) genre booklets
- Children's revised poems from the previous session
- Upper KS2 editing checklist (ITR and PCM, p273)
- Tips and Tricks cards
- Electronic spell checkers
- Access to online dictionaries
- Thesauruses
- Reading books

MINI-LESSON

Choose from the suggested mini-lessons for this writing project, which cover aspects of writing study, grammar and punctuation.

The following mini-lessons may be particularly useful at the editing stage:

- How to edit your writing for capitals
- How to edit your writing for use of vocabulary
- How to edit your writing for punctuation
- How to check and correct your unsure spellings

CLASS WRITING SESSION

Explain that children are to use this session to edit their poems and prepare them for publishing. Children begin to edit their poems using their editing checklists, along with the relevant Tips and Tricks cards to help them understand the correct use of grammar, punctuation and spelling. Remind children that they can use a dictionary to look up any spellings they are unsure of. They can also use their reading books to check the spellings of common words.

Encourage children to work with a talk partner and discuss their work.

Some children may be ready to publish their poems. Ensure that these children have access to the necessary material and the 'Presentation tips' PCM, p274 or ITR.

> ### Conferencing focus
>
> Encourage children to request a conference with you if they get stuck. Also encourage them to read any 'sticky' bits to a partner to get advice before asking you.
>
> A 'sticky' bit is any bit of writing that doesn't sound right. It sounds strange when read out loud. It confuses your reader. Children are very quick to identify 'sticky' bits. You will notice some recurring themes: verb tense, cohesion, switching of pronouns, inability to identify a pronoun's noun.

PLENARY

Show some examples of thoughtful editing. If you and your class that feel they need another editing session, please add one in. Alternatively, if children are confident with the writing processes, you can let them to move on to the next stage independently.

DEEPEN

Suggest that children use a thesaurus to expand vocabulary.

SUPPORT

You could model editing a poem you have written.

Writing lesson 6: Publish

Class writing goal
To publish our poems

OVERVIEW

Most children should now be ready to publish their pieces and you should be ready to begin assessing their outcomes. Any children who have finished publishing their poems can work on their personal writing projects.

PREPARATION AND RESOURCES

- Children's edited poems from the previous session
- A variety of stationery and art materials
- Presentation tips (ITR and PCM, p274)
- Ask your class librarians to display a variety of poetry books
- A recording device
- You may want to invite families or the wider community to an exhibition of the artefacts and accompanying poems the children have written.

MINI-LESSON

Choose from the suggested mini-lessons for this writing project, which cover aspects of writing study, grammar and punctuation.

The following mini-lessons may be particularly useful at the publishing stage:

- Jot for one week: write the next week
- Ways of publishing

CLASS WRITING SESSION

Explain that children should use this session to publish and present their poems. Refer back to the original class writing goal of creating a collection of 'where poetry hides' poems. Ensure children have access to the 'Presentation tips' (PCM, p274) or that you have the 'Presentation tips' ITR displayed on the whiteboard. Children can take this opportunity to present their writing, adding colour, artwork and photographs.

Some children may have published their poems already and so they can continue with their personal writing projects.

Conferencing focus

Encourage children to explore how they want their poem to look on the page or how they could perform their poem most effectively.

Share examples of how poems can be presented on the page with the class. Ask questions such as:

- Does your presentation reflect the emotion expressed in your poem?
- Are there any words / lines / phrases that you want to emphasise? How could you achieve this?
- Have you considered accompanying your poem with a picture, drawing or music?
- What medium will you use to present your poem? E.g. artwork, handwritten, typed, read aloud or recorded.

PLENARY

Invite children to read their poems aloud or share their work with a partner, following the established class sharing routine. Encourage children to use expression when reading aloud.

You may want to record children performing their poems to play during your exhibition.

Class writing project: Explanation texts

Why write explanation texts?

By Year 5, children will be very familiar with reading and writing information texts. Explanation texts are very similar, but where an information text simply tells you what something is like, an explanation text tells you this and then goes on to explain *how* and *why* things happen. Explanation texts are probably the type of non-fiction that children will read most as they go through school.

Children know how to do many things that their peers or adults around them know nothing about. It can be very rewarding and self-affirming to share this knowledge through writing. Children will become aware that they have expertise of value to pass on to others.

This class writing project will show children that sharing knowledge is often an enjoyable, social and satisfying thing to do. You and your class will begin to appreciate the pockets of 'communities' that make up a writing classroom, with children talking and sharing with others their passions, interests and parts of their lives. This is important not only for children understanding the power of writing to inform but also as a social resource.

THINGS TO BEAR IN MIND

- Non-fiction can and should give a sense of personal presence. Children should be able to show their personality and use their 'voice'. It's important to encourage children to choose a topic they are not only interested in but also for which they have some knowledge to share.

- Non-fiction texts should be kept short. Keep them to a page or a page and a half. Children shouldn't strain for ideas. Rather, they should have to make decisions on what to leave out.

- Children's enthusiasm for this writing project can often result in them wanting to write on too general a theme. Direct them to focus on something specific. They will often struggle with the generality and sheer size of their initial topic ideas. For example, if they choose computer games children will often try to explain how *all* types of computer games work. Instead, encourage them to focus on their favourite computer game – or better still, a particular aspect of this.

- Often children will assume that others hold the same knowledge that they have on their subject. This results in them failing to give enough *basic* information to orientate their reader at the start of their text. They will also often fail to describe technical or subject specific vocabulary.

- You are looking for more experienced writers to not only explain something they know a lot about but also to reveal something of themselves. One way of doing this is for children to infuse their explanation text with aspects of memoir writing, such as beginning the text with a personal note about why the topic interests them.

- Don't be surprised to see instruction, information, memoir and poetry coming together in a single piece during this project.

Writing explanation texts

Use these ideas to help you write your own explanation texts for use in class or to introduce the genre to the children.

Why write an explanation text for yourself or your class?

Every day we explain things so that other people can understand them. This can be something physical in the world (such as geography), things people do, or even an idea.

What are the basics of an explanation text?

An information text tells you what something is like whereas an explanation text tells you this and then goes on to explain *how* and *why* things happen.

(FIELD) What is your explanation text going to be about?

It is best to write an explanation text on a topic you know a lot about. Think: do I know exactly *why* something happens? Or exactly *how* something works?

Your text will do two things. It will:

- tell your reader what the topic is that you'll be explaining
- step-by-step explain *how* or *why* something happens.

(TENOR) What is your role as the writer?

You might need to think about these things:

- Your readers may know nothing about your topic.
- You will probably have to explain the meaning of some special words (**technical vocabulary**).
- You can talk to your reader directly by using the word *you*.

(MODE) What should your explanation text look like?

Your text will be **multi-modal**. This means you will use lots of different modes to show off what you know. Some examples of modes are:

- pictures, photos, diagrams, fact-boxes and headings
- different text sizes and colours.

You may want to use A3 paper and spread your different modes across the page.

Headings might be extremely useful to you. You might want to write down a few possible headings on your plan.

(SEMANTICS) How can you make your explanation text clear and interesting?

You can:

- write in the **third person**, e.g. *it, they, them, their, they're*
- write in the **present tense**, e.g. *is, are, have, be, -ing*.

(LEXIS) How can your word choices help?

Because you will be describing and explaining things, you will find these **coordinating and subordinating conjunctions** particularly helpful. They will make it easy to explain things to your reader.

- **Cause** – *because, so, therefore, even though, but, however*
- **Condition** – *if, then, provided that, as long as, may even, even then*
- **Means** – *by*

Genre study I: Introducing explanation texts

> ## Class writing goal
> To learn what our next class writing project will be

OVERVIEW

In this lesson, children will learn about the explanation genre and will discuss why writers write explanation texts. You will then reveal that this is the next class writing project and that the class will be publishing an anthology of texts to place in the class library and beyond. Children will then continue to work on their personal writing projects.

PREPARATION AND RESOURCES

- Ask your class librarians to start displaying a variety of explanation texts. Ensure that your class library has a rich and varied stock of explanation texts.
- Video: 'How I write explanation texts'
- Writing wheel (ITR and PCM, p272)

STUDY

Show children the video 'How I write explanation texts'.

The video shows the writer Rob Lloyd Jones, speaking about how and why he writes explanation texts. He also talks about his favourite explanation text, who he wrote it for, and why it's important to make explanation texts entertaining.

Explain to the class that their class project will be to write their own explanation text.

DISCUSS

Ask the children what they think explanation is and what thoughts they have about the video they have just watched.

Display the 'Writing wheel' ITR on the whiteboard, and hand out printed copies.

Ask the following questions:

- *Why do you think people write explanation (purpose)?*
- *Who do they write it for (audience)?*
- *How are these texts the same as, but also different from, information texts or instruction texts?*
- *Who is an expert on something in our class?*
- *Do we have groups of experts?*

PLENARY

Children share writing from their personal projects, following the established class sharing routine.

PERSONAL WRITING PROJECTS

Throughout the class writing project, once the class writing goal for each session is complete, children carry on with their personal writing projects at their own pace and using their preferred writing processes. See pages 17–19 for more information on personal writing projects and pages 26–30 for more information on pupil conferencing.

Genre study 2: What makes an effective explanation text?

Class writing goal
To discover what makes an effective explanation text

OVERVIEW

In this lesson, children will look at explanation text examples and discuss what topics were chosen, why the writer might have chosen them and what the exemplars do well. They will then continue working on their personal writing projects.

PREPARATION AND RESOURCES

- Explanation texts genre booklets
- Pre-written exemplar explanation texts:
  - *Why does the moon change shape?* (genre booklet p2–3, ITR)
  - *How does a glider fly?* (genre booklet p4–5, ITR)
  - *Effective genre example (ITR)*
- Gather together some explanation exemplars created by children from previous years
- Flip-chart paper

> As you develop your confidence as a writer-teacher, you should aim to create your own explanation text exemplar using the writing project's opening guidance. This should be about something you know a lot about.

STUDY

Children look at and read the explanation texts in your class library, and discuss the following questions in pairs or groups:

- *What did you like about the explanation text you're reading?*   • *What ideas did it give you for your explanation text?*

Children then read and discuss the exemplar explanation texts and discuss the questions again.

DISCUSS

Explain to children that effective explanation texts have a specific focus rather than a general focus. You can use the analogy of mining for diamonds. Children should focus on finding a single diamond from all of their 'rocky' ideas and make that diamond shine. These diamonds are the moments that writers care about the most. In pairs, children discuss the following.

- *Why do writers write explanation texts?*
- *Can you see differences between the examples?*
- *What sort of diamond moments were chosen by the writers? Why?*
- *Who could we write explanation texts for?*
- *What makes for an effective explanation text?*

CREATE

As a class, and using the information on page 1 of the Explanation texts genre booklet, start creating your poster of product goals. These goals should indicate what is needed to publish a great explanation text.

PLENARY

Children share their personal projects following the established class sharing routine.

Place exemplars used in the class library for children to continue reading at their leisure.

DEEPEN

In preparation for tomorrow's lesson, you could challenge children to write their own ineffective explanation text – using their Explanation texts genre booklets to help them.

PERSONAL WRITING PROJECTS

Throughout the class writing project, once the class writing goal for each session is complete, children carry on with their personal writing projects at their own pace and using their preferred writing processes. See pages 17–19 for more information on personal writing projects and pages 26–30 for more information on pupil conferencing.

Genre study 3: Where can explanation texts go wrong?

Class writing goal
To understand where explanation texts can go wrong

OVERVIEW

In this lesson, children will learn about critiquing ineffective examples using the information in their Explanation texts genre booklets. They will then continue working on their personal writing projects.

PREPARATION AND RESOURCES

- Explanation texts genre booklets
- Pre-written ineffective explanation text exemplar (ITR)
- Anonymised ineffective examples of explanation texts taken from previous years

STUDY

As a class, read the ineffective exemplars of explanation texts.

DISCUSS

In pairs, using your class product goals poster from the previous lesson and the information on page 1 of their Explanation texts genre booklets, children discuss and explain for themselves why the examples are ineffective. They could consider the following questions.

- *Is the introduction effective and is it clear what the text is going to be about?*
- *Is the text organised clearly into paragraphs or sections?*
- *Does the text focus on why or how something happens?*
- *Is it easy to follow the explanation?*
- *Are there any instructions?*
- *Does the writer explain how the instructions are connected with the topic?*

Write your own ineffective explanation text using the following as a guide:

- Don't introduce your topic.
- Don't organise your explanation into paragraphs or use headings.
- Don't focus on 'how' or 'why' things happen.
- Make it difficult to follow and understand.
- Use technical language your reader is unfamiliar with.
- Don't address your reader as 'you'.
- Don't include any pictures, diagrams or photos.
- Don't write about why you chose the topic.

CREATE

You could invite children, in writing time, to write their own ineffective explanation texts.

PLENARY

Children share writing from their personal projects, following the established class sharing routine.

PERSONAL WRITING PROJECTS

Throughout the class writing project, once the class writing goal for each session is complete, children carry on with their personal writing projects at their own pace and using their preferred writing processes. See pages 17–19 for more information on personal writing projects and pages 26–30 for more information on pupil conferencing.

Genre study 4: Where do writers get their ideas from?

> ## Class writing goal
> To generate an idea for each child's class writing project

OVERVIEW

In this lesson, using their Explanation texts genre booklets, children will learn about and try out a number of techniques for generating ideas for explanation text writing. They will then choose one idea to use for their class writing project.

PREPARATION AND RESOURCES

- Explanation text genre booklets
- Flip-chart paper

STUDY

Children turn to page 6 of their Explanation text genre booklets. Read and discuss some of the techniques used by writers to generate ideas for writing biographies.

DISCUSS

As a class, create a poster that showcases all the areas of interest or expertise in your class. This will create pockets or 'clubs' within your writing community. Children learn that they can share what they are expert in with others. Children should also discuss who they are planning to write for.

CREATE

As a class, in groups or pairs, children generate a list of potential writing ideas. They can use the suggestions from page 6 of their Explanation text genre booklets to help them come up with ideas.

PLENARY

Children share writing from their personal projects, following the established class sharing routine.

SUPPORT

If children can't think of anything to write about, you can bring in the writing community to help! For example, what would the community like Samir to write about? What is he known for? What can he teach us? What is he really good at?

PERSONAL WRITING PROJECTS

Throughout the class writing project, once the class writing goal for each session is complete, children carry on with their personal writing projects at their own pace and using their preferred writing processes. See pages 17–19 for more information on personal writing projects and pages 26–30 for more information on pupil conferencing.

> ### Conferencing focus
> Bring certain children with similar topics together.
>
> Ensure children focus on a particular diamond within their topic. Encourage them to avoid too broad a theme.
>
> If a child is struggling to form an idea, encourage them to ask their peers for a topic suggestion that the class would be interested in reading about.

> ### Top tip
> Children are always talking about the things they enjoy and know a lot about. Not only with you but with their peers too. How often do you hear them discussing the latest computer game craze, the must-have toy or something they all seem to be doing at the weekends? We need to show them that there is power in putting the knowledge they possess to paper. They will feel important and influential if they are able to explain something about which they know a lot, to others who know nothing.

Genre study 5: What you need to know

Class writing goal
To find out what research we need to do

OVERVIEW

In this lesson, children will use the 'webbing' planning technique and look at the Explanation texts planning grid to consider whether they need to research any aspect of their topic before planning in the next lesson.

PREPARATION AND RESOURCES

- Explanation texts genre booklets
- Planning web (ITR)
- A selection of non-fiction texts
- Internet access
- Explanation texts planning grid (PCM, p281)
- Flip-chart paper

STUDY

Model the webbing technique either by using flip-chart paper or by using the completed 'Planning web' ITR. Pick a topic that you would like to explore further. Consider how the topic could be split into sections and use a flip-chart to model creating a web. This will illustrate to children the knowledge you have about your topic. When you have completed your web, circle three or four of the sub-categories that you would like to focus on. A completed web can be found on screen 1 of the 'Planning web' ITR.

Now use your web to look for important questions about your subject along with questions your readers might want answers to. Screen 2 of the 'Planning web' ITR demonstrates what this should look like. Using your web, tell children what you might need to research in preparation for planning your own explanation text.

Provide each child with an Explanation texts planning grid (PCM, p281). Talk about what you might need to research in preparation for your own explanation text. Model how you would research some information and write your notes as bullet points. Ensure children are clear about how they should use the planning grid to plan their explanation text.

DISCUSS

Explain to children that they will have a go at using this webbing technique for their writing projects. Ask if they have any questions before they start. Offer the choice of trying this technique, writing a list or drawing their webs and questions instead.

CREATE

Children repeat for themselves the same processes you went through, first by webbing their topic for sub-categories. Then they use webbing for questions their reader might want answers to. Finally, they look at the Explanation texts planning grid (PCM, p281) with a partner and consider what they might need to research before they can begin planning their explanation text. Children create notes while researching, using bullet points.

Conferencing focus
If necessary, probe children's knowledge and understanding of their topic. This should include whether they will be able to explain the basics of their topic effectively and which aspects they will focus on.

PLENARY

Children share their ideas for the class writing project, following the established class sharing routine. Ask children the following questions.

- *What would you like to include but don't know enough about yet?*
- *What are you going to research?*
- *What might your readers enjoy reading about the most?*

Encourage children, as homework, to research or bring in material from home about their project idea.

PERSONAL WRITING PROJECTS

Throughout the class writing project, once the class writing goal for each session is complete, children carry on with their personal writing projects at their own pace and using their preferred writing processes. See pages 17–19 for more information on personal writing projects and pages 26–30 for more information on pupil conferencing.

Writing lesson I: Plan

Class writing goal
To plan our explanation texts

OVERVIEW

Children plan or draft their explanation text.

PREPARATION AND RESOURCES

- Explanation texts genre booklets
- Research homework
- Explanation texts planning grid (ITR and PCM, p281)

MINI-LESSON

Choose from the suggested mini-lessons for this writing project, which cover aspects of writing study, grammar and punctuation.

The following mini-lessons may be particularly useful at the planning stage:

- I'm an expert in
- Have you ever wondered … ?
- Write about topic lessons
- Thinking 'faction'
- Webbing

CLASS WRITING SESSION

Before you begin your writing week, tell children that they have ten writing sessions in which to publish their explanation text. Remind them of the different writing styles writers often use. These include being a discoverer, planner, drafter, paragraph piler and sentence stacker. Explain that, depending on their preferred writing style, they are likely to be planning or drafting today.

Conferencing focus
Encourage children to talk through their plans or drafts in pairs and with you throughout this session. Their partner should let the writer know if they are assuming too much prior knowledge from their reader and whether any technical vocabulary needs defining to help their reader understand.

Children start to plan their explanation texts. Remind them what a plan is for – to help them organise ideas and research so they know what their text will include. You could show a plan of your own, or display the example 'Explanation texts planning grid' ITR. Children may also find it useful to look at the planning advice on pages 7–8 of their Explanation texts genre booklet.

If children choose to plan their pieces, they are free to use their 'Explanation texts planning grid' (PCM, p281) if they wish to. Other children may leap straight into drafting their explanation text. Encourage these children to refer to the drafting rules and advice on pages 9–10 of their Explanation texts genre booklets.

PLENARY

Children who have planned their explanation texts turn over their plans and 'tell' their explanation text to someone in the class.

DEEPEN

Tell children that when planning an opening for their explanation text, they should start off with a short story from their own experience or by painting a descriptive scene. They should personalise the text by speaking straight to their reader as 'you'.

SUPPORT

Provide children with an A3-size copy of the 'Explanation texts planning grid' (PCM, p281). Alternatively these children can talk their plan through with an adult and go straight to drafting, or they can draw their plan.

Writing lesson 2: Plan

Class writing goal
To plan our explanation texts

OVERVIEW

Children continue to plan or draft their explanation texts.

PREPARATION AND RESOURCES

- Explanation texts genre booklets
- Research homework
- Explanation texts planning grid (ITR and PCM, p281)

MINI-LESSON

Choose from the suggested mini-lessons for this writing project, which cover aspects of writing study, grammar and punctuation.

The following mini-lessons may be particularly useful at the planning stage:

- Mindmaps
- Webbing
- Using a planning grid

CLASS WRITING SESSION

Children who haven't finished will continue to plan their pieces of writing started the previous day. Remind children to consider what the diamond moment of their piece is and to discuss this with a partner.

If helpful, display your completed 'Explanation texts planning grid' ITR on the whiteboard for reference.

Other children may begin or continue to draft their explanation text. Encourage these children to refer to the drafting rules and advice on pages 9–10 of their Explanation texts genre booklets.

Top tip
If a child is fanatical about a particular hobby or topic, they might want to write about all of it. This can result in a text that is very superficial, without much detail at all. It is better to encourage children to focus on only one aspect of the topic and explain its nuances and intricacies. This will result in a much richer explanation text for the class to enjoy.

Conferencing focus
Encourage children to talk through their plans or drafts in pairs and with you throughout this session. Partners should let the writers know if they are assuming too much prior knowledge from their reader. Is there any technical vocabulary that needs defining to help their reader understand?

PLENARY

Children who have planned their explanation text turn over their plans and tell their explanation text to someone in the class. If you and your class feel they need another planning session, please add one in. Alternatively, if children are confident with the writing processes, you can let them move on to the next stage independently.

DEEPEN

Tell children that when planning an opening for their explanation text, they should start off with a short story from their own experience or by painting a descriptive scene. They should personalise the text by speaking straight to their reader as 'you'.

SUPPORT

Provide children with an A3-size copy of the 'Explanation texts planning grid' (PCM, p281). Alternatively these children can talk their plan through with an adult and go straight to drafting, or they can draw their plan.

Writing lesson 3: Draft

> ## Class writing goal
> To draft our explanation texts

OVERVIEW

Children use the plans they created in previous sessions to start or continue drafting their explanation text. Some children may have finished their drafts at this point and can move on to revising their pieces.

PREPARATION AND RESOURCES

- Explanation texts genre booklets
- Planning grids from the previous lesson
- Drafting rules (ITR)
- Tips and Tricks cards

MINI-LESSON

Choose from the suggested mini-lessons for this writing project, which cover aspects of writing study, grammar and punctuation.

The following mini-lessons may be particularly useful at the drafting stage:
- Using the drafting rules
- Sticky bits and yawny bits

CLASS WRITING SESSION

Explain to the class that they are now going to start drafting their piece of writing based on the plan they have completed.

Remind them to use the drafting rules and advice on pages 9–10 of their Explanation texts genre booklets and to talk it through with a partner if they get stuck. Children should write on the left-hand side of the page, leaving the right-hand side blank for revision in future lessons.

Some children may have finished drafting their explanation text at this point and can move on to revising their pieces using the Upper KS3 non-fiction revision checklist on page 12 of their Explanation texts genre booklets if necessary.

PLENARY

Children share their drafts, following the established class sharing routine. It could work as follows.

1 The writer 'warms up' their text.

2 The writer reads the text.

3 One listener describes what the piece was about.

4 Listeners offer compliments.

5 The writer asks for advice.

6 Listeners offer suggestions and ask questions.

SUPPORT

Encourage children to paragraph pile or sentence stack until they are confident.

> ### Conferencing focus
> Encourage children to request a conference with you if they get stuck. Ask them to regularly reread their pieces as they write them.
>
> Provide intervals in which children share their writing in pairs. Partners should focus on any 'sticky' bits they hear.
>
> A 'sticky' bit is any bit of writing that doesn't sound right. It sounds strange when read aloud. It confuses your reader. Children are very quick to identify 'sticky' bits. You will notice some recurring themes: verb tense, cohesion, switching of pronouns, inability to identify a pronoun's noun.

> ### Top tip
> Sometimes it's helpful to suggest that children leave it a couple of days before they decide to revise or edit their pieces. This means they can look at their writing with fresh and objective eyes.

Writing lesson 4: Draft

Class writing goal
To draft our explanation texts

OVERVIEW
Children continue drafting their explanation text. Some children may have finished their drafts at this point and can move on to revising their pieces.

PREPARATION AND RESOURCES
- Explanation texts genre booklets
- Planning grids from the previous lesson
- Drafting rules (ITR)
- Tips and Tricks cards

MINI-LESSON
Choose from the suggested mini-lessons for this writing project, which cover aspects of writing study, grammar and punctuation.

The following mini-lessons may be particularly useful at the drafting stage:
- Using the drafting rules
- Sticky bits and yawny bits
- Find the 'how'

CLASS WRITING SESSION
Children continue to develop their drafts. Remind them to use the drafting rules and advice on pages 9–10 of their Explanation texts genre booklets.

Some children may have finished drafting their explanation text at this point and can move on to revising their pieces using the revision information and checklist on pages 11–12 of their Explanation texts genre booklets if necessary.

PLENARY
Children share their drafts, following the established class sharing routine. It could work as follows.

1 The writer 'warms up' their text.
2 The writer reads the text.
3 One listener describes what the piece was about.
4 Listeners offer compliments.
5 The writer asks for advice.
6 Listeners offer suggestions and ask questions.

SUPPORT
Encourage children to paragraph pile or sentence stack until they are confident.

Conferencing focus
Encourage children to request a conference with you if they get stuck. Ask them to regularly reread their pieces as they write them. Provide intervals in which they can share their writing in pairs. Partners should focus on any 'sticky' or 'yawny' bits they hear.

A 'sticky' bit is any bit of writing that doesn't sound right. It sounds strange when read out loud. It confuses your reader. Children are very quick to identity 'sticky' bits. You will notice some recurring themes: verb tense, cohesion, switching of pronouns, inability to identify a pronoun's noun.

A 'yawny' bit is any bit of writing that seems unnecessary or repetitive.

Top tip
Sometimes it's helpful to suggest that children leave it a couple of days before they decide to revise or edit their pieces. This means they can look at their writing with fresh and objective eyes.

Writing lesson 5: Draft

> ## Class writing goal
> To draft our explanation texts

OVERVIEW

Children continue drafting their explanation text. Some children may have finished their drafts at this point and can move on to revising their pieces.

PREPARATION AND RESOURCES

- Explanation texts genre booklets
- Planning grids from the previous lessons
- Drafting rules (ITR)
- Tips and Tricks cards

MINI-LESSON

Choose from the suggested mini-lessons for this writing project, which cover aspects of writing study, grammar and punctuation.

The following mini-lessons may be particularly useful at the drafting stage:

- Using the drafting rules
- Sticky bits and yawny bits

CLASS WRITING SESSION

Children continue to develop their drafts. Remind them to use the drafting rules and advice on pages 9–10 of their Explanation texts genre booklets and to talk it through with a partner as necessary.

PLENARY

Children share their drafts, following the established class sharing routine. It could work as follows:

1 The writer 'warms up' their text.

2 The writer reads the text.

3 One listener describes what the piece was about.

4 Listeners offer compliments.

5 The writer asks for advice.

6 Listeners offer suggestions and ask questions.

> ### Conferencing focus
>
> Encourage children to request a conference with you if they get stuck. Ask children to regularly reread their pieces as they write them. Provide intervals in which they share their writing in pairs. Children could refer back to your product goals poster.
>
> Partners should focus on any 'sticky' or 'yawny' bits they hear.
>
> A 'sticky' bit is any bit of writing that doesn't sound right. It sounds strange when read out loud. It confuses your reader. Children are very quick to identity 'sticky' bits. You will notice some recurring themes: verb tense, cohesion, switching of pronouns, inability to identify a pronoun's noun.
>
> A 'yawny' bit is any bit of writing that seems unnecessary or repetitive.

If you and your class feel they need another drafting session, please add one in. Alternatively, if children are confident with the writing processes, you can let them move on to the next stage independently.

SUPPORT

Encourage these children to paragraph pile or sentence stack until they are confident.

Writing lesson 6: Revise

Class writing goal
To revise our explanation texts

OVERVIEW

Children begin the important process of rereading and revising their writing. Focus should be on ensuring that the text makes sense and they have included everything in their plans. Some children may have finished revising their explanation texts at this point and can move on to editing their pieces.

PREPARATION AND RESOURCES

- Explanation texts genre booklets
- Upper KS2 non-fiction revision checklist (ITR and PCM, p278)
- Upper KS2 editing checklist (ITR and PCM, p273)
- Tips and Tricks cards

MINI-LESSON

Choose from the suggested mini-lessons for this writing project, which cover aspects of writing study, grammar and punctuation.

The following mini-lessons may be particularly useful at the revision stage:

- First reread and improve
- Second reread and improve
- Third reread and improve
- Too fast

CLASS WRITING SESSION

Explain to children that many of them are now going to start revising their piece of writing, whilst others will be ready to move on to editing their pieces. Remind them that if they have many changes to make they can create a new version opposite their draft in their English book. This is particularly the case for children whose preferred writing process is that of 'discoverer'.

Conferencing focus

Encourage children to request a conference with you if they get stuck while revising. Also ask them to talk with a partner about where certain revisions would be effective.

Provide intervals in which children share their writing in pairs. Partners should focus on any revisions made.

Remind children to use the revision advice and checklist on pages 11–12 of their Explanation texts genre booklet. They should also use the relevant Tips and Tricks cards to help them with grammar, punctuation and spelling.

Some children may have finished revising their explanation text at this point and can move on to editing their pieces using the 'Upper KS2 editing checklist' (PCM, p273).

PLENARY

Children share their revisions, following the established class sharing routine.

SUPPORT

Encourage children to paragraph pile or sentence stack until they are confident.

Writing lesson 7: Revise

> ## Class writing goal
> To revise our explanation texts

OVERVIEW

Most children will still be revising their writing at this stage.

Once children are happy with their revised text, they move on to editing the text and developing their transcription skills by checking spelling, punctuation and grammar. Some children may have finished editing their explanation texts at this point and can move on to publishing their pieces.

PREPARATION AND RESOURCES

- Explanation texts genre booklets
- Upper KS2 non-fiction revision checklist (ITR and PCM, p278)
- Upper KS2 editing checklist (ITR and PCM, p273)
- Presentation tips (ITR and PCM, p274)
- Tips and Tricks cards
- Reading books

MINI-LESSON

Choose from the suggested mini-lessons for this writing project, which cover aspects of writing study, grammar and punctuation.

The following mini-lessons may be particularly useful at the revision stage:

- First reread and improve
- Second reread and improve
- Third reread and improve
- Find the 'how'

CLASS WRITING SESSION

Children will continue to revise their explanation texts. Remind them that if they have a lot of changes they can create a new version opposite their draft in their English book. This is particularly the case for children whose preferred writing process is that of discoverer.

Remind children to use the revision advice and checklist found on pages 11–12 of their Explanation texts genre booklets. Ask children to use the relevant Tips and Tricks cards to help them with spelling, grammar and punctuation. They can also use their reading books to check the spellings of common words.

Some children may have finished editing their explanation texts at this point and can move on to publishing their pieces using the 'Presentation tips' (PCM, p274).

> ### Conferencing focus
> Encourage children to request a conference with you if they get stuck. Ask them to talk with their partners about where certain revisions would be effective.
>
> Provide intervals in which to share their writing in pairs. Partners should focus on any 'sticky' bits they hear.
>
> A 'sticky' bit is any bit of writing that doesn't sound right. It sounds strange when read out loud. It confuses your reader. Children are very quick to identity 'sticky' bits. You will notice some recurring themes: verb tense, cohesion, switching of pronouns, inability to identify a pronoun's noun.

PLENARY

Children share their revised drafts, following the established class sharing routine. If you or your class feel they need another revision session, please add one in. Alternatively, if children are confident with the writing processes, you can let them move on to the next stage independently.

SUPPORT

If children have finished their drafts, you or another adult could publish it on their behalf.

Writing lesson 8: Edit

Class writing goal
To edit our explanation texts

OVERVIEW

Once children are happy with their revised text, they move on to editing the text and developing their transcription skills by checking spelling, punctuation and grammar.

PREPARATION AND RESOURCES

- Explanation texts genre booklets
- Upper KS2 editing checklist (ITR and PCM, p273)
- Presentation tips (ITR and PCM, p274)
- Tips and Tricks cards
- Electronic spell checkers
- Access to online dictionaries
- Reading books

MINI-LESSON

Choose from the suggested mini-lessons for this writing project, which cover aspects of writing study, grammar and punctuation.

The following mini-lessons may be particularly useful at the editing stage:

- How to edit your writing for capitals
- How to edit your writing for use of vocabulary
- How to edit your writing for punctuation
- How to check and correct your unsure spellings

CLASS WRITING SESSION

Children begin to edit their explanation texts using their editing checklists, along with the relevant Tips and Tricks cards to help them understand the correct use of grammar, punctuation and spelling. Remind children that they can use a dictionary, electronic spell checkers or go online to look up any spellings they are unsure of. They can also use their reading books to check the spellings of common words.

Conferencing focus

Encourage children to request a conference with you if they get stuck.

Encourage children to read any 'sticky' bits to a partner to get advice before asking you.

A 'sticky' bit is any bit of writing that doesn't sound right. It sounds strange when read out loud. It confuses your reader. Children are very quick to identity 'sticky' bits. You will notice some recurring themes: verb tense, cohesion, switching of pronouns, inability to identify a pronoun's noun.

PLENARY

Show some examples of thoughtful editing. If you and your class feel they need another editing session, please add one in. Alternatively, if children are confident with the writing processes, you can let them to move on to the next stage independently.

SUPPORT

If children have finished their editing, you or another adult could publish their text on their behalf.

Writing lesson 9: Publish

Class writing goal
To publish our explanation texts

OVERVIEW

Most children should now be ready to publish their pieces and you should be ready to begin assessing their outcomes. Any children who have finished publishing their explanation texts can work on their personal writing projects.

PREPARATION AND RESOURCES

• A variety of stationery and art materials
• Presentation tips (ITR and PCM, p274)

MINI-LESSON

Choose from the suggested mini-lessons for this writing project, which cover aspects of writing study, grammar and punctuation.

The following mini-lessons may be particularly useful at the publishing stage:
• Ways of publishing

CLASS WRITING SESSION

Refer back to the original class writing goal of creating a collection of explanation texts. Ensure children have access to the 'Presentation tips' (PCM, p274) or that you have the 'Presentation tips' ITR displayed on the whiteboard.

Conferencing focus
Take this opportunity to discuss your assessment of children's pieces and set writing goals for their future class and personal writing projects. Place these goals on the working wall.

Children can take this opportunity to present their writing, adding colour, artwork and photographs.

PLENARY

Children perform their pieces for the class. This can be done as a whole class listening, in table groups or in pairs. It is important that you provide a variety of class sharing opportunities.

Writing lesson 10: Publish

Class writing goal
To publish our explanation texts

OVERVIEW

Most children should now be ready to publish their pieces and you should be ready to begin assessing their outcomes. Any children who have finished publishing their explanation texts can work on their personal writing projects.

PREPARATION AND RESOURCES

- A variety of stationery and art materials
- Presentation tips (ITR and PCM, p274)

MINI-LESSON

Choose from the suggested mini-lessons for this writing project, which cover aspects of writing study, grammar and punctuation.

The following mini-lessons may be particularly useful at the publishing stage:

- Ways of publishing

CLASS WRITING SESSION

At this stage, all children should be nearing the end of publishing. You should begin assessing their outcomes and sharing any writing goals with individual children or with the class as a whole. Continue to refer children to the 'Presentation tips' (PCM, p274) or have the ITR displayed.

Conferencing focus

Take this opportunity to discuss your assessment of children's pieces. Set whole class writing goals for future class and personal writing projects and place these on the working wall.

PLENARY

Children perform their pieces for the class, for other year groups, for parents, for the wider community or in a local library.

Class writing project: Memoir

Why write a memoir?

Teaching memoir in Year 5 is a real joy. Children are beginning to get to grips with it as a genre, having been introduced to it in Years 3 and 4. However, they have also been developing their narrative writing with you too. They are really starting to understand the skills required for developing characters and settings. This project will show them how they can bring all these skills together to create possibly some of the finest writing you will ever receive.

THINGS TO BEAR IN MIND

- Children will have already learned about how poetry can be used to tap into their senses and memories for creating rich description.

- They should continue to consider how they can contrast and compare in poetic ways and sometimes, as memoirists, bend the truth and use hyperbole to blur memory with telling a good story.

- Children will know from Year 4 that they need to engage their reader with a strong opening and a thoughtful ending to make their reader reflect.

- In this project, children will focus their memoirs on the people involved. They will move away from plot-driven narrative to look instead at the thoughts and feelings of the people they are writing about. This means you can use a lot of the lessons and resources that served your children well during their short-story writing.

- The same can be said for setting descriptions. Harness your children's growing expertise in creating vivid settings to transform their memoirs into stunning pieces of writing.

- Finally, you can continue to work on children's ability to 'show' and not 'tell' their narrative.

Writing a memoir

Use these ideas to help you write your own memoir for use in class or to introduce children to the genre.

Why write a memoir for yourself or your class?

Memoirs are a great tool to help you reflect on and share your experiences. When writing stories about your life you will use many of the same tricks you use when writing fiction. You write a memoir to share an interesting event that has happened to you or that you have observed. They are also a way of making sure your memories don't disappear. You can share them in the future with family and friends, and relive the event(s) yourself. Memoirs can also help you to understand the things that have happened to you.

What are the basics of a memoir?

When writing memoirs for your class, you may want to recall an event that children can relate to. This could be something similar to what they may have experienced themselves. Not only does this model the purpose of the writing, but they will be fascinated to hear about your memories, especially if they relate to your childhood.

(FIELD) What is your memoir going to be about?

What is great about memoirs is that they can be about anything you or someone else has done in real life! There is a focus in this unit on experiences that your peers can relate to.

The best memoirs are about an event or experience that was really important to you, and that you will always remember. These can be happy, sad or funny moments in your life.

A good memoir describes an event in an interesting way.

- Your memoir should start by introducing the place and the event to readers.
- Include who, what, where, why and when.
- Explain why this event was significant. Share with readers your reflections on what happened. What was the value of this experience? What did you learn, gain or understand?

(TENOR) What is your role as the writer?

Make sure you choose an event that people will want to read about and that they may relate to.

Readers are often less interested in the event itself but rather **your thoughts and feelings** during the event you are describing. Set your reader up for the experience in your very first sentence or paragraph, e.g. *You may not believe this, but this really happened to me.*

(MODE) What should your memoir look like?

Your memoir will look a lot like a story. Make sure key events are written in order and in paragraphs. You may want to add pictures of important moments so your reader can build an image of your event or experience in their mind.

(SEMANTICS) How can you make your memoir clear and interesting?

You can:

- write in the **third person**, e.g. *it, they, them, their, they are*
- write in the **first person**, e.g. *I, me, my, we, us, our*
- write in the **past tense**, e.g. *was, were, had, been, -ed*
- use **adverbials of time**. Time openers can ensure your memoir has a speedy pace and does not get boring, e.g. *the next day, meanwhile, in the end, once upon a time, soon after, a little later, finally, after that.*

(LEXIS) How can your word choices help?

- Use **noun phrases** to describe the important nouns, such as characters, places or things.
- Try not to always use the first **verbs** that come into your head, see if you can think of interesting alternatives.
- Use **adverbs** to describe *how* characters do things.

Genre study I: Introducing memoir

> ## Class writing goal
> To learn what our next class writing project will be

OVERVIEW

In this lesson, children will recap the memoir genre and will discuss why writers write them. You will then reveal that this is the next class writing project with a specific focus on developing their characters and settings. The class will be publishing an anthology of texts to give to the Year 4 classes to help them write their own memoirs. Children will then continue to work on their personal writing projects.

PREPARATION AND RESOURCES

- Ask your class librarians to start displaying a variety of memoir texts. Ensure that your class library has a rich and varied stock of memoir, poetry and realistic fiction that shows hybridising between these different genres.
- Video: 'How I write memoirs'
- Writing wheel (ITR and PCM, p272)

STUDY

Show children the video 'How I write memoirs'.

The video shows the writer Michael Rosen, speaking about how he writes memoir, how he collects ideas for memoirs and how an editor helped him revise and improve his memoir.

Explain to the class that their class project will be to write their own memoir.

DISCUSS

Ask the children to recall what memoir is, what it shares with story writing and what thoughts they have about the video they have just watched.

Display the 'Writing wheel' ITR on the whiteboard, and hand out printed copies.

Ask the following questions:

- *Why do you like writing memoir (purpose)?*
- *Who have you written memoirs for before (audience)?*
- *What can we learn from our story-writing projects when we write our memoirs?*
- *How do we develop characters when we write stories?*
- *How do we write a vivid setting?*
- *Does anyone have any ideas for their memoirs already?*

PLENARY

Children share writing from their personal projects, following the class sharing routine.

PERSONAL WRITING PROJECTS

Throughout the class writing project, once the class writing goal for each session is complete, children carry on with their personal writing projects at their own pace and using their preferred writing processes. See pages 17–19 for more information on personal writing projects and pages 26–30 for more information on pupil conferencing.

Genre study 2: What makes a good memoir?

Class writing goal
To understand what makes a good memoir

OVERVIEW

In this lesson, children will look at a variety of memoir examples and discuss what topics were chosen, how the writer developed their characters and described their settings. They will then continue working on their personal writing projects.

PREPARATION AND RESOURCES

- Memoir genre booklets
- Pre-written exemplar memoir texts (genre booklet and ITRs)
- Memoir text exemplars created by children from previous years
- Flip-chart paper to generate your memoir product goals

> As you develop your confidence as a writer-teacher, you should aim to create your own memoir text exemplar using the writing project's opening guidance. Focus on character development and setting description.

STUDY

Children look at and read the memoirs in your class library and the pre-written exemplar texts. Discuss the following.
- *What did you like about the memoir you are reading?*
- *What do you know about the characters involved?*
- *What do you know about the setting?*
- *What sorts of ideas did it give you for your memoir?*

DISCUSS

Explain to children that good memoirs have a specific focus rather than a general focus. You can use the analogy of mining for diamonds. Children should focus on finding a single diamond from all of their 'rocky ideas' and make that diamond shine.

In pairs, children discuss the following questions:

- Why do writers write memoir?
- Why do you think I chose my topic(s)? What was my diamond moment?
- Can you see differences between the examples?
- What sort of diamond moments were chosen by the other writers? Why?
- What are we going to have to do to write some good memoirs?

CREATE

As a class, and using the information on page 1 of the Memoir genre booklet, start creating your poster of product goals. These goals should indicate what is needed to publish a great memoir. You will add to these over subsequent sessions as children's understanding of the genre develops.

PLENARY

Children share writing from their personal projects, following the established class sharing routine. Place exemplars into the class library for children to continue reading at their leisure.

DEEPEN

In preparation for tomorrow's ineffective example lesson, you could challenge your more experienced writers to write their own ineffective memoir, using their Memoir genre booklets to help them.

PERSONAL WRITING PROJECTS

Throughout the class writing project, once the class writing goal for each session is complete, children carry on with their personal writing projects at their own pace and using their preferred writing processes. See pages 17–19 for more information on personal writing projects and pages 26–30 for more information on pupil conferencing.

Genre study 3: Where can memoir go wrong?

Class writing goal
To understand where memoir texts can go wrong

OVERVIEW

In this lesson, children will learn about critiquing an ineffective example of a memoir. They will consider the writer's character development and setting description. They will then continue working on their personal writing projects.

PREPARATION AND RESOURCES

- Memoir genre booklets
- Pre-written ineffective exemplar memoir text (ITR)
- Anonymised ineffective examples taken from previous years

STUDY

As a class, read the ineffective examples of memoirs (your own and / or the pre-written example).

DISCUSS

In pairs, using your class product goals poster and page 1 of the Memoir genre booklet, ask children to discuss and explain why the examples are not effective.

Write your own ineffective memoir using the following as a guide:

- Write it like a recount with no sense of feeling or storytelling.
- Write about something which is not important or significant.
- Make it difficult to follow and understand.
- Use no poetic language.
- Your ending should leave your reader wondering why you even chose to write it.
- Do not share anything about your character in terms of their appearance, dialogue or monologue nor through their actions.
- Do not create a vivid setting.

CREATE

You could invite children, in writing time, to write their own ineffective memoirs.

PLENARY

Children share writing from their personal projects, following the established class sharing routine. Place exemplars into the class library for children to continue reading at their leisure.

PERSONAL WRITING PROJECTS

Throughout the class writing project, once the class writing goal for each session is complete, children carry on with their personal writing projects at their own pace and using their preferred writing processes. See pages 17–19 for more information on personal writing projects and pages 26–30 for more information on pupil conferencing.

Genre study 4: Where do writers get their ideas from?

Class writing goal
To generate an idea for our memoirs

OVERVIEW

In this lesson, children will learn and try out a number of techniques for generating ideas for memoir writing. They will then choose one idea to use for their class writing project.

PREPARATION AND RESOURCES

- Memoir genre booklets
- Your own list of potential memoir ideas
- Access to the internet
- A selection of non-fiction texts
- Flip-chart paper

STUDY

Children turn to page 7 of their Memoir genre booklets. Read and discuss some of the techniques used by writers to generate ideas for writing memoirs.

DISCUSS

As a class, in groups or in pairs, talk about the sorts of questions memoirists ask themselves. What sorts of things are they looking to find from their lives?

CREATE

As a class, in groups or in pairs, ask children to generate a list of potential writing ideas.

- Ensure children focus on a particular diamond within their topic.
- Encourage them to avoid too broad a theme.
- Discuss any shared memories the class may have together.
- Bring certain children with similar themes together so they can briefly talk about their ideas.
- If a child is struggling to form an idea, encourage them to ask their peers for a topic that they might be interested in.

PLENARY

Children share their ideas, following the established class sharing routine.

SUPPORT

If children cannot think of any ideas, bring the writing community in to help by sharing what they plan to write about. Alternatively, ask children to bring in an artefact or photograph from home that could spark a memoir idea.

PERSONAL WRITING PROJECTS

Throughout the class writing project, once the class writing goal for each session is complete, children carry on with their personal writing projects at their own pace and using their preferred writing processes. See pages 17–19 for more information on personal writing projects and pages 26–30 for more information on pupil conferencing.

Writing lesson 1: Plan

Class writing goal
To plan our memoirs

OVERVIEW

Children plan or draft their memoirs.

PREPARATION AND RESOURCES

- Memoir genre booklets
- Memoir planning grid (ITR and PCM, p282)

MINI-LESSON

Choose from the suggested mini-lessons for this writing project, which cover aspects of writing study, grammar and punctuation.

The following mini-lessons may be particularly useful at the planning stage:

- Questions for memoirists
- Special moments
- Important people
- Memoir with strong feelings
- When I was younger…

CLASS WRITING SESSION

Before you begin your writing week, tell children that they have ten writing sessions in which to publish their memoir. Remind them of the different writing styles writers often use. These include being a discoverer, planner, drafter, paragraph piler and sentence stacker. Explain that, depending on their preferred writing style, they are likely to be planning or drafting today.

> ### Conferencing focus
> Encourage children to talk through their plans or drafts in pairs and with you throughout this session. Partners should let the writer know if they are simply telling their reader what happened without any sense of feeling or story-telling.

If children choose to plan their pieces, they are free to use their 'Memoir planning grid' (PCM, p282) if they wish to. Other children may leap straight into drafting their memoir. Encourage these children to refer to the 'Drafting rules' ITR and the information on pages 11–13 of their Memoir genre booklets.

PLENARY

Children who have planned their memoir turn over their plans and 'tell' their memoir to someone in the class.

DEEPEN

When planning their memoir, ask children to think about how they might not explicitly explain what happened, but rather allude to it and allow their reader to come to their own conclusions.

SUPPORT

Provide children with an A3-size copy of the 'Memoir planning grid'. Alternatively, ask children to talk their plan through with an adult and go straight to drafting, or they can draw their plan.

Writing lesson 2: Plan

Class writing goal
To plan our memoirs

OVERVIEW

Children continue to plan or draft their memoir.

PREPARATION AND RESOURCES

- Memoir genre booklets
- Memoir planning grid (ITR and PCM, p282)
- Drafting rules (ITR)

MINI-LESSON

Choose from the suggested mini-lessons for this writing project, which cover aspects of writing study, grammar and punctuation.

The following mini-lessons may be particularly useful at the planning stage:

- Favourite places
- Something different happened this time
- Show don't tell
- How to write a vivid setting
- Don't start too far upstream

CLASS WRITING SESSION

Children who have not yet finished their plans will continue to plan their piece of writing. Remind children to consider what the focus of their piece is and discuss this in pairs. If helpful, display the completed 'Memoir planning grid' ITR on the whiteboard for reference.

Once their plan is complete, children can continue with their personal writing projects, at their own pace and using their preferred writing process.

Conferencing focus

Encourage children to talk through their plans or drafts in pairs and with you throughout this session.

Partners should let the writer know where they could describe a setting or character more fully. They should also suggest where they might have an opportunity to be poetic. Could they use a simile or a metaphor to deepen the description?

Ask partners to say if there are any parts which might need explaining to their reader to avoid them getting confused.

Other children may begin or continue to draft their memoirs. Encourage these children to refer to the 'Drafting rules' ITR and the information on pages 11–13 of their Memoir genre booklets.

PLENARY

Children who have planned their memoir turn over their plans and 'tell' their memoir to someone in the class. If you and your class feel they need another planning session, please add one in. Alternatively, if children are confident with the writing processes, you can let them move on to the next stage independently.

DEEPEN

When planning their memoir, ask children to think about using flashbacks and moving around in time to surprise their reader. They should also think about what they can borrow from some of their favourite stories or poems.

SUPPORT

Provide children with an A3-size copy of the 'Memoir planning grid'. Alternatively, ask children to talk their plan through with an adult and go straight to drafting, or they can draw their plan.

Writing lesson 3: Draft

Class writing goal
To draft our memoirs

OVERVIEW

Children use the plans they created in previous sessions to start or continue drafting their memoirs. Some children may have finished their drafts at this point and can move on to revising their pieces.

PREPARATION AND RESOURCES

- Memoir genre booklets
- Planning grids from the previous lesson
- Upper KS2 narrative revision checklist (ITR and PCM, p277)

- Drafting rules (ITR)
- Tips and Tricks cards

MINI-LESSON

Choose from the suggested mini-lessons for this writing project, which cover aspects of writing study, grammar and punctuation.

The following mini-lessons may be particularly useful at the drafting stage:

- Great openings
- See things like a poet

CLASS WRITING SESSION

Explain to children that many of them are now going to start drafting their memoir based on the plan they have completed.

Remind them to use the 'Drafting rules' ITR, and to talk through their drafts in pairs if they get stuck. They may also find it useful to look at the drafting advice on pages 11–13 of their Memoir genre booklet.

Children should write on the left side of their books leaving the right blank for revision in future lessons.

Some children find it hard to write an opening. Ask them to read through the suggested openings on page 11 of their Memoir genre booklet. Ask them to try out different openings on their edit page and to pick their favourite.

Some children may have finished drafting their memoir at this point and can move on to revising their pieces using the revision information and checklist on pages 14–15 in their Memoir genre booklets if necessary.

Conferencing focus

Encourage children to request a conference with you if they get stuck. Also encourage them to regularly reread their pieces as they write them. Provide intervals during which children can share their writing in pairs. Pairs focus on any 'sticky' or 'yawny' bits they hear.

A 'sticky' bit is any bit of writing that doesn't sound right. It sounds strange when read aloud. It confuses their reader. Children are very quick to identify 'sticky' bits. You will notice some recurring themes: verb tense, cohesion, switching of pronouns, inability to identify a pronoun's noun.

A 'yawny' bit is any bit of writing that seems unnecessary or repetitive.

Top tip

Sometimes it's helpful to suggest that children leave it a couple of days before they decide to revise or edit their pieces. This means they can look at their writing with fresh and objective eyes.

PLENARY

Children share their drafts, following the established class sharing routine.

DEEPEN

Ask children to add metaphor and simile to enhance descriptions.

SUPPORT

Encourage children to paragraph pile or sentence stack until they are more confident.

Writing lesson 4: Draft

Class writing goal
To draft our memoirs

OVERVIEW

Children continue drafting their memoir. Some children may have finished their drafts at this point and can move on to revising their pieces.

PREPARATION AND RESOURCES

- Memoir genre booklets
- Planning grids from the previous lesson
- Upper KS2 narrative revision checklist (ITR and PCM, p277)
- Tips and Tricks cards
- Drafting rules (ITR)

MINI-LESSON

Choose from the suggested mini-lessons for this writing project, which cover aspects of writing study, grammar and punctuation.

The following mini-lessons may be particularly useful at the drafting stage:

- Strong endings
- Using nouns and pronouns for cohesion
- Fronted adverbials: moving between time and place
- Parenthesis
- Punctuating dialogue

CLASS WRITING SESSION

Children continue to develop their drafts.

Remind them to use the 'Drafting rules' ITR, and to talk through their drafts in pairs if they get stuck. They may also find it useful to look at the drafting advice on pages 11–13 of their Memoir genre booklet.

Some children may have finished drafting their memoir at this point and can move on to revising their pieces using the revision information and checklist on pages 14–15 of their Memoir genre booklets if necessary.

PLENARY

Children share their drafts, following the established class sharing routine.

DEEPEN

Ask children to add metaphor and simile to enhance descriptions.

SUPPORT

Encourage children to paragraph pile or sentence stack until they are more confident.

Conferencing focus

Encourage children to request a conference with you if they get stuck. Also encourage them to regularly reread their pieces as they write them. Provide intervals during which children can share their writing in pairs. Pairs focus on any 'sticky' or 'yawny' bits they hear.

A 'sticky' bit is any bit of writing that doesn't sound right. It sounds strange when read aloud. It confuses their reader. Children are very quick to identify 'sticky' bits. You will notice some recurring themes: verb tense, cohesion, switching of pronouns, inability to identify a pronoun's noun.

A 'yawny' bit is any bit of writing that seems unnecessary or repetitive.

Top tip

Sometimes it's helpful to suggest that children leave it a couple of days before they decide to revise or edit their pieces. This means they can look at their writing with fresh and objective eyes.

Writing lesson 5: Draft

Class writing goal
To draft our memoirs

OVERVIEW

Children continue drafting their memoirs. Some children may have finished their drafts at this point and can move on to revising their pieces.

PREPARATION AND RESOURCES

- Memoir genre booklets
- Planning grids from the previous lesson
- Upper KS2 narrative revision checklist (ITR and PCM, p277)
- Drafting rules (ITR)
- Tips and Tricks cards

MINI-LESSON

Choose from the suggested mini-lessons for this writing project, which cover aspects of writing study, grammar and punctuation.

The following mini-lessons may be particularly useful at the drafting stage:

- Building atmosphere: Suspense and tension
- Replacing *and* with ; for rhythm
- Determiners
- Simple and multiclause sentences

CLASS WRITING SESSION

Children continue to develop their drafts.

Remind them to use the 'Drafting rules' ITR, and to talk through their drafts in pairs if they get stuck. They may also find it useful to look at the drafting advice on pages 11–13 of their Memoir genre booklet.

Some children may have finished drafting their memoir at this point and can move on to revising their pieces using the revision information and checklist on pages 14–15 of their Memoir genre booklets if necessary.

Conferencing focus

Encourage children to request a conference with you if they get stuck. Ask them to regularly reread their pieces as they write them. They could refer back to your product goals poster.

Provide intervals during which children can share their writing in pairs. Partners should focus on where certain revisions could be effective and on any revisions made. They should also check that their partner can relate to their writing.

Top tip

Sometimes it's helpful to suggest that children leave it a couple of days before they decide to revise or edit their pieces. This means they can look at their writing with fresh and objective eyes.

PLENARY

Children share their drafts, following the established class sharing routine. If you and your class feel they need another drafting session, please add one in. Alternatively, if children are confident with the writing processes, you can let them move on to the next stage independently.

DEEPEN

Children could practise intentionally leaving information out in order to create mystery or interest for their reader.

SUPPORT

Encourage children to paragraph pile or sentence stack until they are more confident.

Writing lesson 6: Revise

Class writing goal
To revise our memoirs

OVERVIEW

Children begin the important process of rereading and revising their writing. Focus should be on ensuring that the text makes sense and that they have included everything in their plans. Some children may have finished revising their memoir at this point and can move on to editing their pieces.

PREPARATION AND RESOURCES

- Memoir genre booklets
- Upper KS2 narrative revision checklist (ITR and PCM, p277)
- Upper KS2 editing checklist (ITR and PCM, p273)
- Tips and Tricks cards

MINI-LESSON

Choose from the suggested mini-lessons for this writing project, which cover aspects of writing study, grammar and punctuation.

The following mini-lessons may be particularly useful at the revising stage:

- First reread and improve
- Second reread and improve
- Third reread and improve
- Five alive!

CLASS WRITING SESSION

Explain to children that many of them are now going to start revising their piece of writing, whilst others will be ready to move on to editing their pieces. Remind them that if they have many changes to make they can create a new version opposite their draft in their English book. This is particularly the case for children whose preferred writing process is that of 'discoverer'.

Remind children to use the revision checklists found on page 15 of their Memoir genre booklets and the relevant Tips and Tricks cards. They may also find it useful to look at the revision advice on page 14 of their Memoir text genre booklet.

Some children may have finished revising their memoir at this point and can move on to editing their pieces using the 'Upper KS2 editing checklist' (PCM, p273).

Conferencing focus

Encourage children to request a conference with you if they get stuck while revising. Ask children to talk with their partners about where certain revisions would be effective.

Provide intervals in which children share their writing in pairs. Partners should focus on any revisions made.

PLENARY

Children share their revised drafts, following the established class sharing routine.

DEEPEN

Children could deepen their revision skills by helping a partner to revise areas of the memoir, using their viewpoint as a reader.

SUPPORT

Encourage children to paragraph pile or sentence stack until they are confident.

Writing lesson 7: Revise

Class writing goal
To revise our memoirs

OVERVIEW

Children continue the important process of rereading and revising their writing. Focus should be on ensuring that the text makes sense and that they have included everything in their plans. Some children may have finished revising their memoirs at this point and can move on to editing their pieces. Some children may have finished editing their memoirs at this point and can move on to publishing their pieces.

PREPARATION AND RESOURCES

- Memoir genre booklets
- Upper KS2 narrative revision checklist (ITR and PCM, p277)
- Upper KS2 editing checklist (ITR and PCM, p273)
- Presentation tips (PCM, p274)
- Tips and Tricks cards

MINI-LESSON

Choose from the suggested mini-lessons for this writing project, which cover aspects of writing study, grammar and punctuation.

The following mini-lessons may be particularly useful at the revising stage:

- First reread and improve
- Second reread and improve
- Third reread and improve
- Five alive!

CLASS WRITING SESSION

Children continue revising their memoirs.

Remind children to use the Upper KS2 narrative revision checklist found on page 15 of their Memoir genre booklets and the relevant Tips and Tricks cards. They may also find it useful to look at the revision advice on page 14 of their Memoir text genre booklet.

Some children may have finished revising their memoir at this point and can move on to editing their pieces using the Upper KS2 editing checklist (PCM, p273).

Conferencing focus

Encourage children to request a conference with you if they get stuck.

Provide intervals during which children can share their writing in pairs. Ask them to talk with their partners about where certain revisions would be effective. Pairs focus on any 'sticky' or 'yawny' bits they hear.

A 'sticky' bit is any bit of writing that doesn't sound right. It sounds strange when read aloud. It confuses their reader. Children are very quick to identify 'sticky' bits. You will notice some recurring themes: verb tense, cohesion, switching of pronouns, inability to identify a pronoun's noun.

Some children may have finished editing their memoir at this point and can move on to publishing their pieces using the 'Presentation tips' (PCM, p274).

PLENARY

Children share their revised drafts, following the established class sharing routine. If you and your class feel they need another revision session, please add one in. Alternatively, if children are confident with the writing processes, you can let them to move on to the next stage independently.

DEEPEN

Children could deepen their revision skills by helping a partner to revise areas of the memoir, using their viewpoint as a reader.

SUPPORT

If children have finished their drafts, you or another adult could publish it on their behalf.

Writing lesson 8: Edit

Class writing goal
To edit our memoirs

OVERVIEW

Once children are happy with their revised text, they move on to editing the text and developing their transcription skills by checking spelling, punctuation and grammar. Some children may have finished editing their memoirs at this point and can move on to publishing their pieces.

PREPARATION AND RESOURCES

- Upper KS2 editing checklist (ITR and PCM, p273)
- Presentation tips (PCM, p274)
- Tips and Tricks cards
- Electronic spell checkers
- Access to online dictionaries
- Reading books

MINI-LESSON

Choose from the suggested mini-lessons for this writing project, which cover aspects of writing study, grammar and punctuation.

The following mini-lessons may be particularly useful at the editing stage:

- How to edit your writing for capitals
- How to edit your writing for use of vocabulary
- How to edit your writing for punctuation
- How to check and correct your unsure spellings

CLASS WRITING SESSION

Children begin to edit their texts using their editing checklists, along with the relevant Tips and Tricks cards to help them understand the correct use of grammar and punctuation. Remind children that they can use a dictionary and the Spelling Tips and Tricks cards to look up any spellings they are unsure of. They can also use their reading books to check the spellings of common words.

Some children may have finished editing their memoirs at this point and can move on to publishing their pieces using the 'Presentation tips' (PCM, p274).

PLENARY

Show some examples of thoughtful editing. If you and your class feel they need another editing session, please add one in. Alternatively, if children are confident with the writing processes, you can let them move on to the next stage independently.

SUPPORT

If children have finished their drafts, you or another adult could publish it on their behalf.

> **Conferencing focus**
>
> Encourage children to request a conference with you if they get stuck.
>
> Provide intervals during which children can share their writing in pairs. Ask them to talk with their partners about where certain revisions would be effective. Pairs focus on any 'sticky' or 'yawny' bits they hear.
>
> A 'sticky' bit is any bit of writing that doesn't sound right. It sounds strange when read aloud. It confuses their reader. Children are very quick to identify 'sticky' bits. You will notice some recurring themes: verb tense, cohesion, switching of pronouns, inability to identify a pronoun's noun.
>
> Children will recognise that it is often easier to edit someone else's work than their own!

Writing lesson 9: Publish

Class writing goal
To publish our memoirs

OVERVIEW

Most children should now be ready to publish their pieces and you should be ready to begin assessing their outcomes. Any children who have finished publishing their memoir can work on their personal writing projects.

PREPARATION AND RESOURCES

- Presentation tips (ITR and PCM, p274)
- A variety of stationery and art materials

MINI-LESSON

Choose from the suggested mini-lessons for this writing project, which cover aspects of writing study, grammar and punctuation.

The following mini-lessons may be particularly useful at the publishing stage:

- Ways of publishing

CLASS WRITING SESSION

Refer back to the original class writing goal of creating a collection of memoirs. Ensure children have access to the 'Presentation tips' (PCM, p274) or that you have the 'Presentation tips' ITR displayed on the whiteboard. Children can take this opportunity to present their writing, adding colour, artwork and photographs.

Conferencing focus
Take this opportunity to discuss your assessment of children's pieces and set writing goals for their future class and personal writing projects. Place these goals on the working wall.

PLENARY

Children perform their pieces to the class. This can be done as a whole class, in small groups or in pairs.

DEEPEN

Children could give detailed feedback as a reader to their peers, ensuring a sensitive response.

Writing lesson 10: Publish

Class writing goal
To publish our memoirs

OVERVIEW

Most children should now be ready to publish their pieces and you should be ready to begin assessing their outcomes. Any children who have finished publishing their memoir can work on their personal writing projects.

PREPARATION AND RESOURCES

- Presentation tips (ITR and PCM, p274)
- A variety of stationery and art materials

MINI-LESSON

Choose from the suggested mini-lessons for this writing project, which cover aspects of writing study, grammar and punctuation.

The following mini-lessons may be particularly useful at the publishing stage:

- Ways of publishing

CLASS WRITING SESSION

Children continue to publish their memoirs. Refer back to the original class writing goal of creating a collection of memoirs. Ensure children have access to the 'Presentation tips' (PCM, p274) or that you have the 'Presentation tips' ITR displayed on the whiteboard. Children can take this opportunity to present their writing, adding colour, artwork and photographs.

Conferencing focus

Take this opportunity to discuss your assessment of children's pieces and set writing goals for their future class and personal writing projects. Place these goals on the working wall.

PLENARY

Children perform their pieces for the class, other year groups, parents, the wider community or in a local library.

DEEPEN

Children could give detailed feedback as a reader to their peers, ensuring a sensitive response.

Class writing project: Graphic novels

Why write a graphic novel?

Graphic novels have become a vital part of contemporary culture. Many of the books children love have taken on the multi-modal nature of graphic novels and indeed children are reading graphic novels in their own right. Not only that, but they are also watching graphic novels come alive on the big screen.

This project is all about narrative writing. Historically, the narrative themes that tend to inspire graphic novels have included: good versus evil, strengths and weaknesses, revenge, betrayal, haunting back-stories, understanding one's self and saving the ones and the things we love. Graphic novels are not neutral. They are based on fundamental themes that have been sources of great writing for centuries.

What will be new and interesting for you and your class is the concept of using pictures to do some of the story-telling for you. You will begin to appreciate how much readers enjoy learning about characters through the images that graphic novelists create. Graphic novelists consider their characters with real care and attention, just as more traditional narrative writers do. The hope is that, as a result of undertaking this writing project, children will consider their characters in more detail in their future narrative writing too.

THINGS TO BEAR IN MIND

- Children will first draft their graphic novels in a traditional way. They will write a short narrative, considering their settings, characters and plots just as they are used to doing. Children will therefore find the guidance on pages 283–286 useful.

- Once written, children will consider how they are going to translate their characters' actions, feelings and thoughts in a visual way. This process is called 'storyboarding'. When their storyboards are complete, they can then publish their story as a graphic novel.

- Children must think about how they will convert their figurative language and sensory detail into an image on the page. They should understand that their drawings will have to show the necessary detail that is usually in their writing. It is important to note that this project is not designed to assess children's artistic ability.

- Children will have to make decisions on what is going to make it into their graphic novel and what will be left out. They must also think about how they will clearly show transitions between place and time.

- When they use captions and speech in their graphic novels, children will need to think hard about what they are going to write. They will need to ask themselves what is essential and what can be left out.

- Children will also have to think about how their story is going to affect their drawing style. Their illustrations should match the tone and theme of the story.

Writing a graphic novel

Use these ideas to help you write your own graphic novel for use in class or to introduce the genre to the children.

Why write a graphic novel for yourself or your class?

Many people have a passion for bringing words and pictures together. Good graphic novelists can use their illustrations to show drama and emotion in characters that they may not be able to show in writing.

What are the basics of a graphic novel?

It tells a story using a mix of pictures and text, with no rules for artwork style or amount of text used.

(FIELD) What is your graphic novel going to be about?

These are some of the typical plots used in graphic novels:

- A supervillain has to steal a number of things to take over the world and needs to be stopped.
- A supervillain is trying to kill a number of people who have something in common and needs to be stopped.
- A supervillain plays on a superhero's weaknesses (e.g. they are trusting of people and loved ones).
- Something or someone from a superhero's past comes back to haunt them.
- A superhero was born with superpowers they don't understand and cannot control.

- Someone that a superhero cares about is in trouble and needs to be saved.
- Someone has been mind-controlled or impersonated by a shape shifter.
- Revenge.
- A victim comes to a superhero for help.
- A superhero has to work with someone they detest to save the world.
- A superhero is betrayed by a friend.

(TENOR) What is your role as the writer / illustrator?

You need to take care that your story is simple enough to be followed using only a small amount of text and detailed illustrations alone. Also consider the following:

- Graphic novels usually show how good defeats evil.
- There is a lack of female heroines in graphic novels and this needs addressing.
- There is lack of ethnic diversity in the heroes in graphic novels and this needs addressing.

(MODE) What should your graphic novel look like?

Before you begin creating a storyboard for your graphic novel, you will first need to write your story. This will look the same as any other short story or flash fiction.

Once you have written your story, you'll turn it into a storyboard. A storyboard is where you write the story as small captions and make quick, rough drawings that will show the descriptions and characters you have created in your story. Once you have created your storyboard, you can begin publishing your graphic novel for real.

(LEXIS) How can your word choices help?

- They can tell your reader where the characters are.
- **Fronted adverbials** signal when and where events happen.

- They can tell us about sound effects.
- Dialogue tells your reader what your character is like and show *how* your character says something.

(GRAPHICS) How should your graphic novel be illustrated?

You will need to decide on an illustration style. This style should match the theme and tone of your story.

Your illustrations provide your reader with information that is not written anywhere on its pages (a raised eyebrow from a character, a tear running down a cheek, etc.)

Graphic novels often don't need long descriptions because the detailed illustrations will show: **feelings, noticing, imagining, hearing, touching, action, asking, tasting** and **smelling**.

Your illustrations must make an impact on your reader and be memorable. They need to show the detail that you would usually include through writing. How can you show your characters' feelings, and create a certain mood with the use of colour and shading?

How to develop a character

Use these ideas to help you develop a powerful and realistic character in your story.

Why develop a character for yourself or your class?

Your character is the centre of your story. Readers will often have their favourites characters. They can only choose a favourite if they know a lot about them so writers work hard to share information about their characters.

Characters might be people, robots, magical creatures or personified animals. Writers such as Roald Dahl would use either the best or worst characteristics of themselves or of others as inspiration for their characters.

(FIELD) How will you develop a character?

Writers develop characters in six ways:

- **Appearance** When introducing a character for the first time, writers will describe how their character looks – facial features, body shape, dress and mannerisms.
- **Action** What a character does and how they do it (**verbs and adverbs**) will tell you a lot about a character. Why do they do the things they do? What do they believe in? Is what they believe in right and wrong? How do they see the world? All of these things have an impact on what a character does.
- **Speech** A writer will think about what their character says and how they say it.
- **Emotions** A writer thinks about the way their character will be feeling and what their emotions will be throughout the story. Their emotions will often be based on what the character cares about the most.
- **Monologue** A great way to let your audience know about your characters is to let the characters themselves tell readers their thoughts and feelings.
- **Poetic metaphor** Some writers will create a character to be a metaphor or a symbol for something else. The character is there to represent an idea, a way of living your life, a way of thinking or behaving. You can disguise this idea by using a character. This also works for settings.

Writers also build **themes** in their writing. A character's emotions and values (the things they believe in) can change during a story. These themes can be things such as friendship, responsibility, courage and kindness to others.

(MODE) When will the character's personality be revealed?

You will often write about a character's qualities when you introduce a new character to your story, and when a character speaks, thinks or does something.

(SEMANTICS) How can you maintain your character?

Writers will often 'dabble' (think and make notes) before they start a plan or a draft for a story. A lot of their dabbling centres on their character(s). They will at least consider and often make notes on some of the following:

- What are you disguising your character as?
- What would you compare them to?
- Sight: *What do they look like?*
- Smell: *What might they smell like?*
- Touch: *What is their mood like and what would they feel like to touch?*
- Sound: *What do they sound like and what might they say?*

- Action: *What might they do and how they might do it?*
- Motives: *Why do they do the things they do?*
- Taste: *If your character had a taste, what would it be?*
- Monologue: *What do they spend their time thinking about? What do other people think of them?*
- *How do they live their life?*

(LEXIS) How can your word choices help?

Use the best **verbs, adverbs, adjectives, noun phrases and poetic devices** to:

- describe characters
- show how a character says something
- write about your character's thoughts
- describe what your character does and how they do it.

The 'best' means the ones that will **really express** what you want to communicate about your character.

How to write a vivid setting

Use these ideas to help you develop an effective setting in your story.

Why write a vivid setting for yourself or your class?

If you are writing about a place your reader is unlikely to have seen or know anything about, you need to provide an effective setting paragraph to make them feel at home. It is also an opportunity to 'paint with words' and bring some poetry to your story.

Some stories barely talk about the setting. Many fairy tales, for example, don't write about the setting very much at all. Instead they often use 'Once upon a time, in a far-away land' to set the stage.

If you're writing about a specific place, it can be important to ensure that your reader understands the historical period or the geographical location your story is set in.

(FIELD) What is your text is going to be about?

Setting doesn't just mean location, though this is one important part of setting. You need:

- location
- weather
- time of day
- historical time
- character's feelings
- setting as a character.

(TENOR) What is your role as the writer?

Think about the following:

- Everyday settings don't often need to be described because your reader will know about them, unless of course you are writing about an ordinary day when something unusual happens. It is the **extraordinary places**, where your reader may never have been, that need to be described well.
- If the weather is a part of your story, you need to describe early what the weather is like, particularly if it is something your reader may **never have witnessed** for themselves.
- The time of day can have a real impact on your reader if you are writing **ghost or scary stories.**
- If your story is set in the **past or future** you need to let your reader know. They may become confused if you include things that would not have been possible in a past era, or if they aren't told that the location is set in the future.
- How you describe your setting can tell your reader a lot about how your character is feeling at the time.
- Finally, you can use your setting as an additional character in your story.

(MODE) What does your setting look like?

Sometimes a paragraph at the start of your story is where you describe your story's setting. Otherwise, it's often when a new setting or scene is first introduced to your readers and this can be at any point in the story.

(SEMANTICS) How do you keep your reader on track?

Using powerful nouns and verbs is an effective way to describe setting. You could use verbs to describe the sights, sounds and smells of a busy street. You do not have to rely on adjectives to write a vivid setting.

(LEXIS) How can your word choices help?

You may find this device helpful:

- Describe places using **adjectives, noun phrases** and **poetic devices** to help your reader create images in their heads.

Genre study I: Why do people write graphic novels?

> **Class writing goal**
> To learn what our next class writing project will be

OVERVIEW

In this lesson, children will learn about graphic novels and will discuss why writers write them. You will reveal that this is the next class writing project and that the class will be publishing an anthology of graphic novels to place in the class library and beyond.

PREPARATION AND RESOURCES

- Graphic novels genre booklets
- Writing wheel (ITR and PCM, p272)
- Ask your class librarians to start displaying a variety of graphic novels and comics – both classic and contemporary

STUDY

Ask children about their experiences of reading graphic novels, or watching film adaptations of graphic novels.

Explain to the class that their class project will be to create their own graphic novel.

DISCUSS

Ask the children what experiences they have of reading, writing and illustrating graphic novels and / or comics. Do children have any thoughts on the video they have just watched? What did they learn about how writers create graphic novels?

Together, look at page 1 of the Graphic novels genre booklet. Ask children to work in pairs or small groups to answer the following questions:

- *What sorts of graphic novels / comics do you, or would you, like to write?*
- *What sorts of comics do you, or would you, like to read? Why?*
- *What do you think would make an effective graphic novel?*
- *Who is good at writing comics in the class? Why? What do they do?*
- *What's your favourite character from a graphic novel? Why?*

PLENARY

Children share writing from their personal projects, following the established class sharing routine.

PERSONAL WRITING PROJECTS

Throughout the class writing project, once the class writing goal for each session is complete, children carry on with their personal writing projects at their own pace and using their preferred writing processes. See pages 17–19 for more information on personal writing projects and pages 26–30 for more information on pupil conferencing.

Genre study 2: What makes an effective graphic novel?

> **Class writing goal**
> To understand what makes an effective graphic novel

OVERVIEW

In this lesson, children will study a variety of graphic novels and discuss what made them effective. They will then continue working on their personal writing projects.

PREPARATION AND RESOURCES

- Graphic novel genre booklets
- Pre-written exemplar graphic novel texts (genre booklet and ITRs)
- Graphic novel examples created by children from previous years
- Flip-chart paper

> As you develop your confidence as a writer-teacher, you should aim to create your own graphic novel exemplar using the writing project's opening guidance. Ensure it has a vivid setting and strong characters.

STUDY

Look at and read examples of graphic novels from your class library. Ask children to discuss them in pairs or small groups.

Display the genre examples on the whiteboard. Also display your own example and any child examples you have collected. Ask children to read the exemplars.

DISCUSS

In groups or pairs, children discuss:

- *What did the writers do that you really liked?*
- *What will we have to do to write a really effective graphic novel?*

CREATE

As a class, and using the information on page 1 of the Graphic novels genre booklet, start creating your poster of product goals. These goals should indicate what is needed to publish a great graphic novel.

PLENARY

Children share their posters, following the established class sharing routine.

PERSONAL WRITING PROJECTS

Throughout the class writing project, once the class writing goal for each session is complete, children carry on with their personal writing projects at their own pace and using their preferred writing processes. See pages 17–19 for more information on personal writing projects and pages 26–30 for more information on pupil conferencing.

Genre study 3: 'Reading' effective illustrations

> **Class writing goal**
> To understand how writers create their illustrations

OVERVIEW

In this lesson, children will look at how writers create their illustrations. They will use the information in their Graphic novels genre booklets to help them with their study. They will then continue working on their personal writing projects.

PREPARATION AND RESOURCES

- Graphic novels genre booklets
- Create your own illustrations for a graphic novel idea you have or use the pre-written exemplar graphic novel texts:
  - *Dad on ice* (genre booklet p2-4, ITR)
  - *Illegal (1)* (genre booklet p5-8, ITR)
  - *Illegal (2)* (ITR)
  - *Isis and the cobra* (ITR)
  - *The arrival* (ITR)

STUDY

Children read and discuss the exemplar graphic novel texts. Ask them to focus particularly on the illustrations and to think about how the novelist has attended to location, weather, time of day, character's feelings and description.

DISCUSS

In pairs, children discuss what should be added to their product goals poster, with the focus on what will make for effective illustration. Prompt them with questions such as:

- *What has the novelist done to develop the location?*
- *How does the weather seem to impact the story?*
- *How has the novelist got their characters' feelings across?*
- *Why has the novelist chosen this time of day?*
- *How has the novelist used their images to describe their character?*

PLENARY

Children share their ideas for effective illustrations, following the established class sharing routine.

PERSONAL WRITING PROJECTS

Throughout the class writing project, once the class writing goal for each session is complete, children carry on with their personal writing projects at their own pace and using their preferred writing processes. See pages 17–19 for more information on personal writing projects and pages 26–30 for more information on pupil conferencing.

Genre study 4: Dabbling characters

> **Class writing goal**
> To dabble our graphic novel character(s)

OVERVIEW

In this lesson, children will take part in some dabbling, focusing on character development. They can then continue with their personal writing projects.

PREPARATION AND RESOURCES

- Graphic novels genre booklets
- Dabbling your character(s) (PCM, p283)
- Developing your character(s) (PCM, p284)
- Flip-chart paper

STUDY

Explain that before writers begin planning or drafting their graphic novels, they will often dabble. Writers will pay particular attention to their characters because they know that this is what their readers often love the most.

Show children the example of writer dabbling on page 11 of their Graphic novels genre booklets. Explain that you are going to try this out together.

DISCUSS

First, very quickly, ask for three typical graphic novel plot ideas. Write these ideas on a flip-chart.

Next, as a class, vote on which one you want to 'dabble' with.

Hand out copies of the 'Dabbling your character(s)' (PCM, p283) and 'Developing your characters' (PCM, p284) and discuss some or all of the questions. You can use these resources to probe the main character in the graphic novel. As you and the class talk, write down some of the things they say as dabbles on the flip-chart, adding little illustrations as you go.

CREATE

In pairs or small groups, children generate two or three potential writing ideas for a graphic novel and practise dabbling. Encourage them to draw as well as write down ideas / dabbles.

Children should use the questions from the 'Dabbling your character(s)' (PCM, p283) to guide them.

PLENARY

Children share their dabbles, following the established class sharing routine.

DEEPEN

Ask a few children to practise dabbling at home so that they could be 'dabble experts' for the next session.

PERSONAL WRITING PROJECTS

Throughout the class writing project, once the class writing goal for each session is complete, children carry on with their personal writing projects at their own pace and using their preferred writing processes. See pages 17–19 for more information on personal writing projects and pages 26–30 for more information on pupil conferencing.

Genre study 5: Dabbling settings

> **Class writing goal**
> To dabble our graphic novel setting(s)

OVERVIEW

In this lesson, children will take part in some dabbling, focusing on setting development. They can then continue with their personal writing projects.

PREPARATION AND RESOURCES

- Graphic novels genre booklets
- Dabbling your setting(s) (PCM, p285)
- Developing your setting(s) (PCM, p286)
- Flip-chart paper

STUDY

Remind children that before writers begin planning or drafting their graphic novels, they will often dabble. Writers will pay particular attention to their settings because they know they are an opportunity to 'paint with words' or share more about their character.

Show children the example of writer dabbling on page 11 of their Graphic novels genre booklets. Explain that you are going to try this out together.

DISCUSS

First, very quickly, ask for three settings typical of graphic novels you've been looking at this week.

Next, as a class, vote on which one you want to 'dabble' with. Ask children to imagine themselves as the character in the setting.

Hand out copies of the 'Dabbling your setting(s)' (PCM, p285) and 'Developing your setting(s)' (PCM, p286) and discuss some or all of the questions. You can use these resources to probe the main setting in the graphic novel. As you and the class talk, write down some of the things they say as dabbles on the flip-chart, adding little illustrations as you go.

CREATE

In groups or pairs, children generate two or three potential settings that a graphic novel story could take place in and practise dabbling. Like yesterday, encourage them to draw and write their dabbles.

Encourage children to use the 'Dabbling your settings' (PCM, p285).

PLENARY

Children share their dabbles, following the established class sharing routine.

SUPPORT

Ask a few children to practise dabbling at home so that they could be dabble experts for the next session.

PERSONAL WRITING PROJECTS

Throughout the class writing project, once the class writing goal for each session is complete, children carry on with their personal writing projects at their own pace and using their preferred writing processes. See pages 17–19 for more information on personal writing projects and pages 26–30 for more information on pupil conferencing.

Genre study 6: Generating ideas

Class writing goal
To generate ideas for our graphic novels

OVERVIEW

In this lesson, children will use a range of techniques for generating graphic novel ideas. They will then decide what their story will be for the class writing project.

PREPARATION AND RESOURCES

- Graphic novels genre booklets
- Published graphic novels
- Flip-chart paper

STUDY

Children read and discuss ways of generating story ideas using the 'Generating good ideas' section on pages 9–10 of their Graphic novels genre booklets.

DISCUSS

As a class, come up with some potential graphic novel ideas. Ask the following questions to probe the ideas further:

- *Do you have an idea of how the story will end?*
- *What is your diamond moment?*
- *How many characters are there, and what is the main character like?*
- *Where is the story set and how many scene changes are there?*

CREATE

In groups, pairs or individually, children generate a list of potential ideas for their graphic novel.

Go around the classroom and hear what the children's ideas are. You can write these up somewhere. Ask:

- *Do you have an idea how it will end?*
- *What's your diamond moment?*
- *How are you going to make sure it's only two pages long?*
- *Tell me a little about your character.*
- *Have you made sure you don't have too many scene changes?*
- *Have you made sure there aren't too many characters?*
- *Have you got a particular story arc in mind?*

PLENARY

Each child can share their idea and ask for any advice or suggestions if they feel they need it. This can be done as a whole class, in groups or in pairs, following the established class sharing routine.

DEEPEN

Ask children to help others to generate ideas for their story or give pupil conferences.

SUPPORT

If children are struggling for an idea, they could ask others what they are planning to write about. Alternatively they may want to ask a friend to generate some ideas with them.

PERSONAL WRITING PROJECTS

Throughout the class writing project, once the class writing goal for each session is complete, children carry on with their personal writing projects at their own pace and using their preferred writing processes. See pages 17–19 for more information on personal writing projects and pages 26–30 for more information on pupil conferencing.

Writing lesson I: Plan

Class writing goal
To plan our graphic novels

OVERVIEW

Children plan or draft their graphic novels.

PREPARATION AND RESOURCES

- Graphic novels genre booklets
- Graphic novel planning grid (PCM, p287)

MINI-LESSON

Choose from the suggested mini-lessons for this writing project, which cover aspects of writing study, grammar and punctuation.

The following mini-lessons may be particularly useful at the planning stage:

- Stories about people
- Fan fiction
- Write a fairy tale
- Rewrite a fairy tale
- Ideas map

CLASS WRITING SESSION

Before you begin your writing week, tell children that they have nine writing sessions in which to publish their graphic novel. Remind them of the different writing styles writers often use. These include being a discoverer, planner, drafter, paragraph piler and sentence stacker. Explain that, depending on their preferred writing style, they are likely to be planning or drafting today.

Children create a plan for their graphic novel. Remind them what a plan needs to include in order to be helpful for the writing process (an opening, introduction of characters, description of setting, a potential ending).

Children may also find it useful to look at the planning advice on page 12 of their Graphic novels genre booklets.

If children choose to plan their pieces, they are free to use their 'Graphic novel planning grid' (PCM, p287) if they wish to. Other children may leap straight into drafting their graphic novel. Encourage these children to refer to the drafting rules on page 13 of their Graphic novel genre booklets.

> ### Conferencing focus
>
> Encourage children to talk through their plans or drafts in pairs and with you throughout this session.
>
> Pairs focus on any 'sticky' bits they hear.
>
> A 'sticky' bit is any bit of writing that doesn't sound right. It sounds strange when read aloud. It confuses your reader. Children are very quick to identify 'sticky' bits. You will notice some recurring themes: verb tense, cohesion, switching of pronouns, inability to identify a pronoun's noun.

PLENARY

Children who have planned their graphic novel turn over their plans and 'tell' their graphic novel to someone in the class.

DEEPEN

Encourage children to think of an alternative ending for their story so they can choose their favourite in the final version.

SUPPORT

Provide children with an A3-size 'Graphic novel planning grid' (PCM, p287). Alternatively, children can talk their plan through with an adult and go straight to the drafting stage or draw their plan.

Writing lesson 2: Plan

Class writing goal
To plan our graphic novels

OVERVIEW

Any children who haven't finished will continue to plan or draft their graphic novels.

PREPARATION AND RESOURCES

- Graphic novels genre booklets
- Graphic novel planning grid (PCM, p287)
- Notes from previous lesson

MINI-LESSON

Choose from the suggested mini-lessons for this writing project, which cover aspects of writing study, grammar and punctuation.

The following mini-lessons may be particularly useful at the planning stage:

- Choosing a story arc
- Create a character
- That's me, I wish that was me, that's the worst of me
- Writing a conversation

CLASS WRITING SESSION

Children continue to plan their graphic novels. Remind them to think really carefully about the setting and character. Prompt them with the following questions.

- *What is your setting like?*
- *If your setting was a person, what would they be like?*
- *Why is the setting behaving the way it is?*
- *If I were there, what would I see, hear or smell?*
- *How does your character feel about this place?*
- *Do you have an idea of what the ending is going to be?*

Other children may begin or continue to draft their graphic novel. Encourage these children to refer to the drafting rules on page 13 of their Graphic novels genre booklets.

Conferencing focus

Encourage children to talk through their plans or drafts in pairs and with you throughout this session. Their partner should let them know if their plan has any 'sticky' bits.

A 'sticky' bit is any bit of writing that doesn't sound right. It sounds strange when read aloud. It confuses your reader. Children are very quick to identify 'sticky' bits. You will notice some recurring themes: verb tense, cohesion, switching of pronouns, inability to identify a pronoun's noun.

PLENARY

Children who have planned their graphic novel turn over their plans and 'tell' their story to someone in the class. If you and your class feel they need another planning session, please add one in. Alternatively, if children are confident with the writing processes, you can let them move on to the next stage independently.

SUPPORT

Provide children with an A3-size 'Graphic novel planning grid' (PCM, p287). Alternatively, children can talk their plan through with an adult and go straight to the drafting stage or draw their plan.

Writing lesson 3: Draft

Class writing goal
To draft our graphic novels

OVERVIEW

Children use the plans they created in previous sessions to start or continue drafting their graphic novels. Some children may have finished their drafts at this point and can move on to revising their pieces.

PREPARATION AND RESOURCES

- Graphic novels genre booklets
- Plans from previous lessons
- Graphic novel planning grid (PCM, p287)
- Drafting rules (ITR)
- Tips and Tricks cards
- Upper KS2 narrative revision checklist (ITR and PCM, p277)

MINI-LESSON

Choose from the suggested mini-lessons for this writing project, which cover aspects of writing study, grammar and punctuation.

The following mini-lessons may be particularly useful at the drafting stage:

- Using body language
- Don't start too far upstream

CLASS WRITING SESSION

Using their plans, children will start to draft their graphic novels. It's important to reiterate this is just a first draft and not the end of the writing process. Children should remember that they are writing *short* stories and that they should limit themselves to only two pages of drafting. Children should write on the left-hand side of the page, leaving the right-hand side blank for revision in future sessions.

Refer children to the drafting rules and advice on page 13 of their Graphic novels genre booklets.

Encourage children, when drafting, to try to make their story as clear as possible just using text. They can then add illustrations later on to enhance the meaning.

Children may find it useful to look at the example openings and endings for stories on pages 14–17 of their Graphic novels genre booklets.

At this point, they should write their graphic novel like a short story. Explain to children that by writing the entire story first in short story format they are able to concentrate on the narrative, making sure that the characters and settings are as fully formed as possible, without being distracted by illustrations. Tell them that once they have written out their story, they will then turn it into a storyboard. This is when they convert their story into a rough draft graphic novel.

Some children may have finished drafting their graphic novel at this point and can move on to revising their pieces using the revision checklist on page 19 of their Graphic novel genre booklets if necessary.

Conferencing focus

Encourage children to request a conference with you if they get stuck. Make sure they continually refer to their plan as they write their draft. Encourage children to regularly reread their writing as they go.

Provide intervals in which children share their writing in pairs. Partners should focus on any 'sticky' bits they hear.

A 'sticky' bit is any bit of writing that doesn't sound right. It sounds strange when read aloud. It confuses your reader. Children are very quick to identify 'sticky' bits. You will notice some recurring themes: verb tense, cohesion, switching of pronouns, inability to identify a pronoun's noun.

Top tip

Sometimes it's helpful to suggest that children leave it a couple of days before they decide to revise or edit their pieces. This means they can look at their writing with fresh and objective eyes.

PLENARY

Children share their drafts, following the established class sharing routine.

SUPPORT

Encourage these children to paragraph pile or sentence stack until they are confident.

Writing lesson 4: Draft

Class writing goal
To draft our graphic novels

OVERVIEW

Children continue drafting their graphic novels in preparation for storyboarding. Some children may have finished their drafts at this point and can move on to revising their pieces.

PREPARATION AND RESOURCES

- Graphic novels genre booklets
- Graphic novel planning grid (PCM, p287)
- Drafting rules (ITR)
- Upper KS2 narrative revision checklist (ITR and PCM, p277)
- Tips and Tricks cards
- Plans from previous lessons

MINI-LESSON

Choose from the suggested mini-lessons for this writing project, which cover aspects of writing study, grammar and punctuation.

The following mini-lessons may be particularly useful at the drafting stage:

- Twenty words
- Parallel stories
- Using body language
- Finding the diamond moment
- Using thoughts and feelings

CLASS WRITING SESSION

Most children will continue to draft their class writing project. Remind them to:

- refer to their plans while writing
- circle any words where they are unsure how to spell.

Also remind children to look at the drafting rules and advice on page 13 of their Graphic novels genre booklets.

Some children may have finished drafting their graphic novel at this point and can move on to revising their pieces using the revision checklist in their Graphic novel genre booklets if necessary.

Conferencing focus

Encourage children to request a conference with you if they get stuck. Ask them to regularly stop and reread their writing.

Provide intervals in which children share their writing in pairs. Partners should focus on any 'sticky' bits they hear.

A 'sticky' bit is any bit of writing that doesn't sound right. It sounds strange when read aloud. It confuses your reader. Children are very quick to identify 'sticky' bits. You will notice some recurring themes: verb tense, cohesion, switching of pronouns, inability to identify a pronoun's noun.

Top tip

Sometimes it's helpful to suggest that children leave it a couple of days before they decide to revise or edit their pieces. This means they can look at their writing with fresh and objective eyes.

PLENARY

Children share their drafts, following the established class sharing routine. If you and your class feel they need another drafting session, please add one in. Alternatively, if children are confident with the writing processes, you can let them move on to the next stage independently.

SUPPORT

Encourage these children to paragraph pile or sentence stack until they are confident.

Writing lesson 5: Revising and editing

Class writing goal

To revise and edit our graphic novels

OVERVIEW

Children begin the important process of rereading and revising their writing. Focus should be on ensuring that the text makes sense and that they have included everything in their plans. Some children may have finished revising their graphic novel at this point and can move on to editing their pieces.

PREPARATION AND RESOURCES

- Graphic novels genre booklets
- Upper KS2 narrative revision checklist (ITR and PCM, p277)
- Upper KS2 editing checklist (ITR and PCM, p273)
- Tips and Tricks cards
- Electronic spell checkers
- Access to online dictionaries
- Reading books

MINI-LESSON

Choose from the suggested mini-lessons for this writing project, which cover aspects of writing study, grammar and punctuation.

The following mini-lessons may be particularly useful at the revision and editing stages:

- Strong endings
- Don't know what to write next?

Conferencing focus

Remind children that all writers find it difficult to identify faults in their own writing, which is why sharing with a partner is helpful. Make sure partners are particularly looking out for:

- a tempting opening
- strong character development
- a diamond moment
- vivid setting description
- a powerful ending.

CLASS WRITING SESSION

Explain to children that many of them are now going to start revising their piece of writing, whilst others will be ready to move on to editing their pieces. Remind them that if they have many changes to make they can create a new version opposite their draft in their English book. This is particularly the case for children whose preferred writing process is that of 'discoverer'.

Revising involves rereading and improving, before moving on to editing. Remind children to use the revision information and checklist on pages 18–19 of their Graphic novels genre booklet. They should also use the relevant Tips and Tricks cards to help them with grammar, punctuation and spelling. Also remind children that they can use a dictionary to look up spellings they are unsure of. They can also use their reading books to check the spellings of common words.

This is a really good opportunity to add in a bit of detail about either the setting or the main character – or both. Encourage children to think about where they can give a bit more insight into where the story is set, or who it is about, so that characters feel more vivid, more alive and more real to readers.

Children should create a new version opposite their draft in their English book if they have a lot of changes to make.

Some children may have finished revising their graphic novel at this point and can move on to editing their pieces using the 'Upper KS2 editing checklist' (PCM, p273).

PLENARY

Children share their revised drafts, following the established class sharing routine. If you or your class feel they need another revision and editing session, please add one in. Alternatively, if children are confident with the writing processes, you can let them move on to the next stage independently.

SUPPORT

Children may require more support in reviewing their own or others' writing and may benefit from adult input.

Writing lesson 6: Storyboarding

Class writing goal
To storyboard our graphic novels

OVERVIEW

Children will continue to turn their short stories into storyboards.

PREPARATION AND RESOURCES

- Graphic novels genre booklets
- Drafts from previous lesson
- Paper and pencils

MINI-LESSON

Choose from the suggested mini-lessons for this writing project, which cover aspects of writing study, grammar and punctuation.

The following mini-lessons may be particularly useful at the storyboarding stage.
- Create a character
- Great openings
- Strong endings
- Moving quickly and slowly in a story

CLASS WRITING SESSION

These next few sessions are for children to storyboard their graphic novels. Storyboarding is when a graphic novelist converts their story into a draft graphic novel.

Together, read the information on storyboarding on page 20 of their Graphic novels genre booklets.

Children will make decisions on how they will use the space. They should limit themselves to around five panels per page.

Children will have to consider how they are going to get their story across using mainly illustrations and some captions. Their captions will focus on changes in location, time and dialogue. Their illustrations will focus on setting description and character development.

Conferencing focus
Ask children the following questions.
- *Which bit are you trying to storyboard?*
- *Is there a bit we could try panelling together?*
- *What's not quite working at the moment?*
- *What do you think of your opening? Have you tried out any other ideas?*
- *What do you think of your ending? Have you tried out any other ideas?*
- *Where have you considered developing your character through illustration?*
- *Where have you considered describing your setting for your reader through illustration?*
- *Tell me a bit more about your character.*

PLENARY

Children share their storyboards, following the established class sharing routine.

DEEPEN

Children may want to include more than five panels per page for their storyboard.

Writing lesson 7: Storyboarding

Class writing goal

To storyboard our graphic novels

OVERVIEW

Children continue to work on their storyboards.

PREPARATION AND RESOURCES

- Graphic novels genre booklets
- Storyboards from previous session
- Paper and pencils

MINI-LESSON

Choose from the suggested mini-lessons for this writing project, which cover aspects of writing study, grammar and punctuation.

The following mini-lessons may be particularly useful at the storyboarding stage.

- Peripheral vision
- Sticky bits and yawny bits
- How to write a vivid setting
- Building atmosphere: Suspense and tension

CLASS WRITING SESSION

Children continue to storyboard their graphic novels. Encourage them to focus on how their illustrations will portray setting description and character development. They should consider how their captions will convey changes in location, time and dialogue.

PLENARY

Show some examples of children's storyboards, following the established class sharing routine. If you and your class feel they need another storyboarding session, please add one in. Alternatively, if children are confident with the writing processes, you can let them move on to the next stage independently.

Conferencing focus

Ask children the following questions.

- *Which bit are you trying to storyboard?*
- *Is there a bit we could try panelling together?*
- *What's not quite working at the moment?*
- *What do you think of your opening? Have you tried out any other ideas?*
- *What do you think of your ending? Have you tried out any other ideas?*
- *Where have you considered developing your character through illustration?*
- *Where have you considered describing your setting for your reader through illustration?*
- *Tell me a bit more about your character.*

SUPPORT

Children may require more adult support in creating their storyboards.

Writing lesson 8: Publish

Class writing goal
To publish our graphic novels

OVERVIEW

Most children should now be ready to publish their pieces and you should be ready to begin assessing their outcomes. Any children who have finished publishing their graphic novels can work on their personal writing projects.

PREPARATION AND RESOURCES

- A variety of stationery and art materials
- Presentation tips (ITR and PCM, p274)

MINI-LESSON

Choose from the suggested mini-lessons for this writing project, which cover aspects of writing study, grammar and punctuation.

The following mini-lessons may be particularly useful at the publishing stage:
- Ways of publishing

CLASS WRITING SESSION

Check children understand what publishing a piece of writing means. Discuss audience and what makes readers interested in a text. In this case, children can create a class collection of short stories.

Ensure children have access to the 'Presentation tips' (PCM, p274) or that you have the 'Presentation tips' ITR displayed on the whiteboard. Children take this opportunity to present their writing, adding colour, artwork and photographs.

PLENARY

Children share their published work and give feedback on how it appeals to readers, following the established class sharing routine.

Conferencing focus

Take this opportunity to discuss your assessment of their graphic novels and then set writing goals for future class and personal projects.

Top tip

Once the graphic novel is finished, it is a good time to think about the title. Children often want to start with a title, but it is actually easier and more effective to come up with something relevant and meaningful once the piece is finished. Encourage them not to be afraid of revising or completely changing titles already chosen.

Writing lesson 9: Publish

Class writing goal
To publish our graphic novels

OVERVIEW

Most children should now be ready to publish their pieces and you should be ready to begin assessing their outcomes. Any children who have finished publishing their graphic novels can work on their personal writing projects.

PREPARATION AND RESOURCES

- A variety of stationery and art materials
- Presentation tips (ITR and PCM, p274)

MINI-LESSON

Choose from the suggested mini-lessons for this writing project, which cover aspects of writing study, grammar and punctuation.

The following mini-lessons may be particularly useful at the publishing stage:
- Ways of publishing

CLASS WRITING SESSION

Children complete the publishing of their graphic novel. Ensure that they continue to refer to the 'Presentation tips' PCM (PCM, p274) or the 'Presentation tips' ITR. Children can take this opportunity to present their writing, adding colour, artwork and photographs.

Conferencing focus

Take this opportunity to discuss your assessment of children's graphic novels and set writing goals for their future class and personal writing projects. Place these goals on the working wall.

Once children have published their graphic novel, they can continue with their personal writing projects, at their own pace and using their preferred writing process.

PLENARY

Children perform their pieces to the class. This can be done as a whole class, in small groups or in pairs.

The class could also share their anthologies with other classes in the school or in the main library.

Class writing project: Persuasive writing (Advocacy journalism)

Why write persuasive articles?

Persuasion is when you advocate for something. It means you champion it, support it and try to stand up for it. This project will give children first-hand experience of undertaking and writing up original research. It will also provide the opportunity for them to learn about local causes and the power of community action. It is a legitimate way for them to see how news / magazine articles are used to inform, entertain *and* persuade people.

This can be a truly collaborative project that brings home and school together. Parents and carers can be involved and children will see their writing 'get to work' by informing others in the local community about their chosen charity. They see what writing an article in a journalistic style can do.

You will be struck by the sheer variety of local charities and the children's personal commitment to them. You may want to compile a list of charities yourself which the children could potentially use. A great many children will, however, be able to choose charities that they, or someone close to them, have been directly involved with or received help from. This will make the project feel even more important to them personally.

THINGS TO BEAR IN MIND

- To make the writing truly purposeful, your school could set up a small charity grant fund and invite the community to top this up. This fund could then be used as a prize for the best three articles. The prize money could be sent along with the articles to the winning charities. Depending on the focus, each article could be placed into one of three groups, for example:
  - helping people
  - helping animals
  - helping the environment.

- The articles could be presented to a group of Year 6 pupils who are then asked to determine which are the most effective in: informing, persuading and providing a personal touch.

- It is a good idea to introduce this project just before a half term. This gives children plenty of time to talk with their families and choose a local charity, organisation or cause that is worthwhile or important to them. They then have the holiday to research details of the charity and bring their information into school. They may be able to visit the charity in person, or could possibly phone to get a quote summing up the role of the charity. Alternatively, they could try getting in touch using email.

- What will become clear to you over the course of this project is what a multi-faceted genre this can be. It requires children to negotiate aspects of informing and persuading as well as recounting a small anecdote relating to the charity.

Writing a persuasive article

Use these ideas to help you write your own persuasive article for use in class or to introduce children to the genre.

Why write a persuasive article for yourself or your class?
To let your readers know about an organisation that you think is worthwhile.

What are the basics of a persuasive article?
When you advocate for something it means you champion it, you support it and you try to stand up for it. You will learn how to take notes, do interviews and write an interesting persuasive article that people will want to read. You will often see these kinds of articles in newspapers, magazines and leaflets, and on websites. You can write about **human**, **animal** or **environmental** problems.

(FIELD) What is your persuasive article going to be about?
Give your readers information about the organisation. **What** it is, **where** it is and its **aims**. This type of writing is best when you choose a charity you have been involved with yourself. You will need to include:

- The problem they are trying to make better.
- What the organisation does.
- The activities they have coming up. What their staff are like and how they raise money.
- A personal story about something the charity has done. Appeal to your reader's emotions.
- End your piece by providing some contact details so people can get involved.

(TENOR) What is your role as the writer?
Use a real **anecdote** from your experience of the charity to really add a personal touch to your piece. It could be amusing, sad or inspirational – but tell it almost like a story to bring your reader in. You could also ask your reader a question about the subject of the charity and then go on to answer it.

Tell your readers how they can be involved by addressing them directly as 'you': *You can get help by …*

At the end of your piece, persuade your reader to find out more, take part or donate money.

(MODE) What does your persuasive article look like?
The piece can be **multi-modal.** Use pictures, photographs, diagrams, maps, logos, fact and figures for interest. Use speech marks when giving a quote from any experts from the charity.

(SEMANTICS) How can you make your persuasive article clear and interesting?
You can:

- Write as a reporter, using the **first person** 'I': *What I did … ; What I saw …; Who I met …*
- Write most of your piece in the **present tense**, e.g. when you are writing about what the charity is doing now.
- Write in the **past tense** when you describe what you saw and did.

(LEXIS) How can your word choices help?
You will need to use **time connectives**, e.g. *later, last year, soon afterwards*. These will allow time to pass in your writing. Time connectives make sure it has a speedy pace and doesn't get boring.

Genre study 1: What do we know about persuasive writing?

> ## Class writing goal
> To learn what our next class writing project will be

OVERVIEW

In this lesson, children will revisit the persuasion genre and will discuss why writers write persuasive articles. The class will be writing, publishing and sending journalistic articles to the charities that they are writing about. As an option, you could let them know that there will be three prizes given out for the best articles. The prize will be sent with their article to their charity.

PREPARATION AND RESOURCES

- Ask your class librarians to display a variety of magazines, leaflets and newspapers
- Video: 'Why I write persuasive articles'
- Writing wheel (ITR and PCM, p272)
- Homework letter (PCM, p292)

STUDY

Show children the video 'Why I write persuasive articles'. The video shows the journalist Eddie de Oliveira, speaking about how and why he writes persuasive articles, how he keeps his audience in mind and how he structures his persuasive writing.

Explain to the class that their class project will be to write their own journalistic article.

DISCUSS

Ask the children what they think persuasive journalism is and what thoughts they have about the video they have just watched.

Display the 'Writing wheel' ITR on the whiteboard, and hand out printed copies.

Ask the following questions:

- *Why do you think people write persuasive journalism (purpose)?*
- *Who do they write it for (audience)?*
- *Why is it important to advocate for things?*
- *What do you care about?*
- *What charities or causes do your families support?*

CREATE

Give out the homework letter and interview questions (PCM, p292) or something similar. Make sure you include the typical questions that will need to be asked about the charity and attach an example of what a finished article looks like. Explain that there are three categories that their charity can come under: helping people, helping animals and helping the environment. You may want to raise some money and turn this project into a competition. The writers of the winning articles could be sent a cheque to support the charity.

PLENARY

Read through the homework letter (PCM, p292) and explain that this homework will be necessary for planning their project. Explain that children might want to supplement their interview answers with material from home.

PERSONAL WRITING PROJECTS

Throughout the class writing project, once the class writing goal for each session is complete, children carry on with their personal writing projects at their own pace and using their preferred writing processes. See pages 17–19 for more information on personal writing projects and pages 26–30 for more information on pupil conferencing.

Genre study 2: What makes a good persuasive article?

Class writing goal

To discover what makes a good persuasive article

OVERVIEW

In this lesson, children will look at a variety of persuasive article examples and discuss what topics were chosen, why they think the writer might have chosen them and what the exemplars do well. They will then continue working on their personal writing projects.

PREPARATION AND RESOURCES

- Persuasive writing (Advocacy journalism) genre booklet
- Pre-written exemplar persuasive articles:
  - *Support Guinea Pig Friends* (genre booklet p3–4, ITR)
  - *The Holiday Fun Club* (genre booklet p5–6, ITR)
- Persuasive article exemplars created by children from previous years
- Flip-chart paper to generate your persuasive article product goals

As you develop your confidence as a writer-teacher, you should aim to create your own persuasive article exemplar about a charity that is significant to you. Use the writing project's opening guidance.

STUDY

Children read and discuss the exemplar persuasive writing articles. Ask these questions:

- *What did you like about the article you are reading?*
- *What ideas did it give you for your article?*

DISCUSS

In pairs, children discuss the following questions.

- *Why do you think the writer chose their topic(s)? What was their diamond?*
- *Can you see differences between the examples?*
- *What sort of diamonds were chosen by the other writers? Why?*
- *What charities do you think deserve to be written about?*
- *What makes a persuasive article a good one?*

CREATE

As a class, and using the information on pages 1–2 of the Persuasive writing (Advocacy journalism) genre booklet, start creating your poster of product goals. These goals should indicate what is needed to publish a great persuasive article.

PLENARY

Children share writing from their personal projects, following the established class sharing routine. Place exemplars into the class library for children to continue reading at their leisure.

DEEPEN

In preparation for tomorrow's ineffective example lesson, you could challenge your more experienced writers to write their own ineffective persuasive article, using their Persuasive writing (Advocacy journalism) genre booklets to help them.

PERSONAL WRITING PROJECTS

Throughout the class writing project, once the class writing goal for each session is complete, children carry on with their personal writing projects at their own pace and using their preferred writing processes. See pages 17–19 for more information on personal writing projects and pages 26–30 for more information on pupil conferencing.

Genre study 3: Where can persuasive articles go wrong?

> ## Class writing goal
> To understand where persuasion articles can go wrong

OVERVIEW

In this lesson, children will learn about critiquing ineffective examples using the genre information in their Persuasive writing (Advocacy journalism) genre booklets. They will then continue working on their personal writing projects.

PREPARATION AND RESOURCES

- Persuasive writing (Advocacy journalism) genre booklets
- Pre-written ineffective persuasive article exemplar (ITR)
- Anonymised ineffective examples of persuasive articles taken from previous years

STUDY

As a class, read the ineffective exemplars of persuasive articles.

DISCUSS

In pairs, using your class product goals poster from the previous lesson and the information on pages 1–2 of their Persuasive writing genre booklets, children discuss and explain for themselves why the examples are ineffective.
Ask questions such as:

- Is it clear what work the charity does?
- Does the writer use emotional language?
- Has the writer made it personal?
- Is there contact information if people want to get involved with the charity?

> Write your own ineffective persuasive article using the following as a guide:
>
> - Choose a charity you know little about.
> - Don't use any persuasive or emotional language – make it solely information based.
> - Don't address your reader using 'you'.
> - Don't provide any personal anecdotes – or if you do make them poor quality.
> - Provide a useless quote – or don't give one at all.
> - Don't write about why the charity is important to you.
> - Don't urge your reader to get involved.

PLENARY

Recap the ineffective features of persuasive journalism so that children understand which features make the articles less persuasive.

PERSONAL WRITING PROJECTS

Throughout the class writing project, once the class writing goal for each session is complete, children carry on with their personal writing projects at their own pace and using their preferred writing processes. See pages 17–19 for more information on personal writing projects and pages 26–30 for more information on pupil conferencing.

Genre study 4: Generating ideas for our persuasive articles

> ## Class writing goal
> To generate ideas for our persuasive articles

OVERVIEW

In this lesson, children will look at each other's notes that they have collected as part of their homework. They will check to see whether they feel their partner has enough information to write their article.

PREPARATION AND RESOURCES

- Persuasive writing (Advocacy journalism) genre booklets
- Research homework
- Persuasive writing planning grid (PCM, p288)
- Access to the internet

STUDY

Children turn to page 7 of their Persuasive writing (Advocacy journalism) genre booklets. Read and discuss some of the techniques used by writers to generate ideas for writing persuasive articles.

DISCUSS

In pairs, ask children to look through each other's homework notes. Ask children to check whether they feel their partner has enough information to write their article. You might want to provide them with a copy of the 'Persuasive writing planning grid' (PCM, p288) so that they can check that they will have everything they need to plan their article. Pairs could ask each other the following questions.

- Do you have enough background information about the charity?
- Do you know what the charity does?
- Do you know about the staff and how the charity is funded?
- Do you have a personal story / anecdote that you can use?
- Have you got a quote from an expert or someone who has used the charity?
- Have you got the charity's contact details?

CREATE

Any children who require more time to gather information could use today's lesson to research their charity using the internet. Alternatively, they could write some notes about what they need and take these home to collect the additional information.

PLENARY

Make sure any children who require more information in preparation for writing know when and how they are going to get hold of this.

PERSONAL WRITING PROJECTS

Throughout the class writing project, once the class writing goal for each session is complete, children carry on with their personal writing projects at their own pace and using their preferred writing processes. See pages 17–19 for more information on personal writing projects and pages 26–30 for more information on pupil conferencing.

Writing lesson I: Plan

> ## Class writing goal
> To plan our persuasive articles

OVERVIEW

Children plan or draft their persuasive articles.

PREPARATION AND RESOURCES

- Persuasive writing (Advocacy journalism) genre booklets
- Homework notes
- Persuasive writing planning grid (ITR and PCM, p288)
- Photographs and / or material from home

MINI-LESSON

Choose from the suggested mini-lessons for this writing project, which cover aspects of writing study, grammar and punctuation.

The following mini-lessons may be particularly useful at the planning stage:

- Use an ideas heart
- Give a voice where none is heard
- Use newspapers and magazines
- General to specific
- What do you believe in?

CLASS WRITING SESSION

Before you begin your writing week, tell children that they have ten writing sessions in which to publish their persuasive article. Remind them of the different writing styles writers often use. These include being a discoverer, planner, drafter, paragraph piler and sentence stacker. Explain that, depending on their preferred writing style, they are likely to be planning or drafting today.

> ### Conferencing focus
> Encourage children to talk through their plans or drafts in pairs and with you throughout this session.
>
> Their partner should let the writer know if they are assuming too much prior knowledge from their reader and whether anything needs explaining to their reader so they can better understand the charity.

You could show children a plan of your own, or display the example 'Persuasive writing planning grid' ITR. Children may also find it useful to look at the planning advice on pages 8–9 of their Persuasive writing (Advocacy journalism) genre booklet.

You may have children who, when planning, notice they don't have the information they need to finish their planning. You can reassure them that they have another planning session in which to sort this out and they can bring in any extra information required the next day.

If children choose to plan their pieces, they are free to use their 'Persuasive writing planning grid' (PCM, p288) if they wish to. Other children may leap straight into drafting their persuasive article. Encourage these children to refer to the Drafting rules on page 10 of their Persuasion genre booklets.

PLENARY

Children who have planned their persuasive articles turn over their plans and 'tell' their article to someone in the class.

DEEPEN

When planning their article, ask children to try to merge it with techniques from story writing. For example can they open their article with a story opening? Can they use: shock / surprise, question, dialogue, monologue, description, action and flashback? Can they describe the setting of the charity and the 'characters' they have met or interviewed? Can they end their article with something that their reader has to think about and reflect on?

SUPPORT

Provide children with an A3-size copy of the 'Persuasive writing planning grid' (PCM, p288). Alternatively, children can talk their plan through with an adult and go straight to drafting, or they can draw their plan.

Writing lesson 2: Plan

Class writing goal
To plan our persuasive articles

OVERVIEW

Children continue to plan or draft their persuasive article.

PREPARATION AND RESOURCES

- Persuasive writing (Advocacy journalism) genre booklets
- Research homework
- Persuasion planning grid (ITR and PCM, p288)
- Photographs and / or material from home

MINI-LESSON

Choose from the suggested mini-lessons for this writing project, which cover aspects of writing study, grammar and punctuation.

The following mini-lessons may be particularly useful at the planning stage:

- What itch needs scratching?
- Make a change!
- Be a reporter
- Paragraphs

CLASS WRITING SESSION

Children can continue their planning started on the previous day. Remind children to consider what the diamond moment of their piece is and discuss this with their talk partners.

Once their plan is complete, children can continue with their personal writing projects, at their own pace and using their preferred writing process.

Other children may begin or continue to draft their persuasive article. Encourage these children to refer to the drafting rules and information on page 10–11 of their Persuasive writing (Advocacy journalism) genre booklets. You could display the 'Drafting rules' ITR.

Conferencing focus

Encourage children to talk through their plans or drafts in pairs, and with you throughout this session.

Partners could let the writer know if they are assuming too much prior knowledge from their reader. Is there anything that needs explaining to their reader so they can better understand the charity?

Top tip

Ask children to think about why this charity matters to them or their family. Can they show this in their article in some way?

PLENARY

Children who have planned their persuasive article turn over their plans and 'tell' their article to someone in the class. If you and your class feel they need another planning session, please add one in. Alternatively, if children are confident with the writing processes, you can let them move on to the next stage independently.

DEEPEN

When planning their article, ask children to try to merge it with techniques from story writing. For example can they open their article with a story opening? Can they use shock / surprise, question, dialogue, monologue, description, action and flashback? Can they describe the setting of the charity and the 'characters' they have met or interviewed? Can they end their article with something that their reader has to think about and reflect on?

SUPPORT

Provide children with an A3-size copy of the 'Persuasive writing planning grid' (PCM, p288). Alternatively, children can talk their plan through with an adult and go straight to drafting, or they can draw their plan.

Writing lesson 3: Draft

Class writing goal
To draft our persuasive articles

OVERVIEW

Children use the plans they created in previous sessions to start or continue drafting their persuasive articles. Some children may have finished their drafts at this point and can move on to revising their pieces.

PREPARATION AND RESOURCES

- Persuasive writing (Advocacy journalism) genre booklets
- Planning grids from the previous lesson
- Drafting rules (ITR)
- Upper KS2 non-fiction revision checklist (ITR and PCM, p278)
- Tips and Tricks cards

MINI-LESSON

Choose from the suggested mini-lessons for this writing project, which cover aspects of writing study, grammar and punctuation.

The following mini-lessons may be particularly useful at the drafting stage:

- Be outrageous
- Support the facts
- Sentences with different forms
- Noun phrases with adjectives and prepositional phrases
- Using modals

CLASS WRITING SESSION

Explain to the class that they are now going to start drafting their piece of writing based on the plan they have completed. Remind them to use the drafting rules and information on pages 10–11 of their Persuasive writing (Advocacy journalism) genre booklets. You could display the 'Drafting rules' ITR. They should talk it through with a partner if they get stuck.

Children should write on the left side of the page, leaving the right side blank for revision in future lessons.

If their draft is complete, children can continue with their personal writing projects, at their own pace and using their preferred writing process.

Some children may have finished drafting their persuasive articles at this point and can move on to revising their pieces using the revision information and checklist on pages 12–14 of their Persuasive writing (Advocacy journalism) genre booklets if necessary.

Conferencing focus

Encourage children to request a conference with you if they get stuck. Ask them to regularly reread their pieces as they write them.

Provide intervals in which to share their writing in pairs. Partners should focus on any 'sticky' bits they hear.

A 'sticky' bit is any bit of writing that doesn't sound right. It sounds strange when read aloud. It confuses your reader. Children are very quick to identify 'sticky' bits. You will notice some recurring themes: verb tense, cohesion, switching of pronouns, inability to identify a pronoun's noun.

Top tip

Sometimes it's helpful to suggest that children leave it a couple of days before they decide to revise or edit their pieces. This means they can look at their writing with fresh and objective eyes.

PLENARY

Children share their drafts, following the established class sharing routine.

SUPPORT

Encourage children to paragraph pile or sentence stack until they are more confident.

Writing lesson 4: Draft

Class writing goal
To draft our persuasive articles

OVERVIEW

Children continue drafting their persuasive articles. Some children may have finished their drafts at this point and can move on to revising their pieces.

PREPARATION AND RESOURCES

- Persuasive writing (Advocacy journalism) genre booklets
- Planning grids from the previous lesson
- Drafting rules (ITR)
- Upper KS2 non-fiction revision checklist (ITR and PCM, p278)
- Tips and Tricks cards

MINI-LESSON

Choose from the suggested mini-lessons for this writing project, which cover aspects of writing study, grammar and punctuation.

The following mini-lessons may be particularly useful at the drafting stage:

- Making information come alive
- Use an anecdote to explain your point
- Circle unsure spellings
- Boxes for punctuation

CLASS WRITING SESSION

Children continue to draft their piece of writing based on the plan they have completed. Remind them to use the drafting rules and information on pages 10–11 of their Persuasive writing (Advocacy journalism) genre booklets. They should talk it through with a partner if they get stuck. You could display the 'Drafting rules' ITR.

Children should write on the left side of the page, leaving the right side blank for revision in future lessons.

Once their draft is complete, children can continue with their personal writing projects, at their own pace and using their preferred writing process.

Some children may have finished drafting their persuasive article at this point and can move on to revising their pieces using the revision information and checklist on pages 12–14 of their Persuasive writing (Advocacy journalism) genre booklets if necessary.

Conferencing focus

Encourage children to request a conference with you if they get stuck. Ask them to regularly reread their pieces as they write them. Provide intervals in which they share their writing in pairs. Partners could focus on any 'sticky' or 'yawny' bits they hear.

A 'sticky' bit is any bit of writing that doesn't sound right. It sounds strange when read aloud. It confuses your reader. Children are very quick to identify 'sticky' bits. You will notice some recurring themes: verb tense, cohesion, switching of pronouns, inability to identify a pronoun's noun.

A 'yawny' bit is any bit of writing that seems unnecessary or repetitive.

Top tip

Sometimes it's helpful to suggest that children leave it a couple of days before they decide to revise or edit their pieces. This means they can look at their writing with fresh and objective eyes.

PLENARY

Children share their drafts, following the established class sharing routine.

SUPPORT

Encourage children to paragraph pile or sentence stack until they are more confident.

Writing lesson 5: Draft

Class writing goal
To draft our persuasive articles

OVERVIEW

Children continue drafting their persuasive articles. Some children may have finished their drafts at this point and can move on to revising their pieces.

PREPARATION AND RESOURCES

- Persuasive writing (Advocacy journalism) genre booklets
- Planning grids from the previous lesson
- Drafting rules (ITR)
- Upper KS2 non-fiction revision checklist (ITR and PCM, p278)
- Tips and Tricks cards

MINI-LESSON

Choose from the suggested mini-lessons for this writing project, which cover aspects of writing study, grammar and punctuation.

The following mini-lessons may be particularly useful at the drafting stage:

- Cohesion
- Can you cut out 'and'?
- Standard English
- Relative clauses and relative pronouns

CLASS WRITING SESSION

The class will continue drafting their class project using the drafting rules. Encourage children to request a conference with you if they get stuck.

Once their draft is complete, children can continue with their personal writing projects, at their own pace and using their preferred writing process.

PLENARY

Children share their drafts, following the established class sharing routine. If any you and your class feel they need another drafting session, please add one in. Alternatively, if children are confident with the writing processes, you can let them move on to the next stage independently.

SUPPORT

Encourage children to paragraph pile or sentence stack until they are confident.

> **Conferencing focus**
>
> Encourage children to regularly reread their pieces as they write them.
>
> Provide intervals in which children share their writing with a partner. They could refer back to their product goals poster.
>
> Partners could focus on any 'sticky' or 'yawny' bits they hear.
>
> A 'sticky' bit is any bit of writing that doesn't sound right. It sounds strange when read aloud. It confuses your reader. Children are very quick to identify 'sticky' bits. You will notice some recurring themes: verb tense, cohesion, switching of pronouns, inability to identify a pronoun's noun.
>
> A 'yawny' bit is any bit of writing that seems unnecessary or repetitive.

Writing lesson 6: Revise

Class writing goal
To revise our persuasive articles

OVERVIEW

Children begin the important process of rereading and revising their writing. Focus should be on ensuring that the article makes sense and they have included everything in their plans. Some children may have finished revising their persuasive article at this point and can move on to editing their pieces.

PREPARATION AND RESOURCES

- Persuasive writing (Advocacy journalism) genre booklets
- Upper KS2 non-fiction revision checklist (ITR and PCM, p278)
- Upper KS2 editing checklist (ITR and PCM, p273)
- Tips and Tricks cards

MINI-LESSON

Choose from the suggested mini-lessons for this writing project, which cover aspects of writing study, grammar and punctuation.

The following mini-lessons may be particularly useful at the revision stage:

- First reread and improve
- Second reread and improve
- Third reread and improve

CLASS WRITING SESSION

Explain to children that many of them are now going to start revising their piece of writing, whilst others will be ready to move on to editing their pieces. Remind them that if they have many changes to make, they can create a new version opposite their draft in their English book. This is particularly the case for children whose preferred writing process is that of discoverer.

Conferencing focus

Encourage children to request a conference with you if they get stuck while revising.

Provide intervals in which children share their writing in pairs. Partners should focus on any revisions made. Ask children to discuss where certain revisions would be effective.

Remind children to use the revision checklist found on page 14 of their Persuasive writing (Advocacy journalism) genre booklets and the relevant Tips and Tricks cards to help with grammar, punctuation and spelling. They may also find it useful to look at the revision advice on pages 12–13 of their Persuasive writing (Advocacy journalism) genre booklet.

Once their revisions are done, children can continue with their personal writing projects, at their own pace and using their preferred writing process.

Some children may have finished revising their persuasive article at this point and can move on to editing their pieces using the 'Upper KS2 editing checklist' (PCM, p273).

PLENARY

Children share their revised drafts, following the established class sharing routine.

SUPPORT

Encourage children to paragraph pile or sentence stack until they are more confident.

Writing lesson 7: Revise

Class writing goal
To revise our persuasive articles

OVERVIEW

Once children are happy with their revised article, they move on to editing the article and developing their transcription skills by checking spelling, punctuation and grammar. Some children may have finished editing their persuasive articles at this point and can move on to publishing their pieces.

PREPARATION AND RESOURCES

- Persuasive writing (Advocacy journalism) genre booklets
- Upper KS2 non-fiction revision checklist (ITR and PCM, p278)
- Upper KS2 editing checklist (ITR and PCM, p273)
- Tips and Tricks cards

MINI-LESSON

Choose from the suggested mini-lessons for this writing project, which cover aspects of writing study, grammar and punctuation.

The following mini-lessons may be particularly useful at the revision stage:

- First reread and improve
- Second reread and improve
- Third reread and improve

CLASS WRITING SESSION

Children will continue to revise their persuasive articles. Remind them that if they have a lot of changes, they can create a new version opposite their draft in their English book. This is particularly the case for children whose preferred writing process is that of 'discoverer'.

Remind children to use the revision advice and checklist found on pages 12–14 of their Persuasive writing (Advocacy journalism) genre booklets. Ask children to use the relevant Tips and Tricks cards to help them with spelling, grammar and punctuation. They can also use their reading books to check the spellings of common words.

Some children may have finished revising and editing their persuasive articles at this point and can move on to publishing their pieces using the 'Presentation tips' (PCM, p274).

> **Conferencing focus**
>
> Encourage children to request a conference with you if they get stuck while revising.
>
> Provide intervals in which children share their writing in pairs. Partners should focus on where certain revisions would be effective and any 'sticky' bits they hear.
>
> A 'sticky' bit is any bit of writing that doesn't sound right. It sounds strange when read aloud. It confuses your reader. Children are very quick to identify 'sticky' bits. You will notice some recurring themes: verb tense, cohesion, switching of pronouns, inability to identify a pronoun's noun.

PLENARY

Children share their revised drafts, following the established class sharing routine. If you and your class feel they need another revision session, please add one in. Alternatively, if children are confident with the writing processes, you can let them move on to the next stage independently.

SUPPORT

Some children may require more support in reviewing their writing and may benefit from adult input.

Writing lesson 8: Edit

> ### Class writing goal
> To edit our persuasive articles

OVERVIEW

Most children will now move on to editing their writing, but those who have finished their edits can move on to publishing their final version.

PREPARATION AND RESOURCES

- Upper KS2 editing checklist (ITR and PCM, p273)
- Tips and Tricks cards
- Electronic spell checkers
- Access to online dictionaries
- Reading books

MINI-LESSON

Choose from the suggested mini-lessons for this writing project, which cover aspects of writing study, grammar and punctuation.

The following mini-lessons may be particularly useful at the editing stage:

- How to edit your writing for capitals
- How to edit your writing for use of vocabulary
- How to edit your writing for punctuation
- How to check and correct your unsure spellings

CLASS WRITING SESSION

Children begin to edit their articles using their editing checklist, along with the relevant Tips and Tricks cards to help them understand the correct use of grammar and punctuation. Remind children that they can use a dictionary and the Spelling Tips and Tricks cards to look up any spellings they are unsure of. They can also use their reading books to check the spellings of common words.

Once their editing is done, children can begin publishing their articles.

> ### Conferencing focus
> Encourage children to request a conference with you if they get stuck.
>
> Ask children to read any 'sticky' bits to a partner to get advice before asking you.
>
> A 'sticky' bit is any bit of writing that doesn't sound right. It sounds strange when read aloud. It confuses your reader. Children are very quick to identify 'sticky' bits. You will notice some recurring themes: verb tense, cohesion, switching of pronouns, inability to identify a pronoun's noun.

PLENARY

Show some examples of thoughtful editing. If you and your class feel they need another editing session, please add one in. Alternatively, if children are confident with the writing processes, you can let them move on to the next stage independently.

SUPPORT

If children have finished their drafts, you or another adult could publish it on their behalf.

Writing lesson 9: Publish

Class writing goal
To publish our persuasive articles to send to our charities

OVERVIEW

Most children should now be ready to publish their pieces and you should be ready to begin assessing their outcomes. Any children who have finished publishing their persuasive articles can work on their personal writing projects.

PREPARATION AND RESOURCES

- A variety of stationery and art materials
- Presentation tips (ITR and PCM, p274)

MINI-LESSON

Choose from the suggested mini-lessons for this writing project, which cover aspects of writing study, grammar and punctuation.

The following mini-lessons may be particularly useful at the publishing stage:
- Ways of publishing

CLASS WRITING SESSION

Refer back to the original class writing goal of writing, publishing and sending journalistic articles to a range of charities. Ensure children have access to the 'Presentation tips' (PCM, p274) or that you have the 'Presentation tips' ITR displayed on the whiteboard.

Conferencing focus

Take this opportunity to discuss your assessment of their piece and set writing goals for their future class and personal writing projects.

Children can present their writing, adding colour, artwork and photographs.

PLENARY

Children perform their pieces to the class. This can be done as a whole class, in small groups or in pairs.

Writing lesson 10: Publish

Class writing goal
To publish our persuasive articles to send to our charities

OVERVIEW

All children should now be nearing the end of publishing their pieces. You should be assessing their outcomes and sharing any writing goals with individual children or with the class as a whole.

PREPARATION AND RESOURCES

- A variety of stationery and art materials
- Presentation tips (ITR and PCM, p274)

MINI-LESSON

Choose from the suggested mini-lessons for this writing project, which cover aspects of writing study, grammar and punctuation.

The following mini-lessons may be particularly useful at the publishing stage:
- Letter of appreciation
- Ways of publishing

CLASS WRITING SESSION

Children continue to publish their articles. Ensure they have access to the 'Presentation tips' (PCM, p274) or that you have the 'Presentation tips' ITR displayed on the whiteboard. Children can take this opportunity to present their writing, adding colour, artwork and photographs.

> **Conferencing focus**
> Take this opportunity to discuss your assessment of children's pieces. Set whole class writing goals for future class and personal writing projects. Place these on the working wall.

Additionally, you may want to announce your winners of the charity prize money. You may want to ask a collection of writers from the year above to judge and choose the three winners and to give their reasons for choosing the articles.

Once children have published their piece, they can continue with their personal writing projects, at their own pace and using their preferred writing process.

PLENARY

Children perform their pieces for the class, for other year groups or for parents. They could also perform them for the wider community in a local library.

Class writing project: Short stories

Why write a short story?

In Year 3, children will have experimented with fairy tales, fables and the typical story arcs that writers employ. Last year, they will have written stories with a greater focus on character development and creating effective settings. The role of this writing project is to build on those experiences and give children an opportunity to bring all they have learned so far together.

THINGS TO BEAR IN MIND

- Children will have a good understanding of plot through their writing projects in Year 4. This writing project should therefore focus on writing intriguing openings that don't have to be overly concerned with orientating their reader – read some short stories and you'll see. Children can also write a variety of endings. Their short stories don't have to be resolved at the end. Indeed, in many short stories there isn't necessarily an absolute resolution at all.

- We suggest that you still limit the children's stories to no more than two pages in length. With less experienced writers, you might want to limit them to just a page. The reason for this is so children continue to use their revision pages more purposefully.

- Children should now be developing their characters through sensory description and dialogue. They will also be aware that, when writers dabble and write, they associate their character with a specific emotion or quality. Children will use what they have learned about comparison, simile, metaphor and symbolism from other projects to develop their characters even further.

- Children will be further aided by their experience in writing memoir. Focus on character occurs quite naturally in children's memoirs because they are talking about their own responses to events. You will find children beginning to use these same skills when developing fictional characters.

- Remind children that settings can be treated as additional 'characters' and take on human traits – this is known as 'pathetic fallacy.' Seeing settings as characters influences how they are described and how they behave.

- Additionally, you should teach children that setting descriptions can be based on how the setting is observed through a character's eyes at the time. For example, two people may well describe the same place in very different ways depending on their mood, morality or intentions.

- This writing project builds on what the children have learned in Year 4 and prepares them for what they will tackle in Year 6. You will continue to see these techniques influencing their other writing, including memoir and poetry.

Writing short stories

Use these ideas to help you write your own short story for use in class or to introduce the genre to the children.

Why write a short story for yourself or your class?

To share an experience, entertain, explain a mystery of the world or teach a lesson about life to other people.

What are the basics of a short story?

Stories are all around us. We tell stories every day when we recount events to others. Storytelling is the same all around the world in every culture, language and among all different ages of people. An effective story has the power to grip your reader's imagination, whether they are adults or children!

(FIELD) What is your short story going to be about?

In a story, something always happens – an event! This event needs to be interesting or exciting for your reader and smaller events lead up to it. At the end of the story, the main event is normally resolved and all ends happily (or not!).

Your story should start by introducing a **place** and your **character(s)** to your audience. Writer Ralph Fletcher uses the metaphor of a waterfall when starting a story. He says that you shouldn't start your story 'too far up stream' away from the roar of the waterfall. **Always start at the roar of the waterfall.**

You then need to think of a **problem** or **main event**. Something could go wrong or someone could make something go wrong or there could be an event that the characters are preparing for. The problem / event could be:

- between your character and nature
- between a character and a powerful person or group of people

- a problem with the character themselves
- something that the character(s) have to prepare for, e.g. a contest.

Your character will have to explain **how they feel** about the problem. They must find a way to solve this problem and any other problems that may present themselves throughout the events. Your story will end when all of the problems have been solved.

You could choose to write a familiar story but from a different character's **point of view**.

(TENOR) What is your role as the writer?

You need an audience, such as younger children, your friends, teachers, family, or maybe just you!

Your role as the writer is to entertain and give enjoyment to your audience. Your story can:

- be funny or serious
- be fast paced (although remember not to tell your audience everything). Use 'big sweeps of time' or fronted adverbials, *e.g. as time went by …; the months and years came and went …; all that time we …*
- teach your reader a life lesson or try to explain something magical that happens in the world.

Remember: your story shouldn't be too long or include unnecessary words! Try to stick to no more than 350 words.

(MODE) What should your short story look like?

Your short story will be written in **paragraphs.** Add illustrations to help your reader understand events further.

(SEMANTICS) How can you make your short story text clear and interesting?

- Write in the **third person** (*he, him, his, she, her, hers, they*) or the first person (*I, me, we, us*) and be consistent.
- Short stories are usually written in the **past tense** (*was, were, had, been*).
- Use **dialogue** when it matters but not too often or unnecessarily.
- Use **adverbs** to explain *how* characters do things.

(LEXIS) How can your word choices help?

You may find these devices helpful:

- Use **fronted adverbials** to signal when and where events are happening.
- Use **adjectives, noun phrases** and **poetic devices** to help your reader create images in their heads.

How to develop a character

Use these ideas to help you develop a powerful and realistic character in your story.

Why develop a character for yourself or your class?

Your character is what your story is centred around. They can only choose a favourite character if they know a lot about them, so writers work hard to share information about their characters.

Characters might be people, robots, magical creatures or personified animals. Writers such as Roald Dahl would use either the best or worst characteristics of themselves or of others as inspiration for their characters.

(FIELD) How will you develop a character?

Writers develop characters in six ways:

- **Appearance** When introducing a character for the first time, writers will describe how their character looks – facial features, body shape, dress, and mannerisms.
- **Action** What a character does and how they do it (**verbs and adverbs**), will tell you a lot about a character. Why do they do the things they do? What do they believe in? What do they believe is right and wrong? How do they see the world? All of these things have an impact on what a character does.
- **Speech** A writer will think about what their character says and how they say it.
- **Emotions** A writer thinks about the way their character will be feeling and what their emotions will be throughout the story. Their emotions will often be based on what the character cares about the most.
- **Monologue** A great way to let your audience know about your characters is to let the characters themselves tell readers their thoughts and feelings.
- **Poetic metaphor** Some writers will create a character to be a metaphor or a symbol for something else. The character is there to represent an idea, a way of living your life, a way of thinking or behaving. You can disguise this idea by using a character. This also works for settings.

Writers also build **themes** in their writing. A character's emotions and values (the things they believe in) can change during a story. These themes can be things such as friendship, responsibility, courage and kindness to others.

(MODE) When will the character's personality be revealed?

You will often write about a character's qualities when you introduce a new character, or a character thinks, speaks or does something:

- you introduce a new character to your story
- a character speaks
- a character thinks
- a character is doing something.

(SEMANTICS) How can you maintain your character?

Writers will often dabble (think and make notes) before they start a plan or a draft for a story. A lot of their dabbling centres on their character(s). They will at least consider, and often make notes on, some of the following:

- *What are you disguising your character as?*
- *What would you compare them to?*
- Sight: *What do they look like?*
- Smell: *What might they smell like?*
- Touch: *What is their mood like and what would they feel like to touch?*
- Sound: *What do they sound like and what might they say?*
- Action: *What might they do and how they might do it?*
- Motives: *Why do they do the things they do?*
- Taste: *If your character had a taste, what would it be?*
- Monologue: *What do they spend their time thinking about? What do other people think of them? How do they live their life?*

(LEXIS) How can your word choices help?

Use the best **verbs, adverbs, adjectives, noun phrases and poetic devices** to:

- describe characters
- show how a character says something
- write about your character's thoughts
- describe what your character does and how they do it.

The 'best' means the ones that will **really express** what you want to communicate about your character.

How to write a vivid setting

Use these ideas to help you develop an effective setting in your story.

Why write a vivid setting for yourself or your class?

If you are writing about a place your reader is unlikely to have seen or known anything about, you need to provide an effective setting paragraph to make them feel at home. It is also an opportunity to 'paint with words' and bring some poetry to your story.

Some stories barely talk about the setting. Many fairy tales, for example, don't write about the setting very much at all. Instead they often use 'Once upon a time, in a far-away land' to set the stage.

If you're writing about a specific place, it can be important to ensure your reader understands the historical period or the geographical location your story is set in.

(FIELD) What is your text is going to be about?

Setting doesn't just mean location, though this is one important part of setting. You need:

- location
- weather
- time of day
- historical time
- character's feelings
- setting as a character.

(TENOR) What is your role as the writer?

Think about the following:

- Everyday settings don't often need to be described because your reader will know about them, unless of course you are writing about an ordinary day when something unusual happens. It is the **extraordinary places**, where your reader may never have been, that need to be described well.
- If the weather is a part of your story, you need to describe early what the weather is like, particularly if it is something your reader may **never have witnessed** for themselves.
- The time of day can have a real impact on your reader if you are writing **ghost or scary stories.**
- If your story is set in the **past or future** you need to let your reader know. They may become confused if you include things that would not have been possible in a past era, or if they aren't told that the location is set in the future.
- How you describe your setting can tell your reader a lot about how your character is feeling at the time.
- Finally, you can use your setting as an additional character in your story.

(MODE) What does your setting look like?

Sometimes a paragraph at the start of your story is where you describe your story's setting. Otherwise, it's often when a new setting or scene is first introduced to your readers and this can be at any point in the story.

(SEMANTICS) How do you keep your reader on track?

Using powerful nouns and verbs is an effective way to describe setting. You could use verbs to describe the sights, sounds and smells of a busy street. You do not have to rely on adjectives to write a vivid setting.

(LEXIS) How can your word choices help?

You may find this device helpful:

- Describe places using **adjectives, noun phrases** and **poetic devices** to help your reader create images in their heads.

Genre study I: Why do people write short stories?

Class writing goal
To learn what our next class writing project will be

OVERVIEW

In this lesson, children will learn about short stories and will discuss why writers write them. You will reveal that this is the next class writing project and that the class will be publishing an anthology of short stories to place in the class library and beyond.

PREPARATION AND RESOURCES

- Short stories genre booklets
- Video: 'Why I love stories'
- Writing wheel (ITR and PCM, p272)
- Display a variety of short story texts

STUDY

Show children the video 'Why I love stories'.

The video shows the writer S. F. Said, speaking about why he loves writing stories. He also talks about where the inspiration for one of his stories comes from and one of the characters he most enjoyed writing.

Explain to children that their class project will be to write their own short story.

DISCUSS

Ask children what experiences they have of reading and writing stories, and what they thought about the video they just watched. What did they learn about how writers create vivid settings and develop their characters?

Display the 'Writing wheel' ITR on the whiteboard, and hand out printed copies (PCM, p272).

Together, look at page 1 of the Short stories genre booklet. Ask children to work in pairs or small groups to answer the following questions:

- *What sorts of stories do you like to write?*
- *What sorts of stories do you like to read?*
- *What makes for a good story?*
- *What sort of characters do you like to read about?*
- *What sort of settings do you think are the most inspiring or intriguing?*

PLENARY

Children share writing from their personal projects, following the established class sharing routine.

PERSONAL WRITING PROJECTS

Throughout the class writing project, once the class writing goal for each session is complete, children carry on with their personal writing projects at their own pace and using their preferred writing processes. See pages 17–19 for more information on personal writing projects and pages 26–30 for more information on pupil conferencing.

Genre study 2: What makes an effective short story?

> ## Class writing goal
> To understand what makes an effective short story

OVERVIEW

In this lesson, children will study a variety of short stories and discuss what makes them effective.

PREPARATION AND RESOURCES

- Short stories genre booklets
- Pre-written exemplar short story texts:
  - *Heat and light* (genre booklet p2–3, ITR)
  - *Ember city* (genre booklet p4–5, ITR)
  - *The painting* (ITR)
- Short story examples created by children from previous years
- Flip-chart paper

> As you develop your confidence as a writer-teacher, you should aim to create your own short story exemplar using the writing project's opening guidance. Ensure it has a vivid setting and strong characters.

STUDY

Look at and read examples of short stories from your class library. Ask children to discuss them in pairs or small groups. Display the genre examples on the whiteboard. Also display your own example and any child examples you have collected. Ask children to read the exemplars.

DISCUSS

In groups or pairs, children discuss:

- *What did the writers do that you really liked?*
- *What will we have to do to write a really good short story?*
- *How do we develop characters?*
- *How can we write vivid settings?*

CREATE

As a class, and using the information on page 1 of the 'Short stories genre booklet', start creating your poster of product goals. These goals should indicate what is needed to publish a great short story.

PLENARY

Children share their posters, following the established class sharing routine.

DEEPEN

You could encourage children to write a very quick short story and compare theirs with a partner. They could discuss what they liked and what they thought was missing.

PERSONAL WRITING PROJECTS

Throughout the class writing project, once the class writing goal for each session is complete, children carry on with their personal writing projects at their own pace and using their preferred writing processes. See pages 17–19 for more information on personal writing projects and pages 26–30 for more information on pupil conferencing.

Genre study 3: Character development and setting description

Class writing goal

To understand how writers develop their characters and create their settings

OVERVIEW

In this lesson, children will look at how writers develop their characters and create their settings.

PREPARATION AND RESOURCES

- Short stories genre booklets
- Pre-written exemplar short story texts:
  - *Heat and light* (genre booklet p2–3 and ITR)
  - *Ember city* (gentre booklet p6–7 and ITR)
  - *The painting* (ITR)
- Your own pre-written short story exemplar (from the previous lesson)
- Short story examples created by children from previous years

STUDY

Children read and discuss the exemplar short story texts and the examples of 'Describing characters' and 'Vivid settings' from pages 6–15 of the Short stories genre booklet. Ask them to focus particularly on:

- the setting description – location, weather, time of day, historical period
- the character development: appearance, action, speech, monologue.

DISCUSS

In pairs, children discuss what should be added to their product goals poster to ensure that their short stories have clear settings and strong characters. Prompt them with questions such as:

- *How does your character speak?*
- *What is your character's mood?*
- *Why should you say what time of day it is?*
- *Does your reader need to know where the action takes place?*

CREATE

Children work on their product goals posters, making any amendments and adjustments needed.

PLENARY

Children share their ideas for a striking setting and memorable characters, following the established class sharing routine.

DEEPEN

Children could write an ineffective example of a short story independently, to include poor character development, and a dull, understated and vague setting.

PERSONAL WRITING PROJECTS

Throughout the class writing project, once the class writing goal for each session is complete, children carry on with their personal writing projects at their own pace and using their preferred writing processes. See pages 17–19 for more information on personal writing projects and pages 26–30 for more information on pupil conferencing.

Genre study 4: Whole-class dabbling

> ### Class writing goal
> To re-cap how to dabble

OVERVIEW

In this lesson, children will take part in some dabbling.

PREPARATION AND RESOURCES

- Short stories genre booklets
- Flip-chart paper

STUDY

Explain that writers will often use dabbling to generate ideas. For stories, writers will spend time dabbling different setting or character ideas to see if anything looks promising. This is a good way to start sometimes because great story writers know that characters are what make for an exceptional story.

Together read through the 'Dabbling advice' section on page 18 of the Short stories genre booklet. Show children the example of writer dabbling and explain that you are going to try this out together.

DISCUSS

First, very quickly, ask for three character ideas. Next, as a class, vote on which one you want to dabble with. Ask children to imagine the character. Probe this character by asking questions, such as:

- *What is their name and how old are they?*
- *Sight: What do they look like?*
- *Smell: What might they smell like?*
- *Touch: What mood are they in, and what would they feel like to touch?*
- *Sound: What sort of voice do they have?*
- *Taste: What can they taste?*
- *Action: What are they doing – and **how** are they doing it?*
- *Motives: **Why** are they doing what they are doing?*
- *Monologue: What are they thinking about?*
- *What could a story plot be?*

CREATE

In groups or pairs, children generate two or three character ideas and choose one to practise dabbling with. Alternatively, they can continue with their personal writing projects.

PLENARY

Children share their final dabbled characters, following the established class sharing routine.

DEEPEN

Ask children to practise dabbling at home tonight with either settings or characters, so that they could be 'dabble experts'.

PERSONAL WRITING PROJECTS

Throughout the class writing project, once the class writing goal for each session is complete, children carry on with their personal writing projects at their own pace and using their preferred writing processes. See pages 17–19 for more information on personal writing projects and pages 26–30 for more information on pupil conferencing.

Genre study 5: Generating ideas

Class writing goal
To generate our short story ideas

OVERVIEW

In this lesson, children will use a range of techniques for generating short story ideas using the Short stories genre booklets. They will then decide what their story will be for the class writing project.

PREPARATION AND RESOURCES

- Short stories genre booklets
- Published short stories
- Flip-chart paper

STUDY

Children read and discuss ways of generating story ideas using the 'Generating good ideas' section on pages 16–17 of the Short stories genre booklet.

DISCUSS

As a class, come up with some potential short story ideas. Ask the following questions to probe the ideas further:

- *Do you have an idea of how the story will end?*
- *What is your diamond moment?*
- *How many characters are there, and what is the main character like?*
- *Where is the story set and how many scene changes are there?*

CREATE

In groups, pairs or individually, children generate a list of potential ideas for their short story.

PLENARY

Children share their story ideas following the established class sharing routine. They should ask for advice or suggestions if they feel they need it. This can be done as a whole class, in groups or in pairs.

SUPPORT

If children are struggling for an idea, they could work in a group with more experienced writers or with you to generate some ideas together.

PERSONAL WRITING PROJECTS

Throughout the class writing project, once the class writing goal for each session is complete, children carry on with their personal writing projects at their own pace and using their preferred writing processes. See pages 17–19 for more information on personal writing projects and pages 26–30 for more information on pupil conferencing.

Writing lesson I: Plan

Class writing goal
To plan our short stories

OVERVIEW

Children plan or draft their short story.

PREPARATION AND RESOURCES

- Short stories genre booklets
- Short stories planning grid (PCM, p289)

MINI-LESSON

Choose from the suggested mini-lessons for this writing project, which cover aspects of writing study, grammar and punctuation.

The following mini-lessons may be particularly useful at the planning stage:

- What if … ?
- Imagine a day when …
- Write about what you're most afraid of
- Read a moment
- Rewrite a Shakespeare play

CLASS WRITING SESSION

Before you begin your writing week, tell children that they have ten writing sessions in which to publish their short story. Remind them of the different writing styles writers often use. These include being a discoverer, planner, drafter, paragraph piler and sentence stacker. Explain that, depending on their preferred writing style, they are likely to be planning or drafting today.

Children start to plan their short story. Remind children what a plan needs to include in order to be helpful for the writing process (an opening, introduction of characters, description of setting, a potential ending). Encourage children to practise their dabbling skills to embellish main characters and settings.

Children may also find it useful to look at the planning advice on page 19 of the Short Stories genre booklets.

If children choose to plan their pieces, they are free to use their 'Short stories planning grid' (PCM, p289) if they wish to. Other children may leap straight into drafting their short story. Encourage these children to refer to the drafting advice and rules on page 20 of their Short story genre booklets.

PLENARY

Children who have planned their short story turn over their plans and 'tell' their story to someone in the class.

DEEPEN

Children could be encouraged to think of an alternative ending involving an unexpected character twist or a dramatic change of scene. They can choose their favourite in the final version.

SUPPORT

Provide children with a copy of the planning grid, which they can either write or draw in. Alternatively, they could talk through their plan with an adult and go straight to the drafting stage or they can draw their plan.

Conferencing focus

Encourage children to talk through their plans or drafts in pairs and with you throughout this session. Pairs focus on any 'sticky' or 'yawny' bits they hear.

A 'sticky' bit is any bit of writing that doesn't sound right. It sounds strange when read aloud. It confuses your reader. Children are very quick to identify 'sticky' bits. You will notice some recurring themes: verb tense, cohesion, switching of pronouns, inability to identify a pronoun's noun.

A 'yawny' bit is any bit of writing that seems unnecessary or repetitive.

Writing lesson 2: Plan

> **Class writing goal**
> To plan our short stories

OVERVIEW

Children continue to plan or draft their short stories.

PREPARATION AND RESOURCES

- Short stories genre booklets
- Short stories planning grid (PCM, p289)
- Drafting rules (ITR)

MINI-LESSON

Choose from the suggested mini-lessons for this writing project, which cover aspects of writing study, grammar and punctuation.

The following mini-lessons may be particularly useful at the planning stage:

- How to write a vivid setting
- How does your character talk?

CLASS WRITING SESSION

Children continue with their plans for their short stories. Remind them to think really carefully about the setting and character. Ask them to think about the following questions:

- *What is your main character like?*
- *What is your main character going to do?*
- *How does your main character look, behave, sound?*
- *What is your setting like? If it were a person, what would it be like?*
- *What can your character see, hear and smell?*

Other children may begin or continue to draft their short stories. Encourage these children to refer to the drafting rules and information on page 20 of their Short stories genre booklets and the 'Drafting rules' ITR.

> **Conferencing focus**
>
> Encourage children to talk through their plans or drafts in pairs and with you throughout this session. Pairs focus on any 'sticky' or 'yawny' bits they hear.
>
> A 'sticky' bit is any bit of writing that doesn't sound right. It sounds strange when read aloud. It confuses your reader. Children are very quick to identify 'sticky' bits. You will notice some recurring themes: verb tense, cohesion, switching of pronouns, inability to identify a pronoun's noun.
>
> A 'yawny' bit is any bit of writing that seems unnecessary or repetitive.

PLENARY

Children who have planned their short story turn over their plans and 'tell' their story to someone in the class. If you and your class feel they need another planning session, please add one in. Alternatively, if children are confident with the writing processes, you can let them move on to the next stage independently.

DEEPEN

Children could write a blurb for their short stories, describing what their story is about, but keeping something back so that readers are intrigued to read it. A good tactic for blurb writing is to start with a brief synopsis of the story and then delete the last sentence or two, perhaps inserting a question instead. This means the whole plot isn't given away, and there's a bit of intrigue to really grab the readers' attention.

Their blurbs should be between 50 and 70 words long and include a gripping tag line, or quote from the main character.

Ask children to read their blurbs aloud to the class or group to demonstrate how to 'sell' an idea to a group of people.

SUPPORT

Provide children with a copy of the planning grid, which they can either write or draw in. Alternatively, they could talk through they plan with an adult and go straight to the drafting stage or they can draw their plan.

Writing lesson 3: Draft

Class writing goal
To draft our short stories

OVERVIEW

Children use the plans they created in previous sessions to start or continue drafting their short stoires. Some children may have finished their drafts at this point and can move on to revising their pieces.

PREPARATION AND RESOURCES

- Short stories genre booklets
- Short stories planning grid (PCM, p289)
- Drafting rules (ITR)
- Tips and Tricks cards
- Upper KS2 narrative revision checklist (ITR and PCM, p278)

MINI-LESSON

Choose from the suggested mini-lessons for this writing project, which cover aspects of writing study, grammar and punctuation.

The following mini-lessons may be particularly useful at the drafting stage:

- Use the senses
- Show don't tell

CLASS WRITING SESSION

Using their plans, children will start to draft their short stories. It is important to reiterate that this is just a first draft and not the end of the writing process and that they are writing *short* stories so should limit themselves to only two pages of drafting.

Ask them to look at the drafting rules and advice on page 20 of their Short Stories genre booklets.

Encourage children to really concentrate on one of the senses when thinking about the main character or story setting, and to really explore it. For example, they could focus on smell and go into lots of detail about what a place smells like or what a character might smell like so that it's as if their reader is in the room.

Children may find it useful to look at the example openings and endings for stories on pages 21–24 of their Short stories genre booklets.

Remind children that once their drafts are complete, they will have their revision pages if they wish to make additions to their stories. Children should write on the left-hand side of the page, leaving the right-hand side blank for revision in future sessions. Encourage children to continually use their plan for their writing, and to regularly reread their writing as they go.

Some children may have finished drafting their short stories at this point and can move on to revising their pieces using the revision checklist on page 26 of their Short stories genre booklets if necessary.

Conferencing focus

Encourage children to request a conference with you if they get stuck. Provide intervals for them to share their writing in pairs. Partners should focus on any 'sticky' or 'yawny' bits they hear.

A 'sticky' bit is any bit of writing that doesn't sound right. It sounds strange when read aloud. It confuses your reader. Children are very quick to identify 'sticky' bits. You will notice some recurring themes: verb tense, cohesion, switching of pronouns, inability to identify a pronoun's noun.

A 'yawny' bit is any bit of writing that seems unnecessary or repetitive.

Top tip

Sometimes it's helpful to suggest that children leave it a couple of days before they decide to revise or edit their pieces. This means they can look at their writing with fresh and objective eyes.

DEEPEN

Children could write another draft from the perspective of a different character. They should think about developing the character. How might this character be different from the previous character? How would the story be different told through their eyes?

SUPPORT

Encourage children to paragraph pile or sentence stack until they are more confident.

162

Writing lesson 4: Draft

Class writing goal
To draft our short stories

OVERVIEW

Children continue drafting their short stories. Some children may have finished their drafts at this point and can move on to revising their pieces.

PREPARATION AND RESOURCES

- Short stories genre booklets
- Short stories planning grid (PCM, p289)
- Drafting rules (ITR)
- Upper KS2 narrative revision checklist (ITR and PCM, p277)
- Tips and Tricks cards

MINI-LESSON

Choose from the suggested mini-lessons for this writing project, which cover aspects of writing study, grammar and punctuation.

The following mini-lessons may be particularly useful at the drafting stage:

- Comb your reading book
- Circle unsure spellings

CLASS WRITING SESSION

Most children will continue to draft their short stories. Remind them to refer to their plans while writing and circle any words where they are unsure of the spelling.

Remind children to use verbs carefully to help build a picture of a character. Describing *specifically* how characters do things gives a lot of their personality away without having to provide long descriptions.

Some children may have finished drafting their short stories at this point and can move on to revising their pieces using the 'Upper KS2 narrative revision checklist' and advice on pages 25–26 of their Short stories genre booklets if necessary.

PLENARY

Children share their drafts, following the established class sharing routine. If you and your class feel they need another drafting session, please add one in. Alternatively, if children are confident with the writing processes, you can let them move on to the next stage independently.

DEEPEN

Children could write another draft from the perspective of a different character. They should think about developing the character. How might this character be different from the previous character? How would the story be different told through their eyes?

SUPPORT

Encourage children to paragraph pile or sentence stack until they are more confident.

Conferencing focus

Encourage children to request a conference with you if they get stuck, and to stop regularly and reread their writing. Provide intervals for children to share their writing in pairs. Partners should focus on any 'sticky' or 'yawny' bits they hear.

A 'sticky' bit is any bit of writing that doesn't sound right. It sounds strange when read aloud. It confuses your reader. Children are very quick to identify 'sticky' bits. You will notice some recurring themes: verb tense, cohesion, switching of pronouns, inability to identify a pronoun's noun.

A 'yawny' bit is any bit of writing that seems unnecessary or repetitive.

Top tip

Sometimes it's helpful to suggest that children leave it a couple of days before they decide to revise or edit their pieces. This means they can look at their writing with fresh and objective eyes.

Writing lesson 5: Revise

Class writing goal
To revise our short stories

OVERVIEW

Children begin the important process of rereading and revising their writing. Focus should be on ensuring that the text makes sense and they have included everything in their plans. Some children may have finished revising their short stories at this point and can move on to editing their pieces.

PREPARATION AND RESOURCES

- Short stories genre booklets
- Upper KS2 narrative revision checklist (ITR)
- Upper KS2 editing checklist (PCM, p273)
- Tips and Tricks cards

MINI-LESSON

Choose from the suggested mini-lessons for this writing project, which cover aspects of writing study, grammar and punctuation.

The following mini-lessons may be particularly useful at the revision stage:

- Great openings
- Strong endings

CLASS WRITING SESSION

Explain to children that many of them are now going to start revising their pieces of writing, whilst others will be ready to move on to editing their pieces. Remind them that if they have many changes to make, they can create a new version opposite their draft in their English book. This is particularly the case for children whose preferred writing process is that of discoverer.

These next few sessions are for the children to revise their pieces. This involves rereading and improving, before moving on to editing. Remind children to use the revision information and checklist on pages 25–26 of the Short stories genre booklet. They should also use the relevant Tips and Tricks cards to help them with grammar, punctuation and spelling.

> **Conferencing focus**
> Encourage children to talk to a partner or request a conference with you if they get stuck. Asking some of these questions might help children get started with their revisions:
> - *Which bit are you trying to revise?*
> - *Is there a bit we could try revising together?*
> - *What's not quite working at the moment?*
> - *What do you think of your opening? Have you tried out any other ideas?*
> - *What do you think of your ending? Have you tried out any other ideas?*
> - *Where have you developed your character?*
> - *Where have you described a setting for your reader?*
> - *Can you tell me a bit more about your setting?*
> - *How well do we know your main character?*

This is a really good opportunity to add in a bit of detail about either the setting or the main character – or both. Encourage children to think about where they can give a bit more insight into where the story is set or who it is about, so that characters feel more vivid, more alive and more real to readers.

Children should create a new version opposite their draft in their English book if they have a lot of changes to make.

Some children may have finished revising their short stories at this point and can move on to editing their pieces using the 'Upper KS2 editing checklist' (PCM, p273).

PLENARY

Children share their revised drafts, following the established class sharing routine.

SUPPORT

Children may require more support in reviewing their own writing and may benefit from adult input.

Writing lesson 6: Revise

> **Class writing goal**
> To revise our short stories

OVERVIEW

Once children are happy with their revised text, they move on to editing the text and developing their transcription skills by checking spelling, punctuation and grammar. Some children may have finished editing their short stories at this point and can move on to publishing their pieces.

PREPARATION AND RESOURCES

- Short stories genre booklets
- Upper KS2 narrative revision checklist (ITR and PCM, p277)
- Presentation tips (ITR and PCM, p274)
- Tips and Tricks cards
- Electronic spell checkers
- Access to online dictionaries

MINI-LESSON

Choose from the suggested mini-lessons for this writing project, which cover aspects of writing study, grammar and punctuation.

The following mini-lessons may be particularly useful at the revision stage:

- First reread and improve
- Second reread and improve
- Third reread and improve
- Show don't tell
- Peripheral vision

CLASS WRITING SESSION

Children continue to make revisions to their work. Encourage children to think carefully about what each section, even sentence, of the story is adding. If it isn't building up the picture of the setting or a character and isn't moving the plot along, is it really needed? If in doubt, cut it out.

Some children may have finished editing their short stories at this point and can move on to publishing their pieces using the presentation tips.

> **Conferencing focus**
> Remind children that all writers find it difficult to identify faults in their own writing, which is why sharing with a partner is helpful. Make sure partners are particularly looking out for:
> - a tempting opening
> - strong character development
> - a diamond moment
> - vivid setting description
> - a powerful ending.

PLENARY

Children share their revised drafts, following the established class sharing routine.

Writing lesson 7: Revise

Class writing goal
To revise our short stories

OVERVIEW

In this lesson, children will continue revising their short stories.

PREPARATION AND RESOURCES

- Short Stories genre booklets
- Upper KS2 narrative revision checklist (ITR and PCM, p277)
- Presentation tips (ITR and PCM, p274)
- Tips and Tricks cards
- Electronic spell checkers
- Access to online dictionaries

MINI-LESSON

Choose from the suggested mini-lessons for this writing project, which cover aspects of writing study, grammar and punctuation.

The following mini-lessons may be particularly useful at the revision stage:

- First reread and improve
- Second reread and improve
- Third reread and improve
- "I'm finished!"
- Mark your own work

CLASS WRITING SESSION

Children continue to make revisions to their work.

Some children may have finished editing their short stories at this point and can move on to publishing their pieces using the 'Presentation tips' (PCM, p274) or display the ITR on the whiteboard.

PLENARY

Children share their revised drafts, following the established class sharing routine. If you or your class feel they need another revision session, please add one in. Alternatively, if children are confident with the writing processes, you can let them move on to the next stage independently.

Conferencing focus
Remind children that all writers find it difficult to identify faults in their own writing, which is why sharing with a partner is helpful. Make sure partners are particularly looking out for:

- a tempting opening
- strong character development
- a diamond moment
- vivid setting description
- a powerful ending.

Writing lesson 8: Edit

Class writing goal
To edit our short stories

OVERVIEW

In this lesson, children should start editing their short stories. This should be the stage at which they polish their writing before it is published. It includes checking spelling, punctuation and grammar.

PREPARATION AND RESOURCES

- Upper KS2 editing checklist (ITR and PCM, p273)
- Presentations tips (ITR and PCM, p274)
- Tips and Tricks cards
- Electronic spell checkers
- Access to online dictionaries

MINI-LESSON

Choose from the suggested mini-lessons for this writing project, which cover aspects of writing study, grammar and punctuation.

The following mini-lessons may be particularly useful at the editing stage:

- How to edit your writing for capitals
- How to edit your writing for use of vocabulary
- How to edit your writing for punctuation
- How to check and correct your unsure spellings

CLASS WRITING SESSION

Children begin to edit their texts using the 'Upper KS2 editing checklist' (PCM, p273) or display the ITR on the whiteboard. They should use the relevant Tips and Tricks cards to help them understand the correct use of grammar, punctuation and spelling. Also remind children that they can use a dictionary to look up spellings they are unsure of. They can also use their reading books to check the spellings of common words.

Conferencing focus

Encourage children to request a conference with you if they get stuck, but to read any 'sticky' and 'yawny' bits to a partner for advice before asking you.

A 'sticky' bit is any bit of writing that doesn't sound right. It sounds strange when read aloud. It confuses your reader. Children are very quick to identify 'sticky' bits. You will notice some recurring themes: verb tense, cohesion, switching of pronouns, inability to identify a pronoun's noun.

A 'yawny' bit is any bit of writing that seems unnecessary or repetitive.

Some children may have finished editing their short stories at this point and can move on to publishing their pieces using the 'Presentation tips' (PCM, p274) or display the ITR on the whiteboard.

PLENARY

Show some examples of thoughtful editing, following the established class sharing routine. If you or your class feel they need another editing session, please add one in. Alternatively, if children are confident with the writing processes, you can let them move on to the next stage independently.

SUPPORT

Children may need more support with their spelling and punctuation. Prompt them to use the high-frequency words they know to help with spelling.

Writing lesson 9: Publish

> ## Class writing goal
> To publish our short stories

OVERVIEW

Most children should now be ready to publish their pieces and you should be ready to begin assessing their outcomes. Any children who have finished publishing their short stories can work on their personal writing projects.

PREPARATION AND RESOURCES

- Presentation tips (ITR and PCM, p274)
- A variety of stationery and art materials

MINI-LESSON

Choose from the suggested mini-lessons for this writing project, which cover aspects of writing study, grammar and punctuation.

- The following mini-lessons may be particularly useful at the publishing stage:
- Ways of publishing

CLASS WRITING SESSION

Check children understand what 'publishing' a piece of writing means. Discuss audience and what makes readers interested in a text. In this case, children can create a class collection of short stories.

Ensure children have access to the 'Presentation tips' (PCM, p274) or display the ITR on the whiteboard. Children take this opportunity to present their writing, adding colour, artwork and photographs.

PLENARY

Children share their published work and give feedback on how it appeals to readers, following the established class sharing routine.

> ### Conferencing focus
> Take this opportunity to discuss your assessment of children's pieces and set writing goals for their future class and personal writing projects. Encourage children to discuss how they want their finished stories to look, what sort of images they would like and what impression they want it to make on their readers.

> ### Top tip
> Once the story is finished, it is a good time to think about the title. Children often want to start with a title, but it is actually easier and more effective to come up with something relevant and meaningful once the piece is finished. Encourage them not to be afraid of revising or completely changing titles already chosen.

Writing lesson 10: Publish

Class writing goal
To publish our short stories

OVERVIEW

In this lesson, children should finish publishing their stories and you should be ready to begin assessing their outcomes.

PREPARATION AND RESOURCES

- Presentation tips (ITR and PCM, p274)
- A variety of stationery and art materials

MINI-LESSON

Choose from the suggested mini-lessons for this writing project, which cover aspects of writing study, grammar and punctuation.

The following mini-lessons may be particularly useful at the publishing stage:
- Ways of publishing

CLASS WRITING SESSION

Children complete the publishing of their short stories. Ensure that they continue to refer to the 'Presentation tips' (PCM, p274) or display the ITR on the whiteboard.

Once children have published their story, they can continue with their personal writing projects, at their own pace and using their preferred writing process.

Conferencing focus
Take this opportunity to discuss your assessment of children's pieces and set writing goals for their future class and personal writing projects. Place these goals on the working wall.

PLENARY

Children perform their story to the class. This can be done as a whole class, in table groups or in pairs. It is important that you provide a variety of class sharing opportunities.

Review what children have learned about short stories.

Class writing project: Biography

Why write biography?

This writing project will show children how they can document the lives of people in their communities. They will discover how the lives of ordinary people they know can be sources of great historical, social and personal interest – not only to themselves as the writer, but to others too. All people's lives are interesting, but we don't always realise it ourselves. Everyone in our society has a story to tell, and by asking the right questions and sharing these stories publicly, children learn that they can give a voice to those people who would never otherwise have had an audience.

Biography writing has strong elements of memoir, although it will be about other people that the writer knows personally or has heard of through family members, friends or the community. At their very best, biographies can carry within them great opportunities for poetic description and rich anecdote. One of the great benefits of this writing project is that the writer can bring in and celebrate stories that can strengthen and enhance the sense of community and connection inside the classroom. There may well be gains, too, for the person being interviewed and written about.

A good biography topic creates the possibility for reflection, empathy or a shared understanding of an experience. Children will come to understand the role biographers have in documenting and preserving people's past.

THINGS TO BEAR IN MIND

- Encourage children to choose someone they have easy access to for interviewing. In your homework letter about interviewing, you are going to want to make it clear that the interviewee is encouraged to share background information about their early life, their main achievement or strongest memory and what happened after this memorable event or moment occurred.

- For your more experienced or enthusiastic writers, you may want to encourage them to dig a little deeper into the era about which they are writing. They can start their biography with a descriptive setting of the scene.

- Additionally, as this is a historical genre, you should encourage children to seek out a historical source that could enhance their biography. The source could be used to directly support the subject of the biography or instead be used to give a greater flavour of the era in general. Sources include photographs, videos, audio, objects, letters, newspaper articles, emails, postcards or direct quotations.

- Have a 'publishing day.' This is where you could invite the community into the classroom to view the artefacts and biographies that the children have written. You may also want to get in touch with your local museum or history centre about showcasing the writing.

Writing biography

Use these ideas to help you write your own biography for use in class or to introduce the genre to the children.

Why write a biography for yourself or your class?
To share with others one of your heroes or heroines from the present or past.

What are the basics of a biography?
Historians and biographers like to tell others about wonderful people: what they did and how they did it. They talk about the impact that person has had on their life, their community or the world.

(FIELD) What is your biography going to be about?
You can write about world-famous people, though often we already know about them. It is often more interesting to choose extraordinary people from your own life or community, whether they are dead or still alive.

A good historical biography describes what someone did, how they did it and the impact this has had on the world, their country, their community or their friends and family. You should seriously consider writing about a woman, because, unfairly, there is less written about women in history compared to men.

- You will need to introduce **who** your biography is about, **when** they were born and when they died (if they have yet!), **where** they are from, and **what** they achieved in their life or their strongest memory.
- Choose the **main event** or **strongest memory** of their life and spend time explaining it. Write something about their **childhood** or **later life** to give more information about them.
- Explain why this person is **significant** or **important** to you and others.

(TENOR) What is your role as the writer?
You have to make sure that you choose someone people will like to hear about but might not know about. You then have to keep the biography interesting throughout:

- Be clear about who they are and why they are worth reading about.
- Only include the most interesting bits of their life.
- Focus on the achievements or memories that make them remarkable to you as the writer.
- Choose someone you know a lot about and can possibly interview.
- You might want to 'paint with words', e.g. you could describe the era at the beginning of your biography.

(MODE) What should your biography look like?
Your biography should have a title and a clear beginning and ending; be organised into paragraphs and have a stand-out title.

You may want to add pictures of important moments. You could also make your biography **multi-modal** by using photographs, maps, letters and newspaper cuttings.

(SEMANTICS) How can you make your biography clear and interesting?
- Write about your subject in the **third person** because the piece isn't about you, e.g. *he, him, his, she, her, hers, they, them, their.*
- Biographies are written in the **past tense**, e.g. *was, were, had, been, -ed.*
- Biographies can be tricky if you have to cover long periods of time. Use **dates** and **places** to help your reader.
- **Contrast and compare** is another good technique to talk about the tough and the good parts of their life.

(LEXIS) How can your word choices help?
You will need **time connectives**. These will allow time to pass in your biography. Time connectives make sure your writing has a speedy pace: *In the 1960s … At that time … until the age of … During those years … Later on … After that …*

You will often talk about the **cause and effect** of an event. Using the connectives **so** or **because** will be very useful.

Genre Study I: Introducing biography

Class writing goal
To learn what our next class writing project will be

OVERVIEW

In this lesson, children will learn about biographies and will discuss why historians write them. You will then reveal that this is the next class writing project and that the class will be publishing an anthology of texts that celebrate the lives of ordinary people. They will then continue to work on their personal writing projects.

PREPARATION AND RESOURCES

- Ask your class librarians to display a variety of history texts. Ensure that your class library has a rich and varied stock of historical texts that share a variety of people's lives. It is also useful to include books that show hybridising between different genres. For example, historical fiction.
- Video: 'Why I write biography'
- Writing wheel (ITR and PCM, p272)

STUDY

Show children the video 'Why I write biography'.

The video shows the writer Michael Rosen, speaking about how he uses biography to make connections with the past as a kind of 'living history'.

Explain to children that their class project will be to write their own biographies.

DISCUSS

Ask the children what they think biography is and what thoughts they have about the video they have just watched.

Display the 'Writing wheel' ITR on the whiteboard, and hand out printed copies.

Ask the following questions:

- *Why do you think people write biographies (purpose)?*
- *Who do they write them for (audience)?*
- *What does memoir have in common with biography?*
- *Who knows someone who has done something interesting in the past?*
- *Who knows someone who has seen an amazing event?*
- *What stories have you been told by members of your family about their past?*
- *What stories have your classmates told you about their past?*

PLENARY

Children share writing from personal projects, following the established class sharing routine.

SUPPORT

Provide children with examples of simpler historical texts of biographies that they can access more easily.

PERSONAL WRITING PROJECTS

Throughout the class writing project, once the class writing goal for each session is complete, children carry on with their personal writing projects at their own pace and using their preferred writing processes. See pages 17–19 for more information on personal writing projects and pages 26–30 for more information on pupil conferencing.

Genre Study 2: What makes a good biography?

Class writing goal
To discover what makes a good biography

OVERVIEW

In this lesson, children will look at a variety of biography examples and discuss what topics were chosen, why they think the writer might have chosen them and what the exemplars do well. Children will then continue working on their personal writing projects.

PREPARATION AND RESOURCES

- Biography genre booklets
- Pre-written exemplar biography texts:
  - *Dan Andrews – defeating fears* (genre booklet p2–3, ITR)
  - *Rachel Williams – giving children a gift* (genre booklet p4–5, ITR)
- Gather together some biography exemplars created by children from previous years
- Flip-chart paper

> As you develop your confidence as a writer-teacher, you should aim to create your own biography text exemplar using the writing project's opening guidance. This should be about someone who is significant to you.

STUDY

Children then read and discuss the exemplar biographies. Ask the following questions:

- *What did you like about the biography you're reading?*
- *What ideas did it give you for your biography?*

DISCUSS

Explain to children that effective biographies have a specific focus rather than a general focus. You can use the analogy of mining for diamonds. Children should focus on finding a single diamond from all of their 'rocky' ideas and make that diamond shine. These diamonds are the moments that writers care about the most.

In pairs, children discuss the following questions:

- *Why do writers write biography?*
- *Why do you think I chose my topic(s)? What was my diamond?*
- *What sort of diamonds were chosen by the other writers? Why?*
- *Who hasn't been written about before? Can we shine a light on them?*
- *Who could we write our biographies about and who would want to read them?*
- *What makes a good biography?*

CREATE

As a class, and using the information on page 1 of the Biography genre booklet, start creating your poster of product goals. These goals should indicate what is needed to publish a great biography.

PLENARY

Children share writing from their personal projects, following the established class sharing routine. Place exemplars into the class library for children to continue reading at their leisure.

DEEPEN

In preparation for tomorrow's ineffective example lesson, you could challenge your more experienced writers to write their own ineffective biography, using their Biography genre booklets to help them.

PERSONAL WRITING PROJECTS

Throughout the class writing project, once the class writing goal for each session is complete, children carry on with their personal writing projects at their own pace and using their preferred writing processes. See pages 17–19 for more information on personal writing projects and pages 26–30 for more information on pupil conferencing.

Genre Study 3: Where can biography go wrong?

> ## Class writing goal
> To understand where biography texts can go wrong

OVERVIEW

In this lesson, children will learn about critiquing ineffective examples, using the information in the Biography genre booklets. They will then continue to work on their personal writing projects.

PREPARATION AND RESOURCES

- Biography genre booklets
- Pre-written ineffective biography exemplar (ITR)
- Anonymised ineffective examples of biography texts taken from previous years

STUDY

As a class, read the ineffective exemplars of biography texts.

> Write your own ineffective biography text using the following as a guide:
>
> - Don't mention who, when and where.
> - Assume too much knowledge in your readers.
> - Tell the events out of chronological order.
> - Make it difficult to follow and understand.
> - Don't write about why it was important to you.

DISCUSS

In pairs, using your class product goals poster from the previous lesson and the information on page 1 of their Biography genre booklets, children discuss and explain for themselves why the examples are ineffective.

If children struggle, you could ask the following questions:

- *Why is this such an ineffective biography?*
- *What advice would you give the writer?*

CREATE

You could invite children, in writing time, to write their own ineffective biography texts.

PLENARY

Children share writing from their personal projects, following the established class sharing routine. Place exemplars into the class library for children to continue reading at their leisure.

PERSONAL WRITING PROJECTS

Throughout the class writing project, once the class writing goal for each session is complete, children carry on with their personal writing projects at their own pace and using their preferred writing processes. See pages 17–19 for more information on personal writing projects and pages 26–30 for more information on pupil conferencing.

Genre study 4: Where do writers get their ideas from?

Class writing goal

To generate an idea for each child's class writing project

OVERVIEW

In this lesson, using their Biography genre booklets, children will learn about a number of techniques for generating ideas for biography writing. They will then be asked to interview someone for homework.

PREPARATION AND RESOURCES

- Biography genre booklets
- Homework letter (PCM, p293)
- Flip-chart paper
- Interview questions

STUDY

Children turn to page 6 of their Biography genre booklets. Read and discuss some of the techniques used by writers to generate ideas for writing biographies.

DISCUSS

As a class, create a poster of people who could be interviewed for your biography project. Then consider what periods of their lives could be asked about. For example, school days, their working or adult lives or old age.

As their teacher, you might consider sharing some memoir moments from your own life as an example. Children may also want to share significant achievements or moments from their lives.

As a class, look at and read the recommended interview questions on page 6 of the Biography genre booklet.

CREATE

Children generate a list of potential people they could interview and what they might ask them about. They can share their ideas with their partner, in groups or with the class.

PLENARY

Read through the homework letter (PCM, p293) and explain that this homework will be necessary for planning their project. Explain that children might want to supplement their interview answers with artefacts or photographs from home.

Conferencing focus

Ask children what stories they have been told about the past by people who are important to them.

Check that children have ready access to the people they would like to talk to.

If still struggling, they may want to do a biography about someone else in the class.

SUPPORT

If a child is struggling to form a list of people they could interview, encourage them to read other children's lists.

PERSONAL WRITING PROJECTS

Throughout the class writing project, once the class writing goal for each session is complete, children carry on with their personal writing projects at their own pace and using their preferred writing processes. See pages 17–19 for more information on personal writing projects and pages 26–30 for more information on pupil conferencing.

Writing lesson 1: Plan

Class writing goal
To plan our biographies

OVERVIEW

Children plan or draft their biographies.

PREPARATION AND RESOURCES

- Biography genre booklets
- Research homework
- Biography planning grid (ITR and PCM, p291)

- Drafting rules (ITR)
- Photographs and / or artefacts from home

MINI-LESSON

Choose from the suggested mini-lessons for this writing project, which cover aspects of writing study, grammar and punctuation.

The following mini-lessons may be particularly useful at the planning stage:

- Using a planning grid
- Finding the diamond moment

Alternatively, you may want to share and discuss how you planned your exemplar.

CLASS WRITING SESSION

Before you begin your writing week, tell children that they have ten writing sessions in which to publish their biography. Remind them of the different writing styles that writers often use. These include being a discoverer, planner, drafter, paragraph piler and sentence stacker. Explain that, depending on their preferred writing style, they are likely to be planning or drafting today.

Children start to plan their biography texts. Remind them what a plan is for (to help them organise ideas and research so that they know what their text will include). You could show a plan of your own, or display the example 'Biography planning grid' (ITR and PCM, p291). Children may also find it useful to look at the planning advice on page 7 of their Biography genre booklets.

Other children may leap straight into drafting their biography. Encourage these children to refer to the drafting information on page 8 of their Biography genre booklets and the 'Drafting rules' ITR.

> ### Conferencing focus
>
> Encourage children to talk through their plans or drafts in pairs and with you throughout this session. Their partner should let them know if they are assuming too much prior knowledge from their reader and whether anything needs explaining so their reader can better understand the event.
>
> You may have children who realise that they do not have the information they need to finish their planning. Reassure them that they have another planning session in which to sort this out and they can bring in any extra information required the next day.

PLENARY

Children who have planned their biography turn over their plans and 'tell' their biography to someone in the class.

SUPPORT

Provide children with an A3-size copy of the 'Biography planning grid' (PCM, p291). Alternatively, children can talk their plan through with an adult and go straight to drafting, or they can draw their plan.

PERSONAL WRITING PROJECTS

Throughout the class writing project, once the class writing goal for each session is complete, children carry on with their personal writing projects at their own pace and using their preferred writing processes. See pages 17–19 for more information on personal writing projects and pages 26–30 for more information on pupil conferencing.

Writing lesson 2: Plan

Class writing goal

To plan our biographies

OVERVIEW

Children continue to plan or draft their biography.

PREPARATION AND RESOURCES

- Biography genre booklets
- Research homework children have completed
- Biography planning grid (ITR and PCM, p291)
- Drafting rules (ITR)
- Photographs and / or artefacts from home

MINI-LESSON

Choose from the suggested mini-lessons for this writing project, which cover aspects of writing study, grammar and punctuation.

The following mini-lessons may be particularly useful at the planning stage:

- Important people
- Don't start too far upstream
- A picture speaks 1000 words
- Use an ideas heart

CLASS WRITING SESSION

Children who have not finished their plans will continue to plan their pieces of writing. Remind children to consider what the focus or diamond moment of their piece is and discuss this in pairs.

If helpful, display your completed 'Biography planning grid' ITR on the whiteboard for reference.

Conferencing focus

Encourage children to talk through their plans or drafts in pairs and with you throughout this session. Their partner should let them know if they are assuming too much prior knowledge from their reader. Is there anything that needs explaining to their reader so they can better understand the event?

Other children may begin or continue to draft their biographies. Encourage these children to refer to the drafting information on page 8 of their Biography genre booklets and to the 'Drafting rules' ITR.

PLENARY

Children who have planned their biography turn over their plans and 'tell' their biographies to someone in the class. If you and your class feel they need another planning session, please add one in. Alternatively, if children are confident with the writing processes, you can let them move on to the next stage independently.

DEEPEN

When planning their biography, challenge children to try to merge it with setting and character description, using the 'painting with words' techniques. For example can they open their biography with a description of the era? You could give them a copy of the 'Biography and story planning grid' (PCM, p291) to help with their planning.

SUPPORT

Provide children with an A3-size copy of the 'Biography planning grid' (PCM, p291). Alternatively, children can talk their plan through with an adult and go straight to drafting, or they can draw their plan.

Writing lesson 3: Draft

Class writing goal
To draft our biographies

OVERVIEW

Children use the plans that they created in previous sessions to start or continue drafting their biographies. Some children may have finished their drafts at this point and can move on to revising their pieces.

PREPARATION AND RESOURCES

- Biography genre booklets
- Planning grids from the previous lesson
- Drafting rules (ITR)
- Tips and Tricks cards

MINI-LESSON

Choose from the suggested mini-lessons for this writing project, which cover aspects of writing study, grammar and punctuation.

The following mini-lessons may be particularly useful at the drafting stage:

- Using the drafting rules
- Determiners
- Fronted adverbials: moving between place and time
- Cohesion
- Sentences with different forms

CLASS WRITING SESSION

Explain to children that many of them are now going to start drafting their biographies based on the plan that they have completed.

Remind them to use the 'Drafting rules' ITR and talk through their drafts in pairs if they get stuck. They may also find it useful to look at the drafting advice on page 8 of their Biography genre booklet.

Children should write on the left side of their books, leaving the right blank for revision in future lessons.

Some children may have finished drafting their biographies at this point and can move on to revising their pieces using the revision information and checklist on pages 9–10 of their Biography genre booklets if necessary.

PLENARY

Children share their drafts, following the established class sharing routine.

SUPPORT

Encourage children to paragraph pile or sentence stack until they are confident.

Conferencing focus

Encourage children to request a conference with you if they get stuck.

Ask children to regularly reread their pieces as they write them. Provide intervals in which they share their writing with a partner. Partners should focus on any 'sticky' bits they hear. A 'sticky' bit is any bit of writing that doesn't sound right. It sounds strange when read aloud. It confuses your reader. Children are very quick to identify 'sticky' bits. You will notice some recurring themes: verb tense, cohesion, switching of pronouns, inability to identify a pronoun's noun.

Top tip

Sometimes it's helpful to suggest that children leave it a couple of days before they decide to revise or edit their pieces. This means they can look at their writing with fresh and objective eyes.

Top tip

Children will find adverbial starters relating to time and place really helpful. They may find themselves stuck because they don't know how to move between space and time. Suggest that they start a new paragraph or use a fronted adverbial.

Writing lesson 4: Draft

Class writing goal
To draft our biographies

OVERVIEW

Children continue drafting their biographies. Some children may have finished their drafts at this point and can move on to revising their pieces.

PREPARATION AND RESOURCES

- Biography genre booklets
- Planning grids from the previous lesson
- Drafting rules (ITR)
- Tips and Tricks cards

MINI-LESSON

Choose from the suggested mini-lessons for this writing project, which cover aspects of writing study, grammar and punctuation.

The following mini-lessons may be particularly useful at the drafting stage:

- Apostrophes to show possession
- Determiners
- Fronted adverbials: moving between place and time
- Cohesion
- Sentences with different forms

CLASS WRITING SESSION

Children continue to develop their drafts.

Encourage children to request a conference with you if they get stuck.

Some children may have finished drafting their biographies at this point and can move on to revising their pieces, using the revision information and checklist on pages 9–10 of their Biography genre booklets if necessary.

PLENARY

Children share their drafts, following the established class sharing routine.

SUPPORT

Encourage children to paragraph pile or sentence stack until they are confident.

Conferencing focus

Encouraging children to regularly reread their pieces as they write them. Provide intervals in which they can share their writing with a partner. Partners should focus on any 'sticky' or 'yawny' bits they hear.

A 'sticky' bit is any bit of writing that doesn't sound right. It sounds strange when read out loud. It confuses your reader. Children are very quick to identify 'sticky' bits. You will notice some recurring themes: verb tense, cohesion, switching of pronouns, inability to identify a pronoun's noun.

A 'yawny' bit is any bit of writing that seems unnecessary or repetitive.

Top tip

Sometimes it is helpful to suggest that children leave it a couple of days before they decide to revise or edit their pieces. This means they can look at their writing with fresh and objective eyes.

Writing lesson 5: Draft

Class writing goal
To draft our biographies

OVERVIEW

Children will continue drafting their class project using the 'vomit draft rules'. Encourage children to request a conference with you if they get stuck.

PREPARATION AND RESOURCES

- Biography genre booklets
- Planning grids from the previous lesson
- Drafting rules (ITR)
- Tips and Tricks cards

MINI-LESSON

Choose from the suggested mini-lessons for this writing project, which cover aspects of writing study, grammar and punctuation.

The following mini-lessons may be particularly useful at the drafting stage:

- Using the drafting rules
- Determiners
- Fronted adverbials: moving between place and time
- Cohesion
- Sentences with different forms

CLASS WRITING SESSION

Children continue to develop their drafts.

Some children may have finished drafting their biographies at this point and can move on to revising their pieces, using the revision information and checklist on pages 9–10 of their Biography genre booklets if necessary.

Encourage children to request a conference with you if they get stuck.

PLENARY

Children share their drafts, following the established class sharing routine. If you and your class feel they need another drafting session, please add one in. Alternatively, if children are confident with the writing processes, you can let them move on to the next stage independently.

SUPPORT

Encourage children to paragraph pile or sentence stack until they are confident.

Conferencing focus

Encouraging children to regularly reread their pieces as they write them. Provide intervals in which they can share their writing with a partner. They could refer back to the class writing goals poster.

Partners should focus on any 'sticky' or 'yawny' bits they hear.

A 'sticky' bit is any bit of writing that doesn't sound right. It sounds strange when read out loud. It confuses your reader. Children are very quick to identify 'sticky' bits. You will notice some recurring themes: verb tense, cohesion, switching of pronouns, inability to identify a pronoun's noun.

A 'yawny' bit is any bit of writing that seems unnecessary or repetitive.

Writing lesson 6: Revise

Class writing goal
To revise our biographies

OVERVIEW

Children begin the important process of rereading and revising their writing. Focus should be on ensuring that the text makes sense and that they have included everything in their plans. Some children may have finished revising their biographies at this point and can move on to editing their pieces.

PREPARATION AND RESOURCES

- Biography genre booklets
- Upper KS2 non-fiction revision checklist (ITR and PCM, p278)
- Upper KS2 editing checklist (ITR and PCM, p273)
- Tips and Tricks cards

MINI-LESSON

Choose from the suggested mini-lessons for this writing project, which cover aspects of writing study, grammar and punctuation.

The following mini-lessons may be particularly useful at the revising stage:

- Sticky bits and yawny bits
- First reread and improve
- Second reread and improve
- Third reread and improve
- Writing your title last

CLASS WRITING SESSION

Explain to children that many of them are now going to start revising their pieces of writing, whilst others will be ready to move on to editing their pieces. Remind them that, if they have many changes to make, they can create a new version opposite their draft in their English book. This is particularly the case for children whose preferred writing process is that of discoverer.

Conferencing focus

Encourage children to request a conference with you if they get stuck while revising. Ask them to talk with their partners about where certain revisions would be effective.

Provide intervals in which children share their writing with a partner. Partners should focus on any revisions made.

Remind children to use the revision checklists found on page 10 of their Biography genre booklets and the relevant Tips and Tricks cards to help them with grammar. They may also find it useful to look at the revision advice on page 9 of their Biography genre booklets.

Some children may have finished revising their biographies at this point and can move on to editing their pieces using the 'Upper KS2 editing checklist' (PCM, p273 and ITR).

PLENARY

Children share their revisions, following the established class sharing routine.

SUPPORT

Encourage children to paragraph pile or sentence stack until they are confident.

Writing lesson 7: Revise

Class writing goal
To revise our biographies

OVERVIEW

Once children are happy with their revised texts, they move on to editing the text and developing their transcription skills by checking spelling, punctuation and grammar. Some children may have finished editing their biographies at this point and can move on to publishing their pieces.

PREPARATION AND RESOURCES

- Biography genre booklets
- Upper KS2 editing checklist (ITR and PCM, p273)
- Presentation tips (PCM, p274)
- Tips and Tricks cards

- Electronic spell checkers
- Access to online dictionaries
- Reading books

MINI-LESSON

Choose from the suggested mini-lessons for this writing project, which cover aspects of writing study, grammar and punctuation.

The following mini-lessons may be particularly useful at the revising stage:

- Sticky bits and yawny bits
- First reread and improve
- Second reread and improve
- Third reread and improve
- Writing your title last

CLASS WRITING SESSION

Children will continue to revise their biographies. Remind them that, if they have a lot of changes, they can create a new version opposite their draft in their English book. This is particularly the case for children whose preferred writing process is that of discoverer.

Remind children to use the revision advice and checklist found on pages 9–10 of their Biography genre booklets. Ask children to use the relevant Tips and Tricks cards to help them with spelling, grammar and punctuation. They can also use their reading books to check the spellings of common words.

Conferencing focus

Encourage children to talk with their partners about where certain revisions would be effective. Provide intervals in which children share their writing with a partner. Partners should focus on any 'sticky' bits they hear.

A 'sticky' bit is any bit of writing that doesn't sound right. It sounds strange when read out loud. It confuses your reader. Children are very quick to identify 'sticky' bits. You will notice some recurring themes: verb tense, cohesion, switching of pronouns, inability to identify a pronoun's noun.

Some children may have finished revising their biographies at this point and can move on to editing their pieces using the 'Upper KS2 editing checklist' (PCM, p273 and ITR).

Some children may have finished editing their biographies at this point and can move on to publishing their pieces using the 'Presentation tips' (PCM, p274).

Encourage children to request a conference with you if they get stuck.

PLENARY

Show some examples of thoughtful editing. If you or your class feel they need another revising session, please add one in. Alternatively, if children are confident with the writing processes, you can let them move on to the next stage independently.

SUPPORT

If children have finished their drafts, you or another adult could publish it on their behalf.

Writing lesson 8: Edit

Class writing goal
To edit our biographies

OVERVIEW

Once children are happy with their revised texts, they move on to editing and developing their transcription skills by checking spelling, punctuation and grammar. Some children may have finished editing their biographies at this point and can move on to publishing their pieces.

PREPARATION AND RESOURCES

- Biography genre booklets
- Upper KS2 editing checklist (ITR and PCM, p273)
- Presentation tips (ITR and PCM, p274)
- Tips and Tricks cards
- Electronic spell checkers
- Access to online dictionaries
- Reading books

MINI-LESSON

Choose from the suggested mini-lessons for this writing project, which cover aspects of writing study, grammar and punctuation.

The following mini-lessons may be particularly useful at the editing stage:

- How to edit your writing for capitals
- How to edit your writing for use of vocabulary
- How to edit your writing for punctuation
- How to check and correct your unsure spellings

CLASS WRITING SESSION

Children begin to edit their biographies using their editing checklists, along with the relevant Tips and Tricks cards to help them understand the correct use of grammar, punctuation and spelling. Remind children that they can use a dictionary to look up any spellings they are unsure of. They can also use their reading books to check the spellings of common words.

Some children may have finished editing their biographies at this point and can move on to publishing their pieces using the 'Presentation tips' (PCM, p274).

Encourage children to request a conference with you if they get stuck.

Conferencing focus

Encourage children to read any 'sticky' bits to a partner to get advice before asking you.

A 'sticky' bit is any bit of writing that doesn't sound right. It sounds strange when read out loud. It confuses your reader. Children are very quick to identify 'sticky' bits. You will notice some recurring themes: verb tense, cohesion, switching of pronouns, inability to identify a pronoun's noun.

PLENARY

Show some examples of thoughtful editing. If you or your class feel they need another editing session, please add one in. Alternatively, if children are confident with the writing processes, you can let them move on to the next stage independently.

SUPPORT

If children have finished their drafts, you or another adult could publish it on their behalf.

Writing lesson 9: Publish

> ## Class writing goal
> To publish our biographies

OVERVIEW

Most children should now be ready to publish their pieces and you should be ready to begin assessing their outcomes. Any children who have finished publishing their biographies can work on their personal writing projects.

PREPARATION AND RESOURCES

- A variety of stationery and art materials
- Presentation tips (ITR and PCM, p274)
- You may want to invite the community into the classroom to view artefacts and the accompanying biographies the children have written.
- You should also consider getting in touch with your local museum or history centre, who may wish to make these biographies publically available.

MINI-LESSON

Choose from the suggested mini-lessons for this writing project, which cover aspects of writing study, grammar and punctuation.

The following mini-lesson may be particularly useful at the publishing stage:

- Ways of publishing

CLASS WRITING SESSION

Refer back to the original class writing goal of creating a collection of biographies. Ensure children have access to the 'Presentation tips' (PCM, p274) or that you have the 'Presentation tips' ITR displayed on the whiteboard. Children can take this opportunity to present their writing, adding colour, artwork and photographs.

> ### Conferencing focus
> Take this opportunity to discuss your assessment of children's pieces and set writing goals for their future class and personal writing projects. Place these goals on the working wall.

PLENARY

Children perform their pieces to the class. This can be done as a whole class, in small groups or in pairs. It is important that you provide a variety of class sharing opportunities.

The class could also share their biographies with other classes in the school or in the main library. You may also want to share the biographies with the wider community or your local library or museum.

Writing lesson 10: Publish

Class writing goal
To publish our biographies

OVERVIEW

All children should now be nearing the end of publishing their pieces. You should be assessing their outcomes and sharing any writing goals with individual children or with the class as a whole.

PREPARATION AND RESOURCES

- A variety of stationery and art materials
- Presentation tips (ITR and PCM, p274)
- You may want to invite the community into the classroom to view artefacts and the accompanying biographies the children have written.
- You should also consider getting in touch with your local museum or history centre – who may wish to make these biographies publically available.

MINI-LESSON

Choose from the suggested mini-lessons for this writing project, which cover aspects of writing study, grammar and punctuation.

The following mini-lesson may be particularly useful at the publishing stage:

- Ways of publishing

CLASS WRITING SESSION

At this stage, all children should be nearing the end of publishing. You should begin assessing their outcomes and sharing any writing goals with individual children or with the class as a whole. Continue to refer children to the 'Presentation tips' (PCM, p274) or have the ITR displayed.

Conferencing focus

Take this opportunity to discuss your assessment of children's pieces. Set whole class writing goals for future class and personal writing projects. Place these on the working wall.

PLENARY

Children perform their pieces for the class, for other year groups, for parents, for the wider community or in a local library or museum.

Class writing project: Poetry 2 (Inspired by ...)

Why write 'inspired by ...' poetry?

Sometimes it can be hard asking children to generate original ideas all the time and this also doesn't represent how published writers always work. Poets and story writers alike find themselves inspired by other things they see, read or hear from other writers, whether consciously or not. This is called 'intertextuality'. You only need to look inside a writer's notebook to see that they are forever collecting, investigating and imitating little diamond moments that they have found lying around in the other texts.

The best way to understand poems is to read a lot of them and to read them often. Children begin to think about what writers are writing and why.

Alongside this writing project, you could read *Love That Dog* by Sharon Creech as your class book. It is written in a free verse diary format, from the perspective of a young boy (Jack) who initially resists poetry assignments from his teacher. As time moves on, Jack's confidence grows, and he is able to respond to and take inspiration from poems, with increasing sophistication. This book makes for an engaging, child-friendly and incredibly valuable demonstration of intertextuality.

THINGS TO BEAR IN MIND

- This is going to be a very lively, sociable and open-ended project. Children should be encouraged to share and perform poems that they like. They should talk about them with one another and ask each other questions about what they take from the poem. You can model this during conferencing.

- If a particular poem attracts them, ask them to read it multiple times. After a few reads, they may start to write notes – little dabblings. They should continue to read the poem again and again until something starts to happen in their mind. Eventually, they will begin to shift away from the poem and concentrate more on their own dabblings. It's at this point that they might want to consider writing a draft.

- Spend some time yourself reading lots of poems and doing the same. Fill a page of your notebook with little snippets, notes, lists and dabbles you've made. Show this to children so that they can see the sorts of things they should be doing too.

- You may find that children write a completely new poem. Or they may change certain elements, cut things out, switch things around or simply add stuff in. All of these processes are legitimate and are used by published writers.

- Tell children that they can do exactly the same thing with the stories they read. They can take parts of a story that they like and turn these into poems.

Writing a poem

Use these ideas to help you write your own 'inspired by ...' poem for use in class or to introduce children to the genre.

Why write a poem for yourself or your class?

Poems help you share thoughts, feelings, experiences and dreams, and say things in new ways. Poetry is writing that comes from the heart.

What are the basics of a poem?

Free-verse poems are the best to start with. You don't have to have regular rhythm, line length or rhyme. Best of all, you can play around with words and put them together in any way you like. You can also play around with punctuation if you like. There are no rules, but below are some tips for writing a strong poem.

(FIELD) What is your poem going to be about?

Poems can be about something ordinary or extraordinary. Try the following:

- Whilst dabbling with your poem idea, write lots of lists of words and phrases.
- When dabbling, write down the feelings you want to express in your poem.
- Try to compare what you are writing about to something else to help you better understand it.

(TENOR) What is your role as the writer?

When writing poems, your aim is to express something or show something to your readers in a new and interesting way. You can write from your own point of view, or imagine things from another point of view – perhaps even the point of view of an object. You role is to express what you have noticed, felt or imagined, and share that feeling with your readers.

(MODE) What should your poem look like?

- Use line breaks or stanzas (groups of lines) to show where you want pauses to be. Try out different possibilities.
- You can be multi-modal. Combine your poem with a picture; accompany it with music or drama in a presentation.

(SEMANTICS) How can you make your poem clear and interesting?

- Once you've written your first attempt, identify your diamond moment and zoom in on it intensely.
- Explore the most passionate part of your poem – where you reveal the most emotion.
- Explore your use of **strong verbs** because this is where your poem is really hiding.
- **Repeat** some of your favourite words or phrases. Maybe repeat the first and last lines.
- Notice your use of **metaphor** and add detail to it.
- Notice where you are playing around with **sounds, rhythm, rhyme** and **repeated lines**.

- Try out **sound effects** such as **alliteration** or **onomatopoeia**.
- Use **line breaks** or **stanzas** (groups of lines) to show where you want your reader to pause in your poem. Try out lots of different possibilities.
- Move lines around until you get the best effect.
- Let your last line leave your readers with something to think about.
- Give a lot of thought to the title.

(LEXIS) How can your word choices help?

- Use **sensory images** – hearing, touch, smell, sight and taste.
- If it works, use **figurative language**, such as **similes** and **metaphors**. If you like, choose a subject and make it a **symbol** for something else: *the sun – kindness; the wind – loneliness; a sword – courage; an eagle – power; a-mountain-- strength*.
- Notice where you've made something not human become human through personification.

Genre study I: Introducing the idea of 'inspired by ...' poems

Class writing goal
To learn what our next class writing project will be

OVERVIEW

In this lesson, children will learn how writers can be inspired by the things that they read. They will learn about the idea of intertexuality and that all writing in some way is inspired by something else.

PREPARATION AND RESOURCES

- Ask your class librarians to display a variety of poetry books.
- Video: 'How I write poetry'
- Writing wheel (ITR and PCM, p272)

STUDY

Show children the video 'How I write poetry'.

The video shows the poet Joseph Coelho, speaking about how he uses poetry to make a change in the world. He also shares some tips for performing poems to an audience.

Tell the class that their class project will be to write their own series of 'inspired by ...' poems. Explain that poets and story writers alike often find themselves inspired by other things they see, read or hear from other writers, whether consciously or not. This is called 'intertextuality'.

It would be valuable to introduce the book *Love That Dog* by Sharon Creech (Bloomsbury) as your class read for the duration of this writing project. The book is a mixture of poems and narrative about a boy (Jack) who learns to be inspired by the poems he reads. It's the perfect way of introducing to children the idea that writers will often write as a result of being inspired by someone else's texts.

DISCUSS

Ask the children what their favourite poems are and what thoughts they have about the video they have just watched.

Display the 'Writing wheel' ITR on the whiteboard and hand out printed copies.

Ask children questions such as:

- *Why do you think people write poetry (purpose)?*
- *Who do they write it for (audience)?*
- *Why are writers inspired by what they read?*
- *Who has a writing idea for an 'inspired by ...' poem already in their minds?*
- *What is your favourite poem? Why do you remember it?*

CREATE

Give children an opportunity to read and perform poems together. If they wish to, after they've finished, they can continue with their personal writing projects.

PLENARY

Children share writing from their personal projects, following the established class sharing routine.

PERSONAL WRITING PROJECTS

Throughout the class writing project, once the class writing goal for each session is complete, children carry on with their personal writing projects at their own pace and using their preferred writing processes. See pages 17–19 for more information on personal writing projects and pages 26–30 for more information on pupil conferencing.

Genre study 2: What makes an effective 'inspired by ...' poem?

> ## Class writing goal
> To understand what makes an effective 'inspired by...' poem

OVERVIEW

In this lesson, children will learn several ways in which to write effective 'inspired by ...' poems. Again, sharing Sharon Creech's *Love That Dog* with your class will further illustrate to children how writers can be inspired by other texts.

PREPARATION AND RESOURCES

- Poetry 2 (Inspired by ...) genre booklets
- Pre-written exemplar poetry texts:
  - *Returning, we hear the larks / Returning from Bonfire Night* (genre booklet p2–3, ITR)
  - *I bit an apple / I chomped a banana* (genre booklet p4–5, ITR)
  - *Remember / Stained* (genre booklet p6–7, ITR)
  - *From a railway carriage / Riding a rollercoaster* (ITR)
- Poetry exemplars created by children from previous years
- Flip-chart paper

> As you develop your confidence as a writer-teacher, you should aim to create your own poem exemplars using the writing project's opening guidance. There are typically five ways poets (including you) are inspired by other poems, these include being inspired by:
>
> - the objects or subjects in the poem
> - the feeling in a poem
> - a word, line or verse in a poem
> - the memories or thoughts the poem reminds you of
> - the rhythm and / or rhyme of a poem.
>
> Prepare two different ways you have been inspired by two different poems. Make sure you have a copy of the original poems too.

STUDY

Children read and discuss the exemplar poetry texts in pairs or groups.

DISCUSS

Show the class the two poems you have written. Ask children if they can tell what it was about the original poem that inspired your poem.

Ask children what makes these poems great and add these points to your product goals poster. Include the ways in which poets can be inspired by the poster, too.

CREATE

As a class, and using the information on page 1 of the Poetry 2 (Inspired by ...) genre booklet, start creating your poster of product goals. These goals should indicate what is needed to publish a great 'inspired by ...' poem.

PLENARY

You may want to continue reading *Love That Dog* with the class.

PERSONAL WRITING PROJECTS

Throughout the class writing project, once the class writing goal for each session is complete, children carry on with their personal writing projects at their own pace and using their preferred writing processes. See pages 17–19 for more information on personal writing projects and pages 26–30 for more information on pupil conferencing.

Genre study 3: What makes an effective 'inspired by ...' poem?

Class writing goal

To understand what makes an effective 'inspired by ...' poem

OVERVIEW

In this lesson, children will be shown a couple of ways in which to write effective 'inspired by ...' poems. Again, sharing Sharon Creech's *Love That Dog* with your class will further illustrate to children how writers can be inspired by other texts.

PREPARATION AND RESOURCES

- Poetry 2 (Inspired by ...) genre booklets
- Pre-written exemplar poetry texts:
  - *Returning, we hear the larks / Returning from Bonfire Night* (genre booklet p2–3, ITR)
  - *I bit an apple / I chomped a banana* (genre booklet p4–5, ITR)
  - *Remember / Stained* (genre booklet p6–7, ITR)
  - *From a railway carriage / Riding a rollercoaster* (ITR)
- Poetry exemplars created by children from previous years
- Flip-chart paper

As you develop your confidence as a writer-teacher, you should aim to create your own poem exemplars using the writing project's opening guidance. There are typically five ways poets (including you) are inspired by other poems, these include being inspired by:

- the objects or subjects in the poem
- the feeling in a poem
- a word, line or verse in a poem
- the memories or thoughts the poem reminds you of
- the rhythm and/or rhyme of a poem.

Prepare two different ways you have been inspired by two different poems. Make sure you have a copy of the original poems, too.

STUDY

Children read and discuss the exemplar poetry texts in pairs or groups.

DISCUSS

Show the class the two poems you have written. Ask children if they can tell what it was about the original poem that inspired your poem.

Ask the children what makes these poems great and add these points to your product goals poster. Include the ways in which poets can be inspired to this on the poster too.

PLENARY

You may want to continue reading *Love That Dog* with the class.

PERSONAL WRITING PROJECTS

Throughout the class writing project, once the class writing goal for each session is complete, children carry on with their personal writing projects at their own pace and using their preferred writing processes. See pages 17–19 for more information on personal writing projects and pages 26–30 for more information on pupil conferencing.

Genre study 4: Where do poets get their ideas from?

Class writing goal
To generate ideas for our 'inspired by ...' poems

OVERVIEW

In this lesson, using their Poetry 2 (Inspired by ...) genre booklets, children will learn and try out a number of techniques for generating ideas for 'inspired by ...' poetry. They will then craft a poem. They may write several poems over the course of this project.

PREPARATION AND RESOURCES

• Poetry 2 (Inspired by ...) genre booklets
• Ask your class librarians to display a variety of poetry books.

STUDY

Ask children to look at page 8 of their Poetry 2 (Inspired by ...) genre booklets to find out how writers generate ideas for 'inspired by ...' poems.

DISCUSS

As a class, in groups or pairs, ask children to talk about, perform and share some of the poems they are enjoying from the class library. Children should consider whether there is something in each poem that is sparking them to write their own.

CREATE

Using the writing techniques on page 8 of their Poetry 2 (Inspired by ...) genre booklets, children read poems until they find one that particularly strikes them. They can then begin crafting their own 'inspired by ...' poem.

PLENARY

Children share with the class what their 'inspired by ...' poem idea is, following the established class sharing routine.

SUPPORT

If a child can't think of anything, you can bring the writing community in to help by sharing what they plan to write about. Alternatively, you could write a poem together based on a poem you or they happen to like.

Conferencing focus
Ask children what particularly strikes them about the poems they are reading. Ask the following questions:

• What do you like?
• What don't you like?
• What do they think works particularly well?
• What doesn't make sense?
• Does the poem remind you of anything from your life?
• Does it remind you of anything else you've seen or read?
• If the poet were here, what might you wish to ask them?

If a child is struggling to feel inspired by a poem, have other children explain the ideas they have chosen from the poems they've been reading.

PERSONAL WRITING PROJECTS

Throughout the class writing project, once the class writing goal for each session is complete, children carry on with their personal writing projects at their own pace and using their preferred writing processes. See pages 17–19 for more information on personal writing projects and pages 26–30 for more information on pupil conferencing.

Writing lesson I: Plan and dabble

Class writing goal
To dabble with our own ideas for an 'inspired by ...' poem

OVERVIEW

Children plan or draft their 'inspired by ...' poems.

PREPARATION AND RESOURCES

- Poetry 2 (Inspired by ...) genre booklets
- Your own dabblings to share with the class
- Children should have an idea of which poem they are inspired by.

MINI-LESSON

Choose from the suggested mini-lessons for this writing project, which cover aspects of writing study, grammar and punctuation.

The following mini-lessons may be particularly useful at the planning stage:

- Answering Michael Rosen's four questions
- Use a spark line

CLASS WRITING SESSION

Before you begin your writing week, tell children that they have ten writing sessions in which to publish their 'inspired by' poem. Remind them

> **Conferencing focus**
> Encourage children to talk through their dabbling or drafts in pairs and with you throughout this session. They should tell their partner what it is that they like about the original poem so much that they feel compelled to try to write their own.

of the different writing styles that writers often use. These include being a discoverer, planner, drafter, paragraph piler and sentence stacker. Explain that, depending on their preferred writing style, they are likely to be planning or drafting today.

Explain to the class that they are going to begin dabbling, expanding on and exploring their ideas for an 'inspired by ...' poem ready for drafting. Ask children to look at the dabbling information on pages 9–10 of their Poetry 2 (Inspired by ...) genre booklets. Dabbling is a type of pre-writing that poets will often do before they begin drafting a poem. Whilst dabbling, they will write lots of lists including words or phrases they might like to use. They may also write down a list of feelings they would like their poem to express to their readers. They may draw pictures with annotations to jog their memories or to make them think. They might write down why the idea is important or what they want their poem to mean. Finally, they will try to compare what they are writing about to other things to help them better understand it. When they feel they have gathered enough dabbles, they will look to turn it into a first draft of a poem.

You could model dabbling your own ideas for a poem.

If children choose to plan their pieces, they can do so now. Other children may leap straight into drafting their 'inspired by ...' poem. Encourage these children to refer to the drafting rules and information on pages 11–12 of their Poetry 2 (Inspired by ...) genre booklets.

PLENARY

Children turn over their dabblings and 'tell' their poem idea to someone in the class.

Children who have planned their 'inspired by ...' poem turn over their plans and 'tell' their poem to someone in the class. If you and your class feel they need another planning session, please add one in. Alternatively, if children are confident with the writing processes, you can let them move on to the next stage independently.

DEEPEN

Ask some children to consider writing a poem that challenges people's treatment of nature.

SUPPORT

Children can talk their dabblings through with an adult and go straight to drafting their poem.

Writing lesson 2: Draft

Class writing goal
To draft our 'inspired by ...' poems

OVERVIEW

Children use the plans that they created in previous sessions to start or continue drafting their poems. Some children may have finished their drafts at this point and can move on to revising their pieces.

PREPARATION AND RESOURCES

- Poetry 2 (Inspired by ...) genre booklets
- Children's dabblings from the previous session
- Copies of poems children are inspired by
- Drafting rules (ITR)
- Upper KS2 poetry revision checklist (ITR and PCM, p279)

MINI-LESSON

Choose from the suggested mini-lessons for this writing project, which cover aspects of writing study, grammar and punctuation.

The following mini-lessons may be particularly useful at the drafting stage:

- Poetry in reading
- Free-writing

CLASS WRITING SESSION

Explain to the class that they are now going to start drafting their poem based on the dabblings they have completed. Remind them to use the drafting rules and advice on pages 11–12 of their Poetry 2 (Inspired by ...) genre booklet. They should talk it through with a partner if they get stuck.

Children should write on the left-hand side of the page, leaving the right-hand side blank for revision in future lessons.

Some children may have finished drafting their 'inspired by ...' poem at this point and can move on to revising their pieces using the revision checklist on page 15 of their Poetry 2 (Inspired by ...) genre booklets if necessary.

Conferencing focus

When conferencing, start your conversations off with something like 'I can see you have ...'. Focus on one of the following:

- Help children to go from the general to the specific. Get them to identify the diamond moment within their poem.
- Help children to explore the passionate part of their poem – where they reveal the most emotion.
- Help them explore their use of strong verbs.
- Look for where they are being playful and ask them questions to bring this out of them more.
- Notice where they have made something not human become human through personification.
- Notice where they are playing around with sounds, rhythm, rhyme and repeated lines.
- Notice their use of metaphor and help them focus on it with a finer detail.
- Notice where they are painting with words – using their senses to create a rich picture.
- If they feel stuck, ask 'What does your poem make you wonder about?'
- If they are unsure whether they have finished, simply ask 'Well, is there anything else you want to say?'
- Ask them to compare what they are writing about to something else to help you better understand it.

PLENARY

Children share their drafts, following the established class sharing routine. You can invite children to briefly explain the theme of their poem and what they want it to make people feel. You can also ask the writers what help they might want from the class to improve it. The child can then read their poem out.

Next, ask the class:

- *How did the poem affect you?*
- *What did it make you wonder?*
- *Did it remind you of anything from your own life?*
- *Did it remind you of anything you've seen, heard or read before?*
- *What words or lines struck you most?*
- *What sounds could you hear?*

DEEPEN

Encourage children to explore the rhythm of their poems. Ask them to practise reading their poems aloud.

Writing lesson 3: Draft

Class writing goal
To draft our 'inspired by ...' poems

OVERVIEW

Children continue drafting their 'inspired by ...' poems. Some children may have finished their drafts at this point and can move on to revising their pieces.

PREPARATION AND RESOURCES

- Poetry 2 (Inspired by ...) genre booklets
- Children's dabblings from the previous session
- Copies of poems children are inspired by
- Drafting rules (ITR)

MINI-LESSON

Choose from the suggested mini-lessons for this writing project, which cover aspects of writing study, grammar and punctuation.

The following mini-lessons may be particularly useful at the drafting stage:

- General to specific
- Finding the diamond moment

CLASS WRITING SESSION

Explain to the class that they are going to continue drafting their poem based on the dabblings they have completed. Remind them to use the drafting rules and advice on pages 11–12 of their Poetry 2 (Inspired by ...) genre booklet. They should talk it through with a partner if they get stuck.

Children should write on the left-hand side of the page, leaving the right-hand side blank for revision in future lessons.

Some children may have finished drafting their 'inspired by...' poems at this point and can move on to revising their pieces using the revision checklist on page 15 of their Poetry 2 (Inspired by ...) genre booklets if necessary.

PLENARY

Children share their drafts, following the established class sharing routine. You can invite children to briefly explain the theme of their poem and what they want it to make people feel. You can also ask the writers what help they might want from the class to improve it. The child can then read their poem out.

Next, ask the class:

- *How did the poem affect you?*
- *What did it make you wonder?*
- *Did it remind you of anything from your own life?*
- *Did it remind you of anything you've seen, heard or read before?*
- *What words or lines struck you most?*
- *What sounds could you hear?*

Top tip

Sometimes it's helpful to suggest that children leave it a couple of days before they decide to revise or edit their pieces. This means they can look at their writing with fresh and objective eyes.

Conferencing focus

When conferencing, start your conversations off with something like *'I can see you have ...'* Focus on one of the following:

- Help children to go from the general to the specific. Get them to identify the diamond moment within their poem.
- Help children to explore the passionate part of their poem – where they reveal the most emotion.
- Help them explore their use of strong verbs.
- Look for where they are being playful and ask them questions to bring this out of them more.
- Notice where they have made something not human become human through personification.
- Notice where they are playing around with sounds, rhythm, rhyme and repeated lines.
- Notice their use of metaphor and help them focus on it with a finer detail.
- Notice where they are painting with words – using their senses to create a rich picture.
- If they feel stuck, ask: *What does your poem make you wonder about?*
- If they are unsure whether they have finished, simply ask: *Well, is there anything else you want to say?*
- Ask them to compare what they are writing about to something else to help you better understand it.

Writing lesson 4: Draft

Class writing goal

To draft our 'inspired by ...' poems

OVERVIEW

Children continue to finish turning their dabblings into a draft poem. If they'd like to, you could encourage children to continue writing more poems.

PREPARATION AND RESOURCES

- Poetry 2 (Inspired by ...) genre booklets
- Children's dabblings from the previous sessions
- Copies of poems children are inspired by
- Drafting rules (ITR)

MINI-LESSON

Choose from the suggested mini-lessons for this writing project, which cover aspects of writing study, grammar and punctuation.

The following mini-lessons may be particularly useful at the drafting stage:

- "I'm finished!"
- Use the senses

CLASS WRITING SESSION

Explain to the class that they are going to continue drafting their poem based on the dabblings they have completed. Remind them to use the drafting rules and advice on pages 11–12 of their Poetry 2 (Inspired by ...) genre booklet. They should talk it through with a partner if they get stuck.

Children should write on the left-hand side of the page, leaving the right-hand side blank for revision in future lessons.

PLENARY

Children share their drafts, following the established class sharing routine. You can invite children to briefly explain the theme of their poem and what they want it to make people feel. You can also ask the writers what help they might want from the class to improve it. The child can then read their poem out.

Next, ask the class:

- *How did the poem affect you?*
- *What did it make you wonder?*
- *Did it remind you of anything from your own life?*
- *Did it remind you of anything you've seen, heard or read before?*
- *What words or lines struck you most?*
- *What sounds could you hear?*

If you and your class feel they need another drafting session, please add one in. Alternatively, if children are confident with the writing processes, you can let them move on to the next stage independently.

Conferencing focus

When conferencing, start your conversations off with something such as *'I can see you have ...'* Focus on one of the following:

- Help children to go from the general to the specific. Get them to identify the diamond moment within their poem.
- Help children to explore the passionate part of their poem – where they reveal the most emotion.
- Help them explore their use of strong verbs.
- Look for where they are being playful and ask them questions to bring this out of them more.
- Notice where they have made something not human become human through personification.
- Notice where they are playing around with sounds, rhythm, rhyme and repeated lines.
- Notice their use of metaphor and help them focus on it with a finer detail.
- Notice where they are painting with words – using their senses to create a rich picture.
- If they feel stuck, ask *'What does your poem make you wonder about?'*
- If they are unsure whether they have finished, simply ask *'Well, is there anything else you want to say?'*
- Ask them to compare what they are writing about to something else to help you better understand it.

Writing lesson 5: Revise

> ## Class writing goal
> To revise our 'inspired by ...' poems

OVERVIEW

Children begin the important process of rereading and revising their writing. Focus should be on ensuring that the text makes sense and they have included everything in their plans. Some children may have finished revising their 'inspired by' poem at this point and can move on to editing their pieces.

PREPARATION AND RESOURCES

- Poetry 2 (Inspired by ...) genre booklets
- Children's draft poems from the previous session
- Upper KS2 poetry revision checklist (ITR and PCM, p279)
- Upper KS2 editing checklist (ITR and PCM, p273)
- Tips and Tricks cards
- Reading books

> ### Top tip
> Children can often wrongly choose their best poem as the one that needs least revising. Encourage children to talk with a partner about which poem would have the most potential if it were revised.

MINI-LESSON

Choose from the suggested mini-lessons for this writing project, which cover aspects of writing study, grammar and punctuation.

The following mini-lessons may be particularly useful at the revision stage:

- The best line
- Writing your title last

CLASS WRITING SESSION

Explain to children that many of them are now going to start revising their poems, whilst others will be ready to move on to editing their pieces. Remind them that if they have many changes to make, they can create a new version opposite their draft in their English book. This is particularly the case for children whose preferred writing process is that of discoverer.

> ### Conferencing focus
> Focus on helping children choose the right poem for revision. Explain and be honest with them about which poem you think has the potential to be great!
>
> Read children's poems aloud. Discuss what it sounds like and what they would like to revise. Ask the following questions:
>
> - *What emotions are you trying to evoke?*
> - *What sounds are evident in your poem?*
> - *Have you used sensory details? Do you want to share the part you like?*
> - *Why not try 'painting with words' on your revision and editing page by using metaphors, similes and symbolism in your writing?*
> - *Which is your favourite line / phrase / word? Why do you like it?*
> - *Are you happy with the line breaks?*
>
> Identify strong word choices together and highlight any words that could be revised.

If they have a variety of poems written, they should discuss with a partner which one they think is most in need of revision.

Direct children to the revision information and checklist on pages 13–15 of the Poetry 2 (Inspired by ...) genre booklet or display this on the whiteboard.

Some children may have finished revising their 'inspired by ...' poem at this point and can move on to editing their pieces using the 'Upper KS2 editing checklist' (PCM, p273).

PLENARY

Children share their drafts, following the established class sharing routine. You can invite children to briefly explain the theme of their poem and what they want it to make people feel. You can also ask the writers what help they might want from the class to improve it. The child can then read their poem out. Ask the class:

- *How did the poem affect you?*
- *What did it make you wonder?*
- *Did it remind you of anything from your own life?*
- *Did it remind you of anything you've seen, heard or read before?*
- *What words or lines struck you most?*
- *What sounds could you hear?*

Writing lesson 6: Revise

Class writing goal
To revise our 'inspired by ...' poems

OVERVIEW

Once children are happy with their revised poems, they move on to editing the text and developing their transcription skills by checking spelling, punctuation and grammar. Some children may have finished editing their 'inspired by ...' poems at this point and can move on to publishing their pieces.

PREPARATION AND RESOURCES

- Poetry 2 (Inspired by ...) genre booklets
- Children's draft poems from the previous session
- Upper KS2 poetry revision checklist (ITR and PCM, p279)
- Upper KS2 editing checklist (ITR and PCM, p273)
- Tips and Tricks cards
- Reading books

MINI-LESSON

Choose from the suggested mini-lessons for this writing project, which cover aspects of writing study, grammar and punctuation.

The following mini-lessons may be particularly useful at the revision stage:

- First reread and improve
- Second reread and improve
- Third reread and improve

CLASS WRITING SESSION

Explain to the class that they are going to continue revising their poems.

Remind children that, if they have a lot of changes, they can create a new version opposite their draft in their English book.

Direct children to the revision information and checklist on pages 13–15 of the Poetry 2 (Inspired by ...) genre booklet or display this on the whiteboard. Ask children to use the relevant Tips and Tricks cards to help them with spelling, grammar and punctuation. They can also use their reading books to check the spellings of common words. They should talk with a partner or request a conference with you if they get stuck.

Some children may have finished editing their 'inspired by ...' poem at this point and can move on to publishing their pieces using the 'Presentation tips' (PCM, p274).

Conferencing focus

Focus on helping children choose the right poem for revision. Explain and be honest with them about which poem you think has the potential to be great!

Read children's poems aloud to them so they have the opportunity to hear their own poem. Discuss what it sounds like and what they would like to revise.

Ask the following questions:

- *What emotions are you trying to evoke?*
- *What sounds are evident in your poem?*
- *Have you used sensory details? Do you want to share the part you like?*
- *Why not try 'painting with words' on your revision and editing page by using metaphors, similes and symbolism in your writing?*
- *Which is your favourite line / phrase / word? Why do you like it?*
- *Are you happy with the line breaks?*

Suggest looking at word choices. Identify strong word choices together and highlight any words that could be revised.

PLENARY

Children share their revisions, following the established class sharing routine.

Writing lesson 7: Revise

Class writing goal
To revise our 'inspired by' poems

OVERVIEW

Once children are happy with their revised poem, they move on to editing the text and developing their transcription skills by checking spelling, punctuation and grammar. Some children may have finished editing their 'inspired by ...' poem at this point and can move on to publishing their pieces.

PREPARATION AND RESOURCES

- Poetry 2 genre booklets
- Children's draft poems from the previous session.
- Upper KS2 poetry revision checklist (ITR and PCM, p279)
- Upper KS2 editing checklist (ITR and PCM, p273)
- Tips and Tricks cards
- Reading books

MINI-LESSON

Choose from the suggested mini-lessons for this writing project, which cover aspects of writing study, grammar and punctuation.

The following mini-lessons may be particularly useful at the revision stage:

- The best line
- Writing your title last

CLASS WRITING SESSION

Explain to the class that they are going to continue revising their poems.

Remind children that if they have a lot of changes they can create a new version opposite their draft in their English book.

Direct children to the revision information and checklist on pages 13–15 of the Poetry 2 (Inspired by ...) genre booklet or display this on the whiteboard. Ask children to use the relevant Tips and Tricks cards to help them with spelling, grammar and punctuation. They can also use their reading books to check the spellings of common words. They should talk with a partner or request a conference with you if they get stuck.

Some children may have finished editing their 'inspired by' poem at this point and can move on to publishing their pieces using the 'Presentation tips' (PCM, p274).

Conferencing focus

Focus on helping children choose the right poem for revision. Explain and be honest with them about which poem you think has the potential to be great!

Read children's poems aloud to them so they have the opportunity to hear their own poem, discuss what it sounds like and what they would like to revise.

Ask the following questions:

- *What emotions are you trying to evoke?*
- *What sounds are evident in your poem?*
- *Have you used sensory details? Do you want to share the part you like?*
- *Why not try 'painting with words' on your revision and editing page by using metaphors, similes and symbolism in your writing?*
- *Which is your favourite line / phrase / word? Why do you like it?*
- *Are you happy with the line breaks?*

Suggest looking at word choices. Identify strong word choices together and highlight any words that could be revised.

PLENARY

Children share their revised drafts, following the established class sharing routine. If you or your class feel they need another revision session, please add one in. Alternatively, if children are confident with the writing processes, you can let them move on to the next stage independently.

Writing lesson 8: Edit

Class writing goal
To edit our 'inspired by ...' poems

OVERVIEW

Once children are happy with their revised poems, they move on to editing the text and developing their transcription skills by checking spelling, punctuation and grammar. Some children may have finished editing their poems at this point and can move on to publishing their pieces.

PREPARATION AND RESOURCES

- Poetry 2 (Inspired by ...) genre booklets
- Children's revised poems from the previous session
- Upper KS2 editing checklist (ITR and PCM, p273)
- Presentation tips (ITR and PCM, p274)
- Tips and Tricks cards

- Electronic spell checkers
- Access to online dictionaries
- Thesauruses
- Reading books

MINI-LESSON

Choose from the suggested mini-lessons for this writing project, which cover aspects of writing study, grammar and punctuation.

The following mini-lessons may be particularly useful at the editing stage:

- Sticky bits and yawny bits

CLASS WRITING SESSION

Explain that children are to use this session to edit their poems and prepare them for publishing. Children begin to edit their poems using their editing checklists, along with the relevant Tips and Tricks cards to help them understand the correct use of grammar, punctuation and spelling. Remind children that they can use a dictionary to look up any spellings they are unsure of. They can also use their reading books to check the spellings of common words.

Encourage children to work with a talk partner and discuss their work.

Some children may be ready to publish their poems. Ensure that these children have access to the necessary material and the 'Presentation tips' (PCM, p274 or ITR).

> ### Conferencing focus
> Encourage children to request a conference with you if they get stuck.
>
> Talk to children about which poems they are considering for publication. Give them your honest opinion on which poem you think has the most merit.
>
> Encourage children to read any 'sticky' bits to a partner to get advice before asking you.
>
> A 'sticky' bit is any bit of writing that doesn't sound right. It sounds strange when read out loud. It confuses your reader. Children are very quick to identify 'sticky' bits. You will notice some recurring themes: verb tense, cohesion, switching of pronouns, inability to identify a pronoun's noun.

PLENARY

Show some examples of thoughtful editing. If you and your class feel they need another editing session, please add one in. Alternatively, if children are confident with the writing processes, you can let them to move on to the next stage independently.

DEEPEN

Suggest that children use a thesaurus to expand vocabulary.

SUPPORT

If children have finished their drafts, you or another adult could publish it on their behalf.

Writing lesson 9: Publish

Class writing goal
To publish our 'inspired by ...' poems

OVERVIEW

Most children should now be ready to publish their pieces, and you should be ready to begin assessing their outcomes. Any children who have finished publishing their 'inspired by ...' poem can work on their personal writing projects.

PREPARATION AND RESOURCES

- Children's edited poems from the previous session
- A variety of stationery and art materials
- Presentation tips (ITR and PCM, p274)
- A recording device
- Ask your class librarians to display a variety of poetry books.

MINI-LESSON

Choose from the suggested mini-lessons for this writing project, which cover aspects of writing study, grammar and punctuation.

The following mini-lessons may be particularly useful at the publishing stage:
- Ways of publishing

CLASS WRITING SESSION

Explain that children should use this session to publish and present their poems. Refer back to the original class writing goal of creating a collection of 'inspired by ...' poems. Ensure children have access to the 'Presentation tips' (PCM, p274) or that you have the 'Presentation tips' ITR displayed on the whiteboard. Children can take this opportunity to present their writing, adding colour, artwork and photographs.

Some children may have published their poems already and so they can continue with their personal writing projects.

PLENARY

Invite children to read their poems aloud or share their work with a partner, following the established class sharing routine. Encourage children to use expression when reading aloud.

You may want to record children performing their poems.

Conferencing focus

Encourage children to explore how they want their poem to look on the page or how they could perform their poem most effectively.

Share examples of how poems can be presented on the page with the class. Ask questions such as:

- Does your presentation reflect the emotion expressed in your poem?
- Are there any words / lines / phrases that you want to emphasise? How could you achieve this?
- Have you considered accompanying your poem with a picture, drawing or music?
- What medium will you use to present your poem, e.g. artwork, handwritten, typed, read aloud or recorded?

Take this opportunity to discuss your assessment of their piece and set writing goals for their future class and personal writing projects.

Writing lesson 10: Publish

Class writing goal
To publish our 'inspired by...' poems

OVERVIEW

Most children should now be ready to publish their pieces and you should be ready to begin assessing their outcomes. Any children who have finished publishing their 'inspired by ...' poems can work on their personal writing projects.

PREPARATION AND RESOURCES

- Children's edited poems from the previous session
- A variety of stationery and art materials
- Presentation tips (ITR and PCM, p274)
- A recording device
- Ask your class librarians to display a variety of poetry books.

MINI-LESSON

Choose from the suggested mini-lessons for this writing project, which cover aspects of writing study, grammar and punctuation.

The following mini-lessons may be particularly useful at the publishing stage:
- Ways of publishing

CLASS WRITING SESSION

At this stage, all children should be nearing the end of publishing. Continue to refer children to the 'Presentation tips' (PCM, p274 or ITR).

Conferencing focus

Take this opportunity to discuss your assessment of children's pieces and set writing goals for their future class and personal writing projects.

PLENARY

Children perform their pieces for the class, for other year groups, for parents or for the wider community.

Class writing project: Information texts

Why write information texts?

Children last encountered information as a class writing project in Year 4. It is likely they will have continued writing information texts in their personal writing projects, and will have been writing traditional or uncomplicated information texts. Now that children know the basics, this project looks to show them how rich and varied this genre can actually be.

There are three likely avenues that children's chosen topics will go down throughout this project:

- **Poetic information text**: This is where children may write a traditional information text but should be encouraged to write it in an entertaining and poetic way. Using figurative language and comparison in their descriptions can really bring an extra dimension to their non-fiction writing.

- **Memoir-infused information text**: This is where children exploit their personal connection with a topic and bring personal anecdotes, feelings, thoughts and information together in their writing. This can also add an extra dimension to their non-fiction writing.

- **'Faction' information text**: This is where children explore the opportunity of mixing their favourite fiction with non-fiction writing.

THINGS TO BEAR IN MIND

- Break the misconception that information texts must be overly formal. Show children how personable and entertaining information writing can be. It can in fact evoke all the senses and leave readers genuinely in awe, entertained, thrilled, emotional, persuaded and informed – often all within the same piece.

- Children's enthusiasm for writing information texts can often result in their chosen theme being too general. Directing them towards a more focused approach is an important writing lesson. Children often struggle with the generality and sheer size of their initial topic ideas. For example, 'animals' is often a popular topic choice. However, you will find that children initially choose to write about all types of animals. Instead, encourage them to narrow down their topic to, for example, 'dogs' and then to a particular breed of dog, or better still their dog!

- You may find that children slide into writing which is more in keeping with explanation texts. This is thoroughly acceptable as it demonstrates the beginnings of 'genre-hybriding', and indeed could make for an interesting teaching point.

- Children's conclusions to their pieces could provide final insight, potential actions, challenges or implications to be considered by their reader.

Writing information texts

Use these ideas to help you write your own information texts in class or to introduce children to the genre.

Why write an information text for yourself or your class?

If you are an expert on a topic, you can tell people about it.

What are the basics of an information text?

When writing an information text, you should focus on the 'whats' and 'hows' of your topic. Avoid writing about *why* things happen, because this is the purpose of an explanation text.

(FIELD) What is your information text going to be about?

Are you an expert on cats, the Vikings, or gymnastics? Tell your audience about it and inspire them too. It is best to write an information text about something you really love or know a lot about and that you would like to share with your readers. Think of things you have done or things you read about because you are likely to be an expert on these topics. Information texts do not have to be factual; they can also be about things that are not real, e.g. mythical creatures.

You should focus on three things: **classifying** what your topic is, **describing** your topic and the **effect** your topic has on the world.

(TENOR) What is your role as the writer?

If you are writing information texts for children, make the facts sound as exciting and as interesting as possible. Often, your role as the writer of an information text is to deliver the facts clearly, so that people can learn from them. It is helpful to use a question as a subheading, and then write a paragraph answering the question. Remember that readers may need some words (**technical vocabulary**) explained to them.

(MODE) What should your information text look like?

Your information text should be **multi-modal**. This means that you will use lots of different ways (or modes) to demonstrate what you know. For example, you could use:

- diagrams, photos, pictures, fact-boxes, lists, bullet points or a key
- different font sizes and colours.

Headings are extremely important too. Write down a few possible headings when you are planning your information text and use them in your writing.

(SEMANTICS) How can you make your information text clear and interesting?

You can:

- write in the third person, e.g. *it, they, them, their, they're*
- write in the present tense, e.g. *is, are, have, be, -ing*
- write about groups of things, e.g. *all, many, most, few*
- compare things, e.g. *biggest, smallest, longer, shorter*
- use colons – these tell your reader that an example or explanation is about to be given.

(LEXIS) How can your word choices help?

Throughout your information text, you will describe things. You may find the following linguistic devices particularly helpful:

- **Co-ordinating conjunctions**, e.g. *and* and *but*
- Vocabulary such as *however, if, then, provided that* and *as long as*
- **Adverbial starters** to introduce a fact, e.g. *amazingly, intriguingly, surprisingly* and *interestingly*
- **Proper nouns** rather than lots of pronouns.

Genre study I: What do we know about information texts?

> ## Class writing goal
> To learn what our next class writing project will be

OVERVIEW

In this lesson, children will revisit the information genre and will discuss why people write information texts. You will then reveal that this is the next class writing project and that the class will be publishing an anthology of information texts to place in the class library and beyond.

PREPARATION AND RESOURCES

- Ask your class librarians to display a variety of information texts, first ensuring that your class library has a rich and varied stock of information texts and texts which show hybridising between different genres.
- Video: 'What makes a good information text?'
- Writing wheel (ITR and PCM, p272)

STUDY

Show children the video 'What makes a good information text?'.

The video shows two writers talking about what they love about writing information texts, how they write them, and how they can use them to change people's minds.

Explain to children that their class project will be to write their own information texts.

DISCUSS

Ask children if they can remember what the information genre is (including 'faction' information texts), and what thoughts they have about the video they have just watched.

Display the 'Writing wheel' ITR on the whiteboard and hand out the printed versions.

Ask the following questions:

- *Why do you think people write information texts (purpose)?*
- *Who do you think writers of information texts write for (audience)?*
- *Who is an expert on something in our class?*
- *Do we have groups of experts on the same topics?*
- *Is there something you have always wanted to find out about?*

PLENARY

Children share writing from their personal projects, following the established class sharing routine.

SUPPORT

Some children will benefit from more support in looking at the features of information texts, and you may choose some simpler information texts that these children are able to access more easily.

PERSONAL WRITING PROJECTS

Throughout the class writing project, once the class writing goal for each session is complete, children carry on with their personal writing projects at their own pace and using their preferred writing processes. See pages 17–19 for more information on personal writing projects and pages 26–30 for more information on pupil conferencing.

Genre study 2: What makes a good information text?

> **Class writing goal**
> To discover what makes a good information text

OVERVIEW

In this lesson, children will look at a variety of information texts and discuss which topics the writers chose, why they chose them and what the exemplars do well. Children will then continue to work on their personal writing projects.

PREPARATION AND RESOURCES

- Information texts genre booklets
- Pre-written exemplar information texts:
  - *Flight* (genre booklet p2–4, ITR)
  - *Different types of knots* (genre booklet p5–6, ITR)
- Exemplars created by children from previous years
- Flip-chart paper

> As you develop your confidence as a writer-teacher, you should aim to create your own information text exemplar using the writing project's opening guidance.

STUDY

Children look at and read the information texts in your class library and discuss the following questions in pairs or groups:

- *What did you like about the information texts you read?*
- *What ideas did they give you for writing your own information text?*

Children then read exemplar information texts (your own, child examples and pre-written exemplars) and discuss the questions again.

DISCUSS

Explain to children that good information texts have a specific focus rather than a general focus. You can use the analogy of mining for diamonds. Children should focus on finding a single diamond from all of their 'rocky' ideas and make that diamond shine. These diamonds are the moments that writers care about the most.

In pairs, children discuss the following questions:

- *Why do you think I / the writers chose my / their topic(s)?*
- *What sort of diamonds were chosen by me / the other writers?*
- *Why do you think I / the other writers chose these diamonds?*
- *Can you see differences between the examples?*
- *Who could you write an information text for?*
- *What makes a good information text?*

CREATE

As a class, and using the information on page 1 of the Information texts genre booklet, start creating your poster of product goals. These goals should indicate what is needed to publish a great information text.

PLENARY

Children share writing from their personal projects, following the established class sharing routine. Place exemplars into the class library for children to continue reading at their leisure.

PERSONAL WRITING PROJECTS

Throughout the class writing project, once the class writing goal for each session is complete, children carry on with their personal writing projects at their own pace and using their preferred writing processes. See pages 17–19 for more information on personal writing projects and pages 26–30 for more information on pupil conferencing.

Genre study 3: Generating ideas for information texts

> ## Class writing goal
> To generate an idea for each child's information text

OVERVIEW

In this lesson, children will learn about and experiment with a number of techniques for generating ideas for their own information texts (including 'faction'). They will then choose one idea to use for their writing project.

PREPARATION AND RESOURCES

- Information texts genre booklets
- Access to the internet
- A selection of non-fiction texts
- Flip-chart paper

STUDY

Children turn to pages 7–8 of their Information texts genre booklets. Read and discuss some of the techniques used by writers to generate ideas for writing information texts.

DISCUSS

As a class, talk about the areas of interest or expertise within the class.

Ask children if there is something that they have always wanted to learn about or been curious about but have never seemed to have the time to research. What would they be interested in reading about?

Once you have a list of suggestions, ask children if they think they could do a good job of tackling one of the topics for the class. Assign topics to willing volunteers.

CREATE

As a class, in small groups or in pairs, ask children to come up with their own list of potential writing ideas. Children could inspire ideas in others by sharing topics they would be interested in reading and learning about. By the end of this lesson, all children should have an idea for their information text.

PLENARY

Children share their ideas, following the established class sharing routine. If children need to do any research for their class writing project, this could be done as homework.

PERSONAL WRITING PROJECTS

Throughout the class writing project, once the class writing goal for each session is complete, children carry on with their personal writing projects at their own pace and using their preferred writing processes. See pages 17–19 for more information on personal writing projects and pages 26–30 for more information on pupil conferencing.

Writing lesson I: Plan

Class writing goal
To plan our information texts

OVERVIEW

Children plan or draft their information texts.

PREPARATION AND RESOURCES

- Information texts genre booklets
- Any research homework children have done in preparation for today's lesson
- Information texts planning grid (ITR and PCM, p294)

MINI-LESSON

Choose from the suggested mini-lessons for this writing project, which cover aspects of writing study, grammar and punctuation.

The following mini-lessons may be particularly useful at the planning stage:

- Webbing
- Using a planning grid
- I'm an expert in …
- Write about topic lessons

CLASS WRITING SESSION

Before you begin your writing week, tell children that they have seven writing sessions in which to publish their information text. Remind them of the different writing styles writers often use. These include being a discoverer, planner, drafter, paragraph piler and sentence stacker. Explain that, depending on their preferred writing style, they are likely to be planning or drafting today.

> **Conferencing focus**
> Encourage children to talk through their plans or drafts in pairs and with you throughout this session. Pairs should let each other know if too much prior knowledge from their reader is being assumed, and whether any technical vocabulary needs to be defined to help their reader understand the text.

You could show children a plan of your own, or display the example 'Information texts planning grid' ITR. Children may also find it useful to look at the planning advice on page 9 of their Information text genre booklet.

If children choose to plan their pieces, they are free to use their 'Information texts planning grid' (PCM, p294) if they wish to. Other children may leap straight into drafting their information texts. Encourage these children to refer to the drafting rules on page 10 of their Information texts genre booklets.

PLENARY

Children who have planned their information texts turn over their plans and 'tell' their information text to someone in the class.

DEEPEN

When planning the opening for their information text, children could start with a short story from their own experience, either descriptive or personalised by speaking straight to their reader. They could also talk about why they chose to write about the topic. Perhaps it is something that a friend wanted to learn about.

SUPPORT

Children could draw their plans into their 'planning grid'. Alternatively, children could talk through their idea or their plan with an adult and move straight to drafting.

Writing lesson 2: Plan

Class writing goal
To plan our information texts

OVERVIEW

Children continue to plan or draft their information text.

PREPARATION AND RESOURCES

- Information texts genre booklets
- Any research homework children have done in preparation for today's lesson
- Information texts planning grid (ITR and PCM, p294)

MINI-LESSON

Choose from the suggested mini-lessons for this writing project, which cover aspects of writing study, grammar and punctuation.

The following mini-lessons may be particularly useful at the planning stage:

- Webbing
- Using a planning grid
- I'm an expert in …
- Lead your reader to the facts

CLASS WRITING SESSION

Children who have not finished their plans will continue to plan their pieces of writing. Remind children to consider what the focus of their piece is and discuss this in pairs. If helpful, display the completed 'Information texts planning grid' ITR on the whiteboard for reference.

> **Conferencing focus**
> Encourage children to talk through their plans or drafts in pairs and with you throughout this session. Pairs should let each other know if too much prior knowledge from the reader is being assumed, and whether any technical vocabulary needs to be defined to help the reader understand the text.

Other children may begin or continue to draft their information texts. Encourage these children to refer to the drafting rules on page 10 of their Information texts genre booklets.

PLENARY

Children who have planned their information texts turn over their plans and 'tell' their information text to someone in the class. If any children feel they need another planning session, please add one in. Alternatively, if children are confident with the writing processes, continue to allow them to move on to the next stage independently.

DEEPEN

When planning the opening for their information text, children could start with a short story from their own experience, either descriptive or personalised by speaking straight to the reader. They could also talk about why they chose to write about the topic. Perhaps it is something that a friend wanted to learn about.

SUPPORT

Children could draw their plans into their planning grids. Alternatively, children could talk through their idea or their plan with an adult and move straight to drafting.

Writing lesson 3: Draft

> ## Class writing goal
> To draft our information texts

OVERVIEW

Children use the plans they created in previous sessions to start or continue drafting their information texts. Some children may have finished their drafts at this point and can move on to revising their pieces.

PREPARATION AND RESOURCES

- Information texts genre booklets
- Planning grids from the previous lesson
- Tips and Tricks cards
- Drafting rules (ITR)

MINI-LESSON

Choose from the suggested mini-lessons for this writing project, which cover aspects of writing study, grammar and punctuation.

The following mini-lessons may be particularly useful at the drafting stage:

- How to be a discoverer
- How to be a planner
- How to be a paragraph piler
- How to be a sentence stacker

CLASS WRITING SESSION

Explain to children that many of them are now going to start drafting their information texts based on the plan they have completed.

Remind them to use the drafting rules found on page 10 of their Information texts genre booklets (or on the 'Drafting rules' ITR) and to talk through their drafts in pairs if they get stuck.

Children should write on the left side of their books leaving the right blank for revision in future lessons.

Some children may have finished drafting their information texts at this point and can move on to revising their pieces using the revision checklist on page 13 of their Information texts genre booklets if necessary.

PLENARY

Children share their drafts, following the established class sharing routine.

SUPPORT

Encourage children to paragraph pile or sentence stack until they are more confident.

Conferencing focus

Encourage children to request a conference with you if they get stuck. Also encourage them to regularly reread their pieces as they write them. Provide intervals during which children can share their writing in pairs. Pairs focus on any 'sticky' or 'yawny' bits they hear.

A 'sticky' bit is any bit of writing that doesn't sound right. It sounds strange when read aloud. It confuses the reader. Children are very quick to identify 'sticky' bits. You will notice some recurring themes: verb tense, cohesion, switching of pronouns, inability to identify a pronoun's noun.

A 'yawny' bit is any bit of writing that seems unnecessary or repetitive.

Top tip

Sometimes it's helpful to suggest that children leave it a couple of days before they decide to revise or edit their pieces. This means they can look at their writing with fresh and objective eyes.

Writing lesson 4: Draft

Class writing goal
To draft our information texts

OVERVIEW

Children continue drafting their information texts. Some children may have finished their drafts at this point and can move on to revising their pieces.

PREPARATION AND RESOURCES

- Information texts genre booklets
- Planning grids from the previous lesson
- Tips and Tricks cards
- Drafting rules (ITR)

MINI-LESSON

Choose from the suggested mini-lessons for this writing project, which cover aspects of writing study, grammar and punctuation.

The following mini-lessons may be particularly useful at the drafting stage:

- Determiners
- Simple and multiclause sentences
- Fronted adverbials: moving between place and time
- Using nouns and pronouns for cohesion
- Sentences with different forms

CLASS WRITING SESSION

Children continue to develop their drafts.

Some children may have finished drafting their information texts at this point and can move on to revising their pieces using the revision checklist on page 13 of their Information texts genre booklets if necessary.

Conferencing focus

Encourage children to request a conference with you if they get stuck. Also encourage them to regularly reread their pieces as they write them. Provide intervals during which children can share their writing in pairs. Pairs focus on any 'sticky' or 'yawny' bits they hear.

PLENARY

Children share their drafts, following the established class sharing routine. If any children feel they need another drafting session, please add one in. Alternatively, if children are confident with the writing processes, continue to allow them to move on to the next stage independently.

Top tip

Sometimes it's helpful to suggest that children leave it a couple of days before they decide to revise or edit their pieces. This means they can look at their writing with fresh and objective eyes.

SUPPORT

Encourage children to paragraph pile or sentence stack until they are more confident.

Writing lesson 5: Revise

Class writing goal
To revise our information texts

OVERVIEW

Children begin the important process of rereading and revising their writing. Focus should be on ensuring that the text makes sense and that they have included everything in their plans. Some children may have finished revising their information texts at this point and can move on to editing their pieces.

PREPARATION AND RESOURCES

- Information texts genre booklets
- Upper KS2 non-fiction revision checklist (ITR and PCM, p278)
- Upper KS2 editing editing checklist (ITR and PCM, p273)
- Tips and Tricks cards

MINI-LESSON

Choose from the suggested mini-lessons for this writing project, which cover aspects of writing study, grammar and punctuation.

The following mini-lessons may be particularly useful at the revision stage:

- Unlike
- Sticky bits and yawny bits
- First reread and improve
- Second reread and improve
- Third reread and improve

You may also wish to consider some of the functional grammar study mini-lessons listed in the previous lessons.

CLASS WRITING SESSION

Explain to children that many of them are now going to start revising their piece of writing, whilst others will be ready to move on to editing their pieces. Remind them that if they have many changes to make they can create a new version opposite their draft in their English book. This is particularly the case for children whose preferred writing process is that of discoverer.

Conferencing focus

Encourage children to request a conference with you if they get stuck. Also encourage them to talk in pairs about where certain revisions could be effective.

Provide intervals during which children can share their writing in pairs. Pairs focus on any revisions made.

Remind children to use the revision checklist found on page 13 of their Information texts genre booklets and the relevant Tips and Tricks cards. They may also find it useful to look at the revision advice on pages 11–12 of their Information text genre booklet.

Some children may have finished revising their information texts at this point and can move on to editing their pieces using the 'Upper KS2 editing editing checklist' (PCM, p273).

PLENARY

Children share their revised drafts, following the established class sharing routine. If any children feel they need another revision session, please add one in. Alternatively, if children are confident with the writing processes, continue to allow them to move on to the next stage independently.

SUPPORT

Some children may require more support in reviewing their writing and may benefit from adult input.

Writing lesson 6: Edit

> ## Class writing goal
> To edit our information texts

OVERVIEW

Once children are happy with their revised text, they move on to editing the text and developing their transcription skills by checking spelling, grammar and punctuation. Some children may have finished editing their information texts at this point and can move on to publishing their pieces.

PREPARATION AND RESOURCES

- Upper KS2 editing checklist (ITR and PCM, p273)
- Presentation tips (PCM, p274)
- Tips and Tricks cards
- Electronic spell checkers
- Access to online dictionaries
- Reading books

MINI-LESSON

Choose from the suggested mini-lessons for this writing project, which cover aspects of writing study, grammar and punctuation.

The following mini-lessons may be particularly useful at the editing stage:

- How to edit your writing for capitals
- How to edit your writing for use of vocabulary
- How to edit your writing for punctuation
- How to check and correct your unsure spellings

You may also want to consider some of the functional grammar study mini-lessons listed in the previous lesson plans.

CLASS WRITING SESSION

Children begin to edit their texts using their editing checklist, along with the relevant Tips and Tricks cards to help them understand the correct use of grammar and punctuation. Remind children that they can use a dictionary and the spelling tips and tricks cards to look up any spellings they are unsure of. They can also use their reading books to check the spellings of common words.

Some children may have finished editing their information texts at this point and can move on to publishing their pieces using the 'Presentation tips' (PCM, p274).

> ### Conferencing focus
> Encourage children to request a conference with you if they get stuck. Also encourage them to read any 'sticky' bits to a partner to get advice before asking you.
>
> Provide intervals during which children can share their writing in pairs. Pairs focus on any revisions made.

PLENARY

Show some examples of thoughtful editing. If any children feel they need another editing session, please add one in. Alternatively, if children are confident with the writing processes, continue to allow them to move on to the next stage independently.

SUPPORT

If children have finished editing their texts, you or another adult could publish it on their behalf.

Writing lesson 7: Publish

Class writing goal

To publish our information texts

OVERVIEW

Most children should now be ready to publish their pieces and you should be ready to begin assessing their outcomes. Any children who have finished publishing their information texts can work on their personal writing projects.

PREPARATION AND RESOURCES

- A variety of stationery and art materials
- Presentation tips (ITR and PCM, p274)

MINI-LESSON

Choose from the suggested mini-lessons for this writing project, which cover aspects of writing study, grammar and punctuation.

The following mini-lesson may be particularly useful at the publishing stage:

- Ways of publishing

You may also want to look at or revisit any areas of grammar or punctuation that have been particularly tricky during this writing project.

CLASS WRITING SESSION

Refer back to the original class writing goal of creating a collection of information texts. Ensure children have access to the 'Presentation tips' (PCM, p274) or that you have the 'Presentation tips' ITR displayed on the whiteboard. Children can take this opportunity to present their writing, adding colour, artwork and photographs.

Conferencing focus

Take this opportunity to discuss your assessment of children's pieces and set writing goals for their future class and personal writing projects. Place these goals on the working wall.

PLENARY

Children share their pieces with the class. This can be done as a whole class, in small groups or in pairs.

If children wrote their information texts in response to something that another child wanted to learn about, ensure that these children share their texts with each other.

The class could also share their anthologies with other classes in the school or in the main library. Over time, your school could create its own self-created encyclopaedia. Parent helpers could even help to publish the texts online for an online school encyclopaedia.

Mini-lessons: Writing study

Use an ideas heart

STUDY

The ideas heart is a way of generating a bank of writing ideas by asking children to focus on the things that matter most to them. Writing down these familiar, best-loved topics will create strong emotions that can then be used to drive a piece of writing.

Using the 'Use an ideas heart' ITR or a piece of flip-chart paper, prepare your own Ideas heart and show it to children as an example before they begin. Ask children to draw a large heart and fill it with the names of people, pets, places, topics and things that are important to them. The ITR also has some suggestions but make it clear to children that they can add whatever details they want at any time.

DISCUSS

- *Has anyone in the class used this technique before?*
- *What do you think of this technique? Is it helpful?*
- *Which topic, or combined topics, might make for a good writing topic?*

CREATE

Encourage children to begin using this technique in their own writing during this lesson.

Use a spark line

STUDY

Explain to children that it can often be helpful to 'use a spark line' to generate ideas for writing. This is where they can take a line that they like from a book that they have read, or are reading at the moment, and turn it into something new (such as a poem, a story, an information text or a memoir). Explain that there should be something about the line that particularly appeals to them such as the use of descriptive words or phrases, the style of the writer, the setting or any character action.

Ask children to imagine that they have chosen the following spark line: '*Fear floods my body, and my blood turns to ice.*'

Discuss with children any ideas for writing that might be inspired by this line. Could it be the opening to a story? The first line of a poem? What about memoir? Ask children whether it reminds them of anything that has happened to them. Ask children to contribute some ideas while you note them down on the board.

DISCUSS

- *Has anyone in the class used this technique before?*
- *What do you think of this technique? Is it helpful?*
- *Can you find any more spark lines in your reading books?*

CREATE

Encourage children to try out this technique during the lesson today.

Favourite objects

STUDY

Ask children to draw their favourite object or bring in a special object from home. Ask children to explain why it is important to them as well as the feelings and emotions the object stirs up in them. Ask children how an object might be defined as 'important'? Is it something they would want to save if their house was on fire? Is it irreplaceable? Why or why not?

Around the drawings of the favourite objects, ask children to write down some of the ideas that the object might give them for different pieces of writing. For example, they may want to write a memoir or an information text about it.

DISCUSS

- *Has anyone in the class used this technique before?*
- *What do you think of this technique? Is it helpful?*
- *Can you think of any special objects that belong to you that might spark some new ideas for writing?*

CREATE

Encourage children to try out using this technique during the time spent writing in the lesson.

What if ...?

STUDY

Ask children to write down a list of 'What if ...?' questions. Explain that 'What if ...?' questions are a great way of stretching your imagination and generating ideas for all forms of writing, though they are particularly suited to fiction and poetry.

Use the example on the 'What if ...?' ITR to explain the technique.

You may find the book *Supposing* by Alastair Reid useful for this mini-lesson.

DISCUSS

- *Has anyone in the class used this technique before?*
- *What do you think of this technique? Is it helpful?*
- *Can you come up with some more 'What if ...?' questions to spark new writing ideas?*

CREATE

Encourage children to try using this technique in the lesson to generate more writing ideas.

When I was younger ...

STUDY

Ask children to write down lots of endings to the sentence: 'When I was younger ...' until they are able to generate a writing idea. Remind children to incorporate feelings and emotions, not just simple facts.

Ask children to give you some suggestions for sentences that begin with 'When I was younger ...' and write them on the board. Explain to children the difference between concrete and the abstract ideas, as well as between facts and emotions, such as:

- When I was younger, I went to Spain on holiday every year.
- When I was younger, I was scared of my neighbour's dog.

Encourage children to use both facts and emotions as well as concrete and abstract ideas in their writing.

DISCUSS

- Has anyone in the class used this technique before?
- What do you think of this technique? Is it helpful?
- Could any of these sentences form the basis for your own writing?

CREATE

Encourage children to begin using this technique in their own writing during this lesson.

Imagine a day when ...

STUDY

Invite children to write down a list of 'Imagine a day when ... ' sentences until an idea appears. This technique can be used to spark new ideas for a variety of writing genres.

Ask children to think about the words 'Imagine a day when ... ' and how they can be used to generate ideas for pieces of writing. Focus children's attention of the word 'imagine'. Explain that this could mean something out of the ordinary, something special, or even a day to remember. Encourage children to reflect their ideas in completed sentences.

DISCUSS

- Has anyone in the class used this technique before?
- What do you think of this technique? Is it helpful?
- Could any of the completed sentences form the basis of a piece of writing?

CREATE

Encourage children to begin using this technique in their own writing during today's lesson.

Free-writing

STUDY

Explain to children that free-writing is a technique that writers often use to generate ideas or to create an early draft of an idea. Our minds are never blank and are always busy, so it is helpful to write down whatever ideas are in your head, however disjointed they might seem. Encourage children to note down whatever comes in and out of their minds as they sit quietly for 10–15 minutes then use this list to come up with a new writing topic. Alternatively, if they have an idea already in their head they can write everything that comes into their mind on that topic for 10–15 minutes.

Prepare an example of your own free-writing for discussion with the class. Explain how free-writing works: even when we say we can't think of anything to write about, our minds are still busily chattering away in the background. That means we can always begin by writing down our thoughts, no matter what those thoughts are. Explain to children how you first read through your free-writing and then pinpoint topics or thoughts that might be worth exploring further. These could be things about the writing that enthused or annoyed you, or simply recurring themes.

DISCUSS

- *Has anyone in the class used this technique before?*
- *What do you think of this technique? Is it helpful?*
- *Are there any words or sentences that you have used in your free-writing, that might be worth building on?*

CREATE

Encourage children to begin using this technique in their own writing from this point onwards.

Have you ever wondered ...?

STUDY

Ask children to choose a subject that they are interested in and that they know something about. It can be about anything from dinosaurs to baking a cake. Explain to children that they will need to talk directly to their reader about the subject they have chosen by providing their reader with useful information and explaining why they are so interested in this subject. Once children have finished writing, encourage them to think about how they can use their notes about this subject area in one or more writing genres.

Explain to children that during the lesson, they will be finding out about the different things that people know about through gathering and sharing information, then pooling their knowledge. Talk through the notes relating to your own writing as an example: how you chose a subject to write about and why you are so interested in it, or why it is of such importance to you. Then show how you might use your notes in one or more writing genres such as an information text relating to a subject or a persuasive piece of text in support of the subject.

DISCUSS

- *Has anyone in the class used this technique before?*
- *What do you think of this technique? Is it helpful?*
- *Which subjects are you interested in that you would like to tell your reader about?*
- *How can these notes be used in five different writing genres?*

CREATE

Encourage children to begin using this technique in their own writing during the lesson.

General to specific

Explain to children that this mini-lesson will drill them down through the general, wider focus of their writing to the specific details of their chosen subject. Encourage children to write about specific people, things, animals, moments or places and avoid talking about general topics. For example, explain to children that they will need to write about a particular autumn day, not all autumn days, or write about one particular starry night, not all nights. Write about your dog or one particular dog.

Explain to children that for most kinds of writing, it is better to focus on a very specific person, place, thing, moment or experience, rather than on a general topic. Show children the 'General to specific' ITR.

Give children the example of a general topic. For example, a trip to the seaside. Now, you could talk about getting in the car, driving to the seaside, getting out of the car, getting the stuff down onto the beach, laying out your towel, eating your sandwiches and everything else that happened that day. However, the part that is most interesting and the part that you really want to talk about is the specific part of the day – the moment you were stung by a jelly fish! This is the valuable lesson you want to put over.

DISCUSS

- *Has anyone in the class used this technique before?*
- *What do you think of this technique? Is it helpful?*

CREATE

Encourage children to begin using the technique of narrowing the focus of their writing in the lesson today.

Answering Michael Rosen's four questions

STUDY

This lesson shows children how inspiration can be drawn from different quarters, and how they can begin 'mining' texts that have already been written, to produce a new diamond moment that can be used as inspiration for their own writing. Explain to children that this is *inspired by* writing. You may want to use Sharon Creech's book *Love That Dog* to help you teach this lesson.

Choose an exemplar text from the class library that is in the same genre as the class writing project. After you have read the text together as a class, ask children the following questions to generate discussion:

- *What does this text remind you of?*
- *Does this text remind you of anything else you have read or seen?*
- *If you could meet the writer, what would you ask them?*
- *Do you think you could write something like that?*

DISCUSS

- *Has anyone in the class used this technique before?*
- *What do you think of this technique? Is it helpful?*

CREATE

Encourage children to begin using this technique in their own writing during this lesson.

Write about what you're most afraid of

STUDY

Ask children what keeps them awake at night. What do you they think about when they are taking a walk? What really gets on their nerves? What do they try to avoid thinking about? American short story writer Donald Barthelme said 'write about what you're most afraid of'. Explain to children that it can be extremely useful, even cathartic, to write down these feelings and emotions.

Begin the lesson with a discussion about the different types of fears that people commonly have and then discuss the specific fears that the children in your class have. Try to move beyond concentrating on nouns / objects (such as ghosts, rats, big scary dogs) and instead encourage discussion about deep feelings and emotions. Explain to children that not everything that they are afraid of is tangible, for example death, worrying about family situations such as parents divorcing, as well as anxiety about global events, such as war and famine.

DISCUSS

- *Has anyone in the class used this technique before?*
- *What do you think of this technique? Is it helpful?*
- *Are there any ideas from this lesson that could be useful in your writing projects?*

CREATE

Encourage children to try using this technique to help them with their writing during the lesson.

Jot for one week, write the next week

STUDY

Introduce to children the idea of jotting down ideas in a small notebook whenever they come up with new ideas so that they can later be used for writing inspiration. Show children the 'Jot for one week, write the next week' ITR.

Explain to children that they might sometimes feel empty handed (or empty headed!) when sitting down to write, when they don't have an idea to get them started. Explain to children that many writers find it helps to carry a pocket-sized notebook around with them and to jot down a key word or phrase when something strikes them in the moment. Explain that this means that they can look back at their work to see why it was important and then they will always have a spark of something waiting for them when they have time to sit down and really write something in depth.

DISCUSS

- *Has anyone in the class used this technique before?*
- *What do you think of this technique? Is it helpful?*
- *Can you think of a time when you had an idea away from your desk? What sparked it?*
- *Have you seen, heard or felt anything in the past few days that you wish you could remember more clearly?*

CREATE

Encourage children to think about where and when they may be able to collect ideas for their own writing before their next writing session.

Use newspapers and magazines

STUDY

Introduce children to the idea of looking through newspapers and magazines to find sparks of ideas for stories.

Explain to children that writers can find ideas in all sorts of places and in all sorts of ways. One way to make a story really believable is to include situations or details from the real world. For example, explain that they could use a real memory or find a true story and change different parts of it to spin it into a fictional story instead. One way to find a wide selection of different real-life stories is to look at newspapers and magazines. There are stories hiding not only in the big world events but also in the little things, such as wedding announcements or 'lost and found' adverts.

DISCUSS

- *Has anyone in the class used this technique before?*
- *What do you think of this technique? Is it helpful?*
- *What news stories or real-life accounts have you read?*
- *What parts of these stories could you use and change in your own work?*

CREATE

Encourage children to look through newspapers and magazines before their next writing session, clipping out stories that interest them and thinking about how these could be adapted.

Give a voice where none is heard

INTRODUCTION

Ask children what they think the wind would say if it were able to talk. What about an abandoned dog? Or a tube train going through the dark tunnel? Who would they want to talk to if they were able to speak? What would their voices sound like? What would they need us to know?

Explain to children that this mini-lesson is all about trying to understand how *things* could feel if they were personified. How can we give life and a voice to the things that can't *actually* speak in our writing?

STUDY

Start a discussion with children about those individuals or things that don't have a voice, for whatever reason. Work with children to add to create a list. This technique is much more effective if children are discouraged from explicitly stating the thing or object whose voice they have chosen to adopt. Instead, children should be encouraged to convey this information through their descriptions of the actions, thoughts and feelings of their chosen persona, as well as through their style and choice of language. Make it clear that this is also much more interesting for their reader.

DISCUSS

- *Has anyone in the class used this technique before?*
- *What do you think of this technique? Is it helpful?*
- *Could this technique help you with your future writing projects when thinking about fictional characters?*

CREATE

Encourage children to try using this technique to help them with their writing during the lesson.

Ideas map

STUDY

Show children the 'Ideas map' ITR. Explain to children that to start drawing their ideas map, they should take two characters, two settings and two problems from a book that they have read and then build their map around them. Invite children to see if they can connect these ideas together to make one story idea. Explain that making connections can be fun and it can throw up all sorts of storylines that they may never, ever have thought of!

DISCUSS

- *Has anyone in the class used this technique before?*
- *What do you think of this technique? Is it helpful?*
- *Do you think this is a useful technique to help deal with writer's block?*

CREATE

Encourage children to try out this technique during the lesson. Allow time for children to search through books they have read, to find characters, settings and problems. Encourage children to keep notes on these for future writing projects.

Read a moment

STUDY

To introduce the topic, ask children to choose a text that they have read or have loved reading, this year. Encourage children to look for a moment in the text that they would like to have a go at rewriting for themselves.

If children have found the text in a story, explain that they could retell the moment from the viewpoint of a different character. Alternatively, if the story is written in the first person, then explain that they could rewrite it in the third person. If the moment is from a different kind of text, ask children to see if they can present the information in another way. They could rewrite the moment in a different order to the original version or use a different descriptive language. Show children the 'Read a moment' ITR.

DISCUSS

- *Has anyone in the class every used this technique?*
- *What do you think of this technique? Is it helpful?*
- *How easy is it to find a 'moment' in a text?*

CREATE

Encourage children to try out this technique in today's lesson and keep any notes on moments that they have found for future writing projects.

Twenty words

STUDY

Introduce the topic to children by explaining that you are giving them just twenty words to write a story! The twenty words that the children have been given make up four or five sentences at the maximum, so explain to children that they will have to think very carefully about what to include. Encourage children to cut out any unnecessary words and also try to engage your reader's attention by adding in some interesting and intriguing details that will make them want to know more about the story.

Once children have written their twenty words, encourage them to build up the words into a longer story. Show children the 'Twenty words' ITR.

DISCUSS

· *Has anyone in the class used this technique?*
· *What do you think of this technique? Is it helpful?*
· *Do you think any of the twenty words stories could generate storylines for longer pieces of writing?*

CREATE

Encourage children to use these techniques during their lesson today.

Write a fairy tale

STUDY

Ask children if they can think of any well-known fairy tales. Explain that traditional fairy tales very often follow story patterns, regardless of where in the world they come from. Many fairy tales include opposite themes such as good versus evil, rich versus poor or creatures versus humans.

Explain to children that the number three is often used in fairy tales (such as three wishes, three chances and the three Billy Goats Gruff). The fairy tales might also be set a long time ago. The characters are usually straightforward in types, such as silly or clever, kind or mean. Fairy tales may include magical characters, royal characters and magical events. There is often a problem to be solved, followed by a happy ending.

Invite children to say as many fairy tales as they can and think of, while you list them on the board. Then encourage children to look for patterns within the fairy tales that appear more than once. Explain to children that this will remind them of the important things that they need to think about when they write their own fairy tales. Explain to children that it is also important to remember that they don't need to use every single one of these points in their own story! Show children the 'Write a fairy tale' ITR.

DISCUSS

· *Has this activity reminded you of the things you need to consider when writing a fairy tale?*
· *Have any of the fairy tales mentioned today inspired any ideas for writing your own story?*

CREATE

Encourage children to use these techniques during their lesson today.

Re-write a fairy tale

STUDY

Ask children to choose a traditional fairy tale. Explain that during this lesson, children will be shaking up the fairy tale a little! For example, children could change something about the traditional story or the characters, in order to be playful! Encourage children to think about a surprising ending to their chosen fairy tale. Perhaps Cinderella doesn't want to marry her Prince Charming straightaway? Or maybe Rapunzel thinks she should get her hair cut off? Ask children whether their fairy tale could be set in the present day. Explain that before they begin work on their fairy tale, it is important to ask themselves exactly what a fairy tale is.

DISCUSS

- *Has anyone in the class used this technique before?*
- *What do you think of this technique? Is it helpful?*
- *Has this task helped you to think differently about fairy tales?*

CREATE

Encourage children to re-write fairy tales during the lesson.

Developing a character

STUDY

Explain to children that writers work hard to share information about their characters because they know this is what their readers often love the most. Explain that there are lots of different ways writers can describe and develop their characters. Show children the 'Developing a character' ITR and talk through the prompts.

DISCUSS

- *Has anyone in the class used this technique before?*
- *What do you think of this technique? Is it helpful?*
- *Has this given you any new ideas for how to describe your character?*

CREATE

Encourage children to try out this technique during the lesson today, to help describe their characters.

Create a character

STUDY

Introduce the idea of creating a character by drawing a picture of a story character that the children already know. Explain to children that drawing a picture of the character living inside their heads before they begin writing is a great way to help their characters come alive.

Give your example character a name but avoid just concentrating on what they look like. Think about their family background, who they are, where they live, their likes and dislikes, their problems, their wants and needs and where they are in their lives right at this moment.

Finally, place your example character in a story moment. Show children the 'Create a character' ITR.

DISCUSS

- *Has anyone in the class every used this technique?*
- *What do you think of this technique? Is it helpful?*
- *Does it matter if you don't use all your character details in your story?*

CREATE

Encourage children to try out this technique in today's lesson.

That's me, I wish that was me, that's the worst of me

STUDY

To introduce the topic, encourage children to look back at books that they have read or have loved reading. Ask children to concentrate on the characters in those stories for this lesson.

Ask children whether the characters in the stories influenced whether or not they liked these books. If so, who were they? What did they do in the story? Choose one or some of these characters that the children have told you about to use in your own example story. The characters should come from one of the following categories: 'That's me', 'I wish that was me' and 'That's the worst of me'. Show children the 'That's me, I wish that was me, that's the worst of me' ITR.

DISCUSS

- *Has anyone in the class used this technique before in their writing?*
- *What do you think of this technique? Is it helpful?*
- *Was it easier to find a 'That's me', 'I wish that was me' or 'That's the worst of me' character to write about?*

CREATE

Encourage children to use these techniques during their lesson today.

Important people

STUDY

Ask children to think about the most important people in their lives. Explain that these people may not always be the people that they see most often but they will be people who they love to spend time with.

Invite children to choose one person who is important to them and to make a list of memories that children have of that person that the two of them share. The memories that they have might be happy or sad and sometimes they are both at the same time. Ask children to choose one of those memories and invite them to write it down as a memoir or a poem.

DISCUSS

- *Has anyone in the class used this technique before in their writing?*
- *What do you think of this technique? Is it helpful?*
- *Is it easy or difficult to write about someone you know very well and are close to?*

CREATE

Encourage children to use these techniques during their lesson today.

Memoir with strong feelings

STUDY

Introduce the topic by explaining to children that feelings and emotions, whether they are happy or sad, are all part of being human. Explain that during the lesson, children will use these feelings and emotions to inspire their writing.

Invite children to think about and say different types of emotions and feelings while you write them on the board. They could be happy, sad, scared, angry and so on. Encourage children to come up with even more descriptive words such as joyful, desperate, miserable, etc. Then ask children to write down a moment when they have felt each of these strong emotions. Then encourage them to turn that moment into a memoir or a poem. Show children the 'Memoir with strong feelings' ITR.

DISCUSS

- *Has anyone in the class used this technique before in their writing?*
- *What do you think of this technique? Is it helpful?*
- *Is starting with a strong feeling a good way to develop a piece of writing?*

CREATE

Encourage children to use these techniques during their lesson today.

Favourite places

STUDY

Introduce the topic by asking children to choose their favourite place, either at home or elsewhere. Explain to children that they will be using these favourite places as inspiration for their writing in the lesson.

Invite children to jot down what they think it is like to be in their favourite place. Explain to children that they should try and capture the look and feel of the place in their writing, for someone who has never been and doesn't know anything about the place. Encourage children to describe all five senses if they can, and think about the emotions that the place stirs in them as well as what is so important about it. Ask children to close their eyes, to help them visualise their favourite place inside their imaginations. If it helps, encourage children to do a quick sketch of what they see when they close their eyes. Then, when they are ready, invite children to turn these thoughts into a memoir or a poem. Show children the 'Favourite places' ITR.

DISCUSS

- *Has anyone in the class used this technique before in their writing?*
- *What do you think of this technique? Is it helpful?*
- *How does describing the five senses help to capture the feeling of a favourite place?*

CREATE

Encourage children to use these techniques during their lesson today. They could swap their work with other children in their class to see if their peers agree that they've chosen the best sense to describe their favourite place.

Something different happened this time

STUDY

Introduce the topic by inviting children to write down a list of 'always times', meaning the things that happen over and over again in their own lives. Explain that these could be things that are repeated year after year. They might even include routines that the children do every day.

Explain to children that the list that they are writing might include happy things such as Christmas and birthdays but they might also include some not-so-happy things such as visiting the dentist! Explain that everyday routines could include eating lunch, playing with their sisters, brothers or friends or even just watching TV.

Encourage children to make their lists as long as they can. Then encourage them to think of a moment in time that really stands out for them because it was different to the 'always', regardless of whether it was good or bad or just 'different'. Explain that it could something different such as something that happened at Christmas or on their birthday. Or it could even be about visiting the dentist, an occasion when they were eating lunch or when they were playing with friends.

Encourage children to look for the extraordinary in the ordinary and then turn it into a memoir.

DISCUSS

- *Has anyone in the class used this technique before in their writing?*
- *What do you think of this technique? Is it helpful?*

CREATE

Encourage children to use these techniques during their lesson today.

A picture speaks 1000 words

STUDY

Explain to children that photographs can speak to us, even pictures from many years ago that were taken well before the age of colour photography and digital cameras!

Ask children to bring in some photographs from home that are important to them. Ask children to make sure that they choose pictures that they particularly like and examine carefully the setting and the people who are in the pictures. If any of the photographs were taken before the children were born, encourage them to ask someone in their family to tell them about that person.

During the lesson, ask children to look at their photos in detail and note down any interesting details that they can see to use as a basis for a memoir.

DISCUSS

- *Has anyone in the class used this technique before in their writing?*
- *What do you think of this technique? Is it helpful?*
- *Is this similar to any other techniques you have tried, such as starting with a drawing?*

CREATE

Encourage children to use these techniques during their lesson today. If possible, allow time for children to share their photographs with the class.

Questions for memoirists

STUDY

Introduce the topic by explaining to children that our memories of our own lives are a great resource to tap into when writing. Explain that writing down our memories gives us a strong link to the past. By writing down your memories, you may find yourself remembering things that you had completely forgotten!

Show children the 'Questions for memoirists' ITR. Explain that one of the best ways to generate ideas for a memoir is to ask yourself questions such as the ones listed in the ITR.

DISCUSS

- *Has anyone in the class used this technique before in their writing?*
- *What do you think of this technique? Is it helpful?*

CREATE

Encourage children to try out this technique during the lesson.

Special moments

STUDY

Introduce the topic by explaining to children that we all have special moments in our lives and these moments are worth remembering. Ask children to make a list of some of these special moments that they can recall in their own lines. Show children the 'Special moments' ITR.

DISCUSS

- *Has anyone in the class used this technique before?*
- *What do you think of this technique? Is it helpful?*
- *Do any of these special moments give you an idea for a new piece of writing?*

CREATE

Encourage children to use these techniques during their lesson today.

Writing your title last

STUDY

Introduce the topic by explaining to children that many writers don't give their work a title until they have finished writing it! Encourage children to reflect on their own writing and ask them to hold off adding the title to their piece until they have finished the draft. When children are ready to write the title invite them to make a list of possible titles, and then ask a class partner to decide which title is most engaging and is really going to draw their reader in.

Ask children to choose a book from the class library that the children are familiar with, or use the example presented in the 'Writing your title last' ITR. Then, begin a class discussion about the title. Ask children:

- *Is this the best title for this book?*
- *Can you think of any other possible titles for this book?*
- *Which title is most engaging?*

DISCUSS

- *Has anyone in the class used this technique before?*
- *What do you think of this technique? Is it helpful?*
- *Look at any other pieces of writing that you have done recently and use this technique to retitle them.*

CREATE

Encourage children to use these techniques during their lesson today.

The best line

STUDY

Explain to children that it is helpful to be their own critic when it comes to looking at their writing!

Using your own writing as an example, read through the text and underline which you think is the best line. Invite children to think about why they have chosen this sentence. Ask children:

- *Is it because of the descriptive language or the style?*
- *Is it because of a character, the setting or a description of the action in the plot?*

Then take the best line and turn it into a paragraph by expanding on it, using more descriptive language. Then invite children to work through the same process, using their own writing.

DISCUSS

- *Has anyone in the class used this technique before?*
- *What do you think of this technique? Is it helpful?*
- *How does it help to be critical of your own work?*

CREATE

Encourage children to use these techniques during their lesson today. Children could even exchange their writing with other children in the class, to see if their peers agree that they have chosen the best line.

Use the senses

STUDY

Introduce the topic by explaining to children that they can use all their senses to bring their writing to life for their readers. As well as the five senses that children already know, there are two additional 'writer's senses' that they can use: their imagination and remembering things or events using their memory. Explain to children that readers really like it when writers give them lots of descriptive language about the senses.

Encourage children to bear this in mind when they are drafting or revising their writing. Suggest to children that they write a list at the top of their draft that includes at least three of the seven writer's senses: seeing, hearing, touching, tasting, smelling, imagining and remembering. Explain that they don't have to use them all; they can choose which senses are most important to that particular piece of writing. Invite children to go back through their draft, underlining the areas of the text where these senses come into play and then expanding on these sections, using additional details.

DISCUSS

- *Has anyone in the class used this technique before?*
- *What do you think of this technique? Is it helpful?*

CREATE

Encourage children to use these techniques during their lesson today.

Show don't tell

STUDY

Introduce the topic by explaining to children that it is easy to provide useful information in a story by telling your reader things about the plot, the characters and the setting.

Encourage children to think about whether this the best way of writing a story. If not, why not?

Explain that when we tell readers something in a piece of writing, they will often use the following words: *is, was, have, had, does, did.* Explain that if children replace those words, they will find themselves showing their reader something, rather than telling them. Readers like this approach. Invite children to look at the examples in the 'Show don't tell' ITR and discuss why one of the examples is much more interesting for both reader and writer than the other.

DISCUSS

- *Has anyone in the class used this technique before?*
- *What do you think of this technique? Is it helpful?*
- *Look back at other pieces of written work you have completed and see if you can spot any moments when you could have used this technique.*

CREATE

Encourage children to use these techniques during their lesson today.

How does your character talk?

STUDY

Introduce the topic by explaining to children that voices and the way people talk are a very important part of someone's character. Invite children to think about the people they know and how they talk. Would they be able to recognise them from just their voices?

Encourage children to think about how the characters in their stories might sound, so that their reader can recognise them. Ask children:

- *What is the character's tone of voice?*
- *What do they sound like?*
- *Do they speak in short or long sentences?*
- *Do they have an accent?*
- *Do they use slang?*
- *Can you show something of their character, in the way they speak? For example, are they happy, gloomy, a joker, stern, jolly, stressed, anxious?*

DISCUSS

- *Has anyone in the class used this technique before?*
- *What do you think of this technique? Is it helpful?*

CREATE

Encourage children to use these techniques during their lesson today.

Five alive!

STUDY

Introduce the topic by inviting children to take one sentence from their piece of writing and then rewrite it in at least five different ways. Explain to children that they will need to keep any characters, settings or information the same. However, encourage them to play around with word order, language and style. Once children have written five new sentences ask them to choose their favourite. Show children the 'Five alive!' ITR.

DISCUSS

- *Has anyone in the class used this technique before?*
- *What do you think of this technique? Is it helpful?*

CREATE

Encourage children to use these techniques during their lesson today. Children could also swap their five sentences with a classmate, to see if they agree with their choice of best sentence.

Mark your own writing

STUDY

Introduce the topic by explaining to children that in their writing, it can be helpful to be their own harshest critic! Explain that after they have finished writing their draft, they can use sticky notes in the margin to mark places where they could improve things such as choice of language, style, description and meaning. Explain that is also important to check spellings and punctuation.

As the teacher, share a draft of your own writing as an example. Model rereading and identifying places to improve, including adding sticky notes into the margin. Take suggestions from the class about what you think you could have done better.

DISCUSS

- *Has anyone in the class used this technique before?*
- *What do you think of this technique? Is it helpful?*
- *Is it helpful to leave a piece of writing for a day or two and look at it with fresh eyes? Why?*

CREATE

Encourage children to use these techniques during their lesson today.

'Inspired by' poems

STUDY

Introduce the topic by explaining to children that the language of poems can be inspirational. It can make you look at everyday things in a way that you have never looked at them before. Invite children to take a poem that they like from the class library and then use it as inspiration to write their own poem. You can also use the "Inspired by' poems' ITR as an example. You may find the book *Love That Dog* by Sharon Creech a useful illustration of this lesson.

DISCUSS

- *Has anyone in the class used this technique before?*
- *What do you think of this technique? Is it helpful?*
- *Have you read any other poems that might inspire you to write a poem in response?*

CREATE

Encourage children to use these techniques during their lesson today.

Poetry in reading

STUDY

Introduce the topic by inviting children to choose a sentence or two from one of their reading books that they could turn into a poem. Explain to children they might think that only certain types of sentences can inspire a poem. This isn't true! Explain that poetry can be about anything and everything from the ordinary and everyday, to the special and magical. Then show children the 'Poetry in reading' ITR.

DISCUSS

- *Has anyone in the class used this technique before?*
- *What do you think of this technique? Is it helpful?*

CREATE

Encourage children to use these techniques during their lesson today.

I'm an expert in ...

STUDY

Introduce the topic by inviting children to write an 'I'm an expert in …' list. This could be a list of anything that you know a great deal about, from ballet to Spain; from model cars to different flavours of crisps! Explain to children that they can turn their passion into an information text.

Ask children to think about how they can present their information clearly and simply for people who may know nothing at all about the topic that they have chosen.

DISCUSS

- *Has anyone in the class used this technique before?*
- *What do you think of this technique? Is it helpful?*

CREATE

Encourage children to use these techniques during their lesson today.

Write about topic lessons

STUDY

Introduce the topic by explaining to students that they can use what they are learning about in other subjects to generate writing ideas. Ask children to think about what they have been studying in other lessons and subject areas during the term so far. Invite children to think of and say a list of topic areas while you write them down on the board. These could be information texts or topics that spark ideas for stories set in specific periods in history such as during the time of the Ancient Egyptians.

DISCUSS

- *Has anyone in the class used this technique before?*
- *What do you think of this technique? Is it helpful?*
- *Is there anything else you would need to find out or research before trying out one of these ideas?*

CREATE

Encourage children to use these techniques during their lesson today.

Thinking 'faction'

STUDY

Introduce the topic to children by explaining that 'faction' is a mash-up of fact and fiction! Explain to children that they could write an information text or an explanation about something from a fictional world that they have read about, or even one that they have invented. Invite children to make a list of potential writing topics by looking back at books that they have read or stories that they have written, that were set in a world different to our own. Explain that in this type of writing, it is important to make sure someone who doesn't know about this imaginary world will learn all about it from your 'faction' text.

DISCUSS

- *Has anyone in the class used this technique before?*
- *What do you think of this technique? Is it helpful?*
- *Do you like the idea of mixing up fact and fiction? Why or why not?*

CREATE

Encourage children to use these techniques during their lesson today.

What itch needs scratching?

STUDY

Introduce the topic by explaining to children that they will often have real events happening in their own lives that can generate ideas for writing. They may find it helpful to write things down and get them out of their heads and off their chests! Be mindful that some children may want to write about difficult or upsetting events.

Invite children to think about some of the things that are happening in their lives right now that might inspire their writing.

DISCUSS

- *Is there a dilemma or awkward situation that is happening in your life right now?*
- *Are there any issues that need solving, correcting or explaining to someone else.*
- *Are there any topics that make you furious or leave you feeling confused?*

CREATE

Encourage children to use these techniques during their lesson today.

Fan fiction

STUDY

Encourage children to think about any books that they have read recently that are by their favourite writer. What do they love about that writer's style? Do they have a favourite character in any of the stories? Is it someone that they admire and are inspired by? Have they read any fiction in settings that intrigued and fascinated them?

Ask children to write down answers to these questions and then encourage them to choose one to write a piece of fan fiction. Show children the 'Fan fiction' ITR.

DISCUSS

- *Has anyone in the class used this technique before?*
- *What do you think of this technique? Is it helpful?*
- *Have you ever read a book that was inspired by another book?*
- *Could any of the ideas be used in your writing?*

CREATE

Encourage children to try to use this technique to help them with their writing during the lesson.

Rewrite a Shakespeare play

STUDY

Ensure your children have access to either Tony Ross' *The Shakespeare Stories,* Angela McAllister's *A Stage Full Of Shakespeare Stories*, Leon Garfield's *Shakespeare Stories* or Marcia Williams *Bravo Mr. William Shakespeare.*

DISCUSS

- *What is your favourite play?*
- *Who is your favourite or most interesting character?*
- *What is your favourite scene?*
- *What scene or play would you like to rewrite for yourself?*
- *Who thinks they could use a character, scene or whole play to write their own Inspired by … story or poem?*

CREATE

Encourage children to try using this technique during writing sessions.

Comb your reading book

STUDY

Invite children to spend a session reading their book and 'combing' or 'skim-reading' it for interesting vocabulary, sentences or passages that really strike them and that they might like to use in their own writing. Remind children that they are searching for exciting, descriptive words and phrases that really leap off the page and grab their attention! Encourage children to check the meanings of any words that they think appear interesting but that they don't understand.

Invite a volunteer to share a page from their reading book or use the example on the 'Comb your reading book' ITR.

DISCUSS

- *Has anyone in the class used this technique before?*
- *What do you think of this technique? Is it helpful?*
- *Is this technique something you think might be useful to you in future?*

CREATE

Encourage children to try using this technique to help them with their writing during the lesson.

How to write a vivid setting

STUDY

Explain to children that if they are writing about a specific place, it is important for them to ensure that their reader can really sense the historical period or the geographical location that their story is set in.

Remind children that the setting doesn't just mean the place of a story. Depending on the story, they might need to describe things other than the place. Show children the 'How to write a vivid setting' ITR.

DISCUSS

- *Has anyone in the class used this technique before?*
- *What do you think of this technique? Is it helpful?*

CREATE

Encourage children to try using this technique to help them with their writing during the lesson.

What do you believe in?

STUDY

Introduce the topic by starting a discussion about what children believe in and what is important to them. Some of the children's ideas might include global themes such as saving the environment and preventing plastic from poisoning the sea, or the ideas might be more locally focused, such as saving a local library from being closed down.

Ask children to think about how they might tell someone about their beliefs and convictions. How might they be able to persuade their reader that the issues are serious and important? Show children the 'What do you believe in?' ITR.

DISCUSS

- *Has anyone in the class used this technique before?*
- *What do you think of this technique? Is it helpful?*
- *Can any of the beliefs or convictions that you have form the basis of a story or another piece of writing?*

CREATE

Encourage children to try using this technique to help them with their writing during the lesson.

Stories about people

STUDY

Explain to children that stories very often involve a person versus someone or something else. This is known as *conflict*. Conflict means a clash of viewpoints, so a conflict within a story can involve a person or group of people standing against others with different opinions from their own, but sometimes conflict can take place inside a person as they struggle to deal with feelings pulling them first one way and then another. Or the opponent in a conflict can be non-human for example a force of nature or even society itself. Ask children to look at the categories and the examples in the 'Stories about people' ITR and add your own ideas to these.

DISCUSS

- *Has anyone in the class used this technique before?*
- *What do you think of this technique? Is it helpful?*
- *Which categories do the conflicts in the stories you are reading fall into?*

CREATE

Encourage children to try using this technique to help them with their writing during the lesson.

Writing a conversation

STUDY

Ask the children to write a conversation between two or three characters for ten minutes. This could be a fantasy conversation between fictional characters they've made up or from the books they have read. Alternatively, it could be a reimagining of a real conversation *they* have had. Once they have finished writing, ask them to think about how they could turn these notes into some kind of story or memoir.

DISCUSS

- *Who would you most like to have a conversation with?*
- *What's the most interesting conversation you've ever had with someone?*
- *Which characters from fiction would really hit it off – or not?!*
- *What conversations do you wish you had had but for whatever reason never did?*
- *What do you think of this technique? Is it helpful?*

CREATE

Encourage children to try using this technique to help them with their writing during the lesson.

Parallel stories

STUDY

Introduce to children the idea that stories can be made richer and more interesting if the events are plotted not only from the central character's point of view but also with relation to a secondary character. Show children the 'Parallel stories' ITR.

Ask children to think back and recall books that they have read that have more than one plotline, or characters that have different experiences. Discuss with children how including these contrasting details can give depth and variety to narratives. Explain that they can map out two characters' storylines in a similar way to mapping out one character's storyline, by drawing story arcs. Different characters might experience the same big events, which you could show with connecting lines between the arcs, but react to them differently or act differently during them.

DISCUSS

- *Has anyone in the class used this technique before?*
- *What do you think of this technique? Is it helpful?*
- *What main events will both of your characters experience?*
- *How will your characters contrast and how will they connect?*

CREATE

Encourage children to map timelines for their stories' main characters and big events before thinking more about another character's experiences.

Lead your reader to the facts

STUDY

Introduce to children the idea that they can engage their reader in a non-fiction text by starting it off with the kind of descriptions that they would usually see in a fiction text. Show children the 'Lead your reader to the facts' ITR.

Explain to children that they may think that vivid descriptions and detailed settings are used only in fiction. However, explain that they can also add lots of interest and impact in non-fiction topics. Remind children that a great way to get their reader interested and immediately involved in what they are explaining is to immerse them in the world of the topic area with a 'scene painting', micro-story, anecdote or a poem. Explain that they can even make the topic a personal one, addressing their introduction directly to the reader.

DISCUSS

- *Has anyone in the class used this technique before?*
- *What do you think of this technique? Is it helpful?*
- *Which part of your text do you think would be fun to describe?*
- *Where can you see an opportunity to write a little story, share an anecdote or include a poem?*

CREATE

Encourage children to try using this technique to help them with their writing during the lesson.

Building atmosphere: Suspense and tension

STUDY

Introduce to children the idea that they can create suspense and tension, and that it is about keeping something back, withholding the climax. Readers like to sense something important is about to happen but without being told what it is straight away. So, to create tension, find the part of the story that appears immediately before the most important or dramatic event and tease it out. This can be done in the following ways.

- You kill the tension in your piece when you *tell* your reader what is happening, so instead 'paint with words' to *show* your reader what it happening – like they were watching it on the cinema screen.
- Use dialogue sparingly, if at all.
- Instead, mention your character's internal monologue – share what they are thinking.
- Use your setting to create a tension and mood before the climactic moment by describing changes to the conditions.
- Choose your verbs and nouns carefully and precisely.
- Sentence construction – use shorter sentences as you lead up to the climactic moment.

DISCUSS

- *What is the climactic moment in your writing? Can you find it?*
- *Has anyone noticed that they've used these techniques already? Could they read out their piece?*
- *What did you think of this technique? Was it helpful?*

CREATE

Ask children to locate the climactic part of their stories and work on the writing that precedes it.

Moving quickly and slowly in a story

STUDY

Introduce to children the idea of changing the speed and level of detail in different parts of a story, depending on the importance of the parts involved.

Explain that it is important for writers to vary the speed at which they tell different parts of their stories: readers need plenty of detail at important moments and not too much detail when the story needs to move along.

Remind children to slow down when they are:

- building up to their climax
- introducing a character for the first time
- changing their setting
- introducing an important object for the first time.

Remind children move quickly when they are:

- wanting to move through time
- wanting to move through a setting
- when they are writing dialogue.

DISCUSS

- *Has anyone in the class used this technique before?*
- *What do you think of this technique? Is it helpful?*
- *Look at where you introduce your characters, setting, special objects for the first time – have you slowed down to reveal more detail about these things for your reader before moving on? If not, think about rereading and improving these parts today.*
- *Where might you be able to cut some of your story to move it on more quickly?*

CREATE

Encourage children to look carefully at their stories and look at how other writers do it in the books they are reading.

See things like a poet

STUDY

Introduce to children the idea that they can add to the descriptions in their writing by using comparison, just like a poet would.

Children already know that they can bring their poetry, fiction or even non-fiction to life by 'painting with words'. Painting with words can include:

- comparing something to something else (through simile and metaphor)
- *showing* what someone or something does instead of simply *telling* them
- using the different senses to describe things in interesting ways
- giving nature or things human characteristics or emotions through personification or pathetic fallacy.

DISCUSS

- *Has anyone in the class used this technique before?*
- *What do you think of this technique? Is it helpful?*
- *Can we find some more examples in the books we are reading?*
- *Has anyone got an example from some of their writing?*

CREATE

In their writing today, ask children to try out one or two of the techniques on their characters, objects, weather or settings.

Using body language

STUDY

Introduce to children the idea of using gestures, movements and facial expressions to tell the reader what a character is like.

Explain to children that body language is made up of the various movements, poses or facial expressions that people use, either purposefully or accidentally, that can tell others about their attitudes, thoughts or feelings. They often secretly reveal something to us as a reader. Ask children to think about which gestures, movements and facial expressions their character might show that tell the reader what they are like, how they are feeling or what they are really thinking.

Ask the class whether anyone can find an example of a writer using this technique in the books they are reading. Someone who is particularly good at this is the children's writer Piers Torday.

DISCUSS

- *Has anyone in the class used this technique before?*
- *What do you think of this technique? Is it helpful?*
- *What body language do people display that gives away how they are feeling?*

CREATE

Encourage children to try out this technique during the lesson today.

Seeing things differently I

STUDY

Introduce to children the idea of finding ideas for a poem by comparing something abstract (such as an emotion, psychological state or philosophical position) to a 'thing'.

Explain to children that poems are often little pieces of writing but about big ideas. One way of writing about big ideas is to compare them to objects, people, creatures or places. We recommend DK's *The Philosophy Book* as a helpful addition to your class library or for this mini-lesson.

They can start with anything concrete and then think about what it could be compared to in the abstract. For example, compare a puddle to loneliness, a sloth to apathy and laziness, a smoker's lungs to environmental protection or a sword to the idea of the ends justifying the means. Alternatively, they could start with the abstract thing and find an object that could represent it. For example pleasure to sweets, comfort seeking to a blanket or, not learning from the past to a shadow.

DISCUSS

- *What do you think of this technique? Is it helpful?*
- *What poems do you know that do this?*
- *Has anyone written a poem that already does this?*

CREATE

Encourage children to read some poetry and try out this technique during the lesson today.

Seeing things differently 2

STUDY

Introduce to children the idea of finding ideas for a poem by comparing two people that they know well.

Ask children to picture two people in their minds that they know and who are different in some way. Ask children how they might describe the differences between the two of them. Comparing two people like this can help to create ideas for poems with conflict or contrast at their hearts. Explain to children that they could write a poem about the people in a straightforward manner. Alternatively, they could use their ideas in an abstract way. For example, this technique could help children write a poem comparing and personifying a puppy and an elderly dog. Alternatively, after thinking about the two people carefully, children might decide that the people could be represented clearly by using comparisons with fireworks and a still lake.

DISCUSS

- *Has anyone in the class used this technique before?*
- *What do you think of this technique? Is it helpful?*
- *What similarities and differences do the two people you describe have?*
- *What do these people you know remind you of?*

CREATE

Invite children to use this technique today.

Where poetry hides

STUDY

Introduce to children the idea of finding ideas for a poem in the things that we own or the places we go.

Encourage children to dash around their home, garden or any other space as quickly as they can, absorbing flashes of all the things that they experience or the things that they see: objects, people, smells, feelings – anything! Then ask children to sit down and quickly jot down everything they can remember. The things that stick most clearly in their minds might be the perfect starting points for their poetry.

DISCUSS

- *Has anyone in the class used this technique before?*
- *What do you think of this technique? Is it helpful?*
- *What places would be ideal for trying out this technique?*

CREATE

Suggest that children try out this technique at home and ask them to bring in their list of potential inspirations to use in class when they next need to find a poetic idea.

Peripheral vision

STUDY

Introduce to children the idea of writing quickly about what is on the edges of the main action in a story. Show children the 'Peripheral vision' ITR.

Explain to children that one way to add details and depth to a scene, especially to a character, is to write about the 'periphery' of the action, meaning things that are on the edges of, and surround, the main subject. Explain that children could write details about what would literally appear in the scene that are visible and happening at that moment. They could also write details about connections with ideas and memories that feel tangential but are also related, and even link these ideas with their own experiences. Explain to children that, when they have finished the exercise, their writing is likely to feel a little unfocused and flooded with ideas that aren't particularly helpful, but that's okay. Explain that children will have lots more background for their character and setting, and their next step will be to slim things down a bit to locate which details you can use.

DISCUSS

- *Has anyone in the class used this technique before?*
- *What do you think of this technique? Is it helpful?*
- *What might your characters be able to see around them at this point?*
- *What would your characters' observations make them think and feel?*

CREATE

Encourage children to perform the exercise, taking single moments from their own stories and free-writing around the main actions.

Letter of appreciation

STUDY

Ask children to think of someone or something that they admire or appreciate. It could be someone or something they know personally, such as their mum or their favourite football team; or it could be someone or something in the wider world, such as a person they have never met but who has inspired them.

Ask children to write a letter to that person, expressing their admiration and appreciation of them, explaining why they feel this way. Show children the 'Letter of appreciation' ITR.

DISCUSS

- *Has anyone in the class used this technique before?*
- *What do you think of this technique? Is it helpful?*
- *How did writing this letter of appreciation make you feel?*

CREATE

Encourage children to try out this technique during the lesson.

Make a change!

STUDY

Introduce to children the idea of choosing a topic by thinking about something they would like to see happen, or that they would like to change. Show children the 'Make a change!' ITR.

Explain to children that writers often produce their most meaningful work when they are trying to convince their reader to take on board a particular idea using persuasion, which is much more powerful when they are passionate about the subject. Explain to children that almost everyone can think of something that they would wish to change, either within our immediate surroundings, such as at school, or within the wider world. Explain that children will also need to think about who has the power to change it and how they might best be reached (by post, email, a poster or through speech). This can help children to keep their audience in mind as they write, and to choose the best form for their writing.

DISCUSS

- *Has anyone in the class used this technique before?*
- *What do you think of this technique? Is it helpful?*
- *What do you wish was different about the world?*
- *What kind of writing do you think would be the most persuasive way to explain your ideas?*

CREATE

Encourage children to plan out a persuasive letter, poster, speech or essay about a change they would genuinely like to see made.

Be a reporter

STUDY

Introduce the topic to children by explaining that, when they are thinking about topics for persuasive writing, they don't have to restrict themselves to something that they want to change. Instead, they could be a reporter, helping someone else change something in the world. Real reporters do this!

Show children the 'Be a reporter' ITR. Ask the class questions, such as: *What do you want to change? What do you wish was different?* Explain that they can ask others these sorts of questions too! Together, write a list of people they could interview and then report on.

DISCUSS

- *Has anyone in the class used this technique before?*
- *What do you think of this technique? Is it helpful?*

CREATE

Encourage children to try out this technique during the week.

Be outrageous

STUDY

Introduce to children the idea of starting a piece of writing with a strong, surprising claim before detailing arguments both for and against it. Show children the 'Be outrageous' ITR.

Tell children that writers who are hoping to create a compelling piece of work often grab attention by starting their essays with bold and controversial statements. These are likely to make people react quickly and strongly, and hook them in. Explain to children that they can also use this technique to make *themselves* react, using an outrageous claim as a springboard to start free-writing and seeing where their pencil takes them! Explain to children that it is okay if they don't believe their claim entirely, as this can actually help them to explore both sides of the argument. Encourage children to try to write without judging themselves, just keeping their pencil moving.

DISCUSS

- *Has anyone in the class used this technique before?*
- *What do you think of this technique? Is it helpful?*
- *What outlandish and attention-grabbing claim could you make?*
- *What arguments could be made for and against your claim?*

CREATE

Encourage children to think of an outrageous claim and use sentence starters to structure the different sides of their arguments.

Support the facts

STUDY

Introduce the idea of explaining facts even more using a definition, example, analogy or story.

Explain to children that you have been looking over a draft of your work for facts that need some further explanation. Explain that you have found one sentence that needs a little more detailed explanation: 'The moon has craters.' Explain to children that if the reader doesn't already know what a crater is, that sentence doesn't really help them! Explain that this particular sentence needs to be added to a little more to support the facts so that the reader can really learn and understand what you are saying. Explain to children that you could add a definition to your writing piece, such as: 'A crater is a bowl-shaped dent in the surface of the moon.' Alternatively, explain that you could also add a story, for example: 'A long time ago, a meteor flew through space and landed on the surface of the moon. When it hit, boom! A big dent was left in its place.'

DISCUSS

- *Has anyone in the class used this technique before?*
- *What do you think of this technique? Is it helpful?*
- *Can you find a fact in your writing that requires a little more detail?*
- *What kind of information do you think would be helpful to add?*

CREATE

Encourage children to look through their own writing and underline any facts that don't provide quite enough detail and plan additional sentences that would help to explain them.

Find the 'how'

STUDY

Ask children to read through their first draft and check that they haven't just focused on what someone or something does but detailed *how* it's done as well. Explain to children that focusing on the 'how' means that they are moving their text on from being a simple information text to one that tries to give explanation. Show children the 'Find the 'how'' ITR.

DISCUSS

- *Has anyone in the class used this technique before?*
- *What do you think of this technique? Is it helpful?*
- *Could this technique be used in other forms of writing?*

CREATE

Encourage children to try out this technique during the lesson.

Unlike

STUDY

Explain to children that 'unlike' is a very useful word that will allow them to compare their subject with its opposite, or with someone or something that is very different. Explain that this technique will allow their readers to understand their work better. Show children the 'Unlike' ITR.

DISCUSS

- *Has anyone in the class used this technique before?*
- *What do you think of this technique? Is it helpful?*
- *Where might you be able to use this technique in your writing today?*

CREATE

Encourage children to try out this technique during the lesson.

Too fast

STUDY

Explain to children that reading non-fiction should be as interesting and as fascinating as reading an exciting fiction story. Discuss with children that, when they are writing non-fiction pieces, they will sometimes share stories or anecdotes to explain more about the people, places, animals or things they have chosen to explain. These stories can be written as carefully as the stories they write for fiction. Encourage children to think about story-telling in their non-fiction texts and show children the 'Too fast' ITR. Ask them whether they have described the subjects, objects or settings in a poetic way.

DISCUSS

- *Has anyone in the class used this technique before?*
- *What do you think of this technique? Is it helpful?*
- *Where have you seen this used in the non-fiction texts in the library?*
- *Where do you think you could use it in your writing today?*

CREATE

Encourage children to try out this technique during the lesson.

Making information come alive

STUDY

Ask children to picture in their minds the thing that they have decided to write about (a quick sketch might help) then write a description of it. Explain to children that it can be challenging to make non-fiction as interesting to read as fiction, so it is important to use all the tools that they have at their disposal! Encourage children to really think about how to order the information in their writing and present it the most interesting way that they can and consider the descriptive language that they are using. Encourage children to use personification and think about sharing real-life situations or stories. Show children the 'Making information come alive' ITR.

DISCUSS

- *Has anyone in the class used this technique before?*
- *What do you think of this technique? Is it helpful?*
- *What aspects of this technique could be used in other types of writing?*

CREATE

Encourage children to try out this technique during the lesson.

Use an anecdote to explain your point

STUDY

Explain to children that anecdotes are the stories we tell each other. Often they are personal to us. For example, children might describe to their friend how they fell off their bike and were rushed into hospital with a broken arm. That is an anecdote. Or children might repeat an anecdote that they have heard about a celebrity, an individual or something else that isn't personal to them. Explain to children that when making a point in a piece of non-fiction writing, they might use a personal anecdote to back up what they are explaining. Show children the 'Use an anecdote to explain your point' ITR.

DISCUSS

- *Has anyone in the class used this technique before?*
- *What do you think of this technique? Is it helpful?*
- *Where might a personal anecdote help you get your point across in your text?*
- *Could any of your favourite anecdotes, such as the ones that you tell over and over, provide ideas for other pieces of writing?*

CREATE

Encourage children to try out this technique during the lesson.

Can you cut out 'and'?

STUDY

Introduce to children the idea of assessing whether or not 'and' is used effectively to join sentences in their writing. Show children the 'Can you cut out 'and'?' ITR.

Explain to children that all writers can get carried away by the flow of events in their writing. Sometimes, this means that sentences get joined together by the word 'and' when they aren't really connected. Remind children that when they read their work, they should keep a look out for any places that they have used 'and' several times in one sentence. Encourage children to look at each sentence and think to themselves: 'Which of the ideas before and after 'and' need to stay connected?' Explain to children that they should keep the 'and' where the ideas are related. Where they are not, ask them to remove the 'and' and put a full stop and capital letter in its place.

DISCUSS

- *Has anyone in the class used this technique before?*
- *What do you think of this technique? Is it helpful?*
- *How many times have you used the word 'and' in one sentence?*
- *When looking at each sentence, are you sure the information before the 'and' relates closely to the information after it?*

CREATE

Encourage children to look through their own work and underline any unnecessary uses of the word 'and'. Then suggest to children that they use a different colour to circle the examples they think they should keep.

Using a planning grid

STUDY

Explain to children that you are going to demonstrate one method of planning writing. Remind children that they need to decide on the purpose, audience and genre for their writing before they begin to plan it and that if they are writing a poem, it is usually better to dabble with ideas instead of creating a formal plan. Select the relevant 'Planning grid' ITR for the class writing project and talk through or model planning your piece of writing, talking through the process as you go and expanding on your ideas. Remind children that plans are only a guide and that they can be changed at any time.

DISCUSS

- *Has anyone in the class used this technique before?*
- *What do you think of this technique? Is it helpful?*
- *What do you think the advantages and disadvantages are of using a planning grid?*

CREATE

Encourage children to begin using this technique in their own writing during this lesson.

Choosing a story arc

STUDY

Explain to children that a story arc is a diagram that can help them plan the high and low points in their story. Explain that stories have high points when things go well for the characters involved and low points when things are not going so well. Encourage children to think about any stories that they have read recently and whether they can spot where the high points and the low points are. Explain that a story arc shows a character's triumphs and success, their problems and conflicts with others, their ups and their downs. Invite children to think about their own stories and ask them to think about what shape their story will take?

DISCUSS

- *How can a story arc help to shape your stories?*
- *What do you think of this technique? Is it helpful?*
- *What are the advantages and disadvantages of using a story arc?*

CREATE

Encourage children to try using a story arc to shape their stories during the lesson.

Finding the diamond moment

STUDY

Explain to children that in any single writing topic you might have lots of ideas but that it is important to focus on just one, to avoid confusing your reader. This is like finding that one shiny diamond in the piles of rocks that are all of your ideas. Children can then observe it carefully, focusing only on that one idea and then writing about it. Model locating the diamond moment by talking through one of your own writing ideas (this could be a topic for a non-fiction piece, a personal story for a memoir, or even an idea for a story or poem). Talk about which bit of your idea shines through the most. This will be the diamond moment of your piece. Explain to children how you can plan your writing so that it focuses on that one central idea. Then encourage children to do the same with their own writing.

DISCUSS

- *Has anyone in the class used this technique before?*
- *What do you think of this technique? Is it helpful?*

CREATE

Encourage children to begin using this technique in their own writing from this point onwards.

Drawing as planning

STUDY

Explain to children that they can draw pictures to help them plan a piece of writing. They might choose to draw a picture of a particular setting, or maybe even draw a map that shows the layout of a house, street or town. Children might choose to draw pictures, characters or objects that are important to the story. They might even draw a series of linked pictures and then use these pictures to tell a story. Show children the 'Drawing as planning' ITR.

DISCUSS

- *Has anyone in the class used this technique before?*
- *What do you think of this technique? Is it helpful?*
- *Do you find it easier to draw first and then start to write, or to start writing straightway? Why?*

CREATE

Encourage children to try drawing pictures to plan their stories during the lesson.

Dabbling

STUDY

Explain to children that dabbling is a type of prewriting that they can do before they begin drafting. Explain that whilst dabbling, children can write lots of lists, including words or phrases that they might like to use in their writing. Children might also like to write down a list of feelings that they would like their writing to convey to their readers. Children might choose to draw pictures with written annotations, to jog their memories or to make them think about their writing a bit more. Children might decide to write down why their idea is important or what they want their writing to mean to their readers. Finally, children can try to compare what they are writing about to other things in their lives, to help them understand the idea better. Explain to children that when they feel as though they have gathered enough dabbles, they can begin to turn their ideas into a first draft. Dabbles can appear almost as a type of plan. Explain to children that dabbling is often used when preparing to draft a poem but writers can dabble for all kinds of writing.

DISCUSS

- *Has anyone in the class used this technique before?*
- *What do you think of this technique? Is it helpful?*

CREATE

Encourage children to try dabbling to help them with their writing during the lesson.

Using thoughts and feelings

STUDY

Explain to children that writing down their thoughts and feelings is a particularly useful technique when writing a personal piece of writing, such as a memoir or a poem. Explain that doing this can help children to gather their thoughts and shape their text. Show children the 'Using thoughts and feelings' (ITR).

Using the class writing project as an example, model choosing a few of the sentence starters and completing the sentences. Ask children whether it helps them to focus on the feeling or thoughts that they want to get across to their reader within each section of their writing.

DISCUSS

- *Has anyone in the class used this technique before?*
- *What do you think of this technique? Is it helpful?*

CREATE

Encourage children to try using this technique to help them with their writing during the lesson.

Webbing

STUDY

Explain to children that when writing a non-fiction text about something they know a lot about, they might sometimes find it difficult to organise their ideas. Explain that webbing is a planning technique that will help them think about how their topic could be split into sub-categories. Model the webbing technique either by using flip-chart paper or by using the completed 'Planning web' ITR.

DISCUSS

· *Has anyone in the class used this technique before?*
· *What do you think of this technique? Is it helpful?*

CREATE

Ask children to consider how their topic could be split into sections. When children have completed their web, ask them to circle three or four of the sub-categories that they would like to focus on in their piece.

Explain to children that they will now be able to use their web to look for important questions about their subject, along with questions their readers might want answers to. Screen 2 of the 'Planning web' ITR demonstrates what this should look like.

Mindmaps

STUDY

Introduce the topic to children by explaining that mindmaps are visual overviews of a topic and another type of planning or idea generation where they can write their title in the middle of their page (or screen) and then write around it, using colours, words and perhaps even images. The sections of information connect to each other using branches and sub-branches. Explain to children that it is a great way to arrange all the information that may be jumbled up inside their heads into a clear, concise form. Show children the 'Mindmaps' ITR.

DISCUSS

· *Has anyone in the class used this technique before?*
· *What do you think of this technique? Is it helpful?*
· *Do you think that mindmapping can make things clearer for you? What about for someone else who might need a summary of the information?*

CREATE

Encourage children to try out this technique during the lesson.

Don't start too far upstream

STUDY

Use the metaphor of a waterfall to discuss good openings with the class. Explain to children that it is better to avoid starting your piece of writing 'too far upstream'. Explain that instead, they should start it at the 'roar of the waterfall', meaning right before the important action. To illustrate this point, show children the example text on the 'Memoir ineffective genre example' ITR. Ask the children whether the example writing piece starts too far upstream. Encourage children to locate the 'roar of the waterfall'. Ask which parts of the writing the children think could be left out.

DISCUSS

- *Has anyone in the class used this technique before?*
- *What do you think of this technique? Is it helpful?*
- *Can you locate the 'roar of the waterfall' in your own writing today?*

CREATE

Encourage children to try using this technique during the lesson.

Great openings

STUDY

Explain to children that there are lots of different ways that they can make the opening to their story seem outstanding. Show children some of the examples of great openings to stories on the 'Great openings' ITR.

DISCUSS

- *Why do you think these are great openings for a story?*
- *Have you seen any other great openings in books you have read? Why were they so special?*
- *Can you think of a great opening for your own story?*

CREATE

Encourage children to think of great openings to their own stories during the lesson. Children might find it helpful to draw inspiration from some of the reading books in the class library.

Strong endings

STUDY

Explain to children that there are lots of different ways that they can end their stories so that they leave their readers with something to think about. Show children a variety of exemplar texts from the genre booklets and ITRs.

DISCUSS

- *What did you like about the endings in these examples?*
- *Are there any other stories that you know of that have strong endings?*
- *Can you think of any strong endings for your own stories?*

CREATE

Encourage children to try out a few different endings on the story edit pages, when they are nearing the end of their story writing process. In pairs, or with a teacher, children discuss the different endings that they have used, and which one they think would work the best.

Using the drafting rules

STUDY

Show children the 'Using the drafting rules' ITR. Emphasise the fact that the most important thing at this stage is for children to write down the things they want to say in their writing. Explain that this should be a quick and easy process. Ask children to take their plan for the class writing project and model drafting from their plan, observing the drafting rules and talking through the process as they go through it.

Remind children to use the left-hand page in their books for drafting, leaving the right-hand page blank for revising.

DISCUSS

- *Has anyone in the class used this technique before?*
- *What do you think of this technique? Is it helpful?*
- *What are the most important things to remember about the drafting rules?*

CREATE

Encourage children to refer to the drafting rules when drafting their writing pieces during the lesson.

Circle unsure spellings

STUDY

Show children the 'Drafting rules' ITR. Remind children that when they are drafting, they should focus on writing down what they want to say quickly; it does not need to be perfect.

Highlight to children the rule about what to do if they are not sure of the spelling of a particular word. Model writing a sentence that includes a tricky spelling and make an attempt at the tricky spelling by talking through the process. Explain to children how you write down the sounds in the syllables that you can hear and then put a circle around the word. Explain that you will look up the spelling in a dictionary later on, when editing your writing.

DISCUSS

- *Has anyone in the class used this technique before?*
- *What do you think of this technique? Is it helpful?*
- *What are some of the tricky spellings you have come across in your writing today?*

CREATE

Encourage children to try using this technique for tricky spellings during the lesson.

Boxes for punctuation

STUDY

Show children 'Drafting rules' ITR. Remind children that when they are drafting their piece of writing, they should focus on writing down what they want to say quickly; it does not need to be perfect.

Highlight to children the point about what they need to do if they are unsure about which punctuation to use. Model writing a sentence with tricky punctuation, talking through how you draw a box where you think a punctuation mark needs to go. Explain to children that you will check the punctuation later, when you are editing your writing.

DISCUSS

- *Has anyone in the class used this technique before?*
- *What do you think of this technique? Is it helpful?*

CREATE

Encourage children to try using this technique for tricky punctuation during the lesson.

'Sticky' bits and 'yawny' bits

STUDY

Show the 'Drafting rules' ITR. Remind children that when they are drafting, they should focus on putting down what they want to say quickly; it does not need to be perfect.

Highlight the point about what to do if they think they may have written a 'sticky' bit (a bit that doesn't make sense) or a 'yawny' bit (adding too much detail so it becomes boring for their reader). Explain that they can underline those bits so that they know to come back to them later when they revise their work. Suggest that their partner may be able to help them spot 'sticky' bits and 'yawny' bits.

DISCUSS

- *Has anyone in the class used this technique before?*
- *What do you think of this technique? Is it helpful?*

CREATE

Encourage children to use this technique in their own writing.

Don't know what to write next?

STUDY

Show children the 'Drafting rules' ITR. Explain to children that when they are drafting their writing, there might come a time when they feel a bit stuck and don't know what to write next.

Refer to the drafting rules listed in the ITR, and encourage children to read their draft to their class to see if their partner has any questions about it. The questions that their partner asks may give them hints and suggestions about what information they might have left out that their reader needs to know. Or it might give them a clue as to where their story might go next.

You could ask a volunteer from the class to read out a piece of their writing where the child feels as though they have become a bit 'stuck'. Model asking one or two questions that you as the reader need to know about the piece of writing to help generate new ideas.

DISCUSS

- *Has anyone in the class used this technique before?*
- *What do you think of this technique? Is it helpful?*
- *Do you have any other ideas about what you could do if you get stuck?*

CREATE

Encourage children to begin using this technique in their own writing from this point onwards.

"I'm finished!"

STUDY

Show children the 'Drafting rules' ITR. Explain to children that when they think they have finished their writing, they can begin or continue with a personal writing project. Before they do this, children should make sure they have really finished! Encourage children to take the following steps, just to make sure that they have finished their writing:

- *Reread your writing, slowly. Imagine you are the reader and are reading it for the first time. Writers will often do this several times so you should do it at least twice.*
- *Ask yourself 'Is there anything else I want to say?'*
- *Read your writing to your partner. Do they have any questions they want to ask?*

DISCUSS

- *Has anyone in the class used this technique before?*
- *What do you think of this technique? Is it helpful?*

CREATE

Encourage children to begin using this technique in their own writing from this point onwards.

How to be a discoverer

STUDY

Explain to children that not all writers plan their writing before they begin. Discoverers like to start drafting straight away, using their first draft almost like a plan; they then do a lot of work on their plan at the revising stage.

Remind children that they will still need to decide on the purpose, audience and genre for their writing before they begin to draft. Use a class writing project as an example, or choose an alternative genre using the 'Writing wheel' ITR. Model how you might make some very brief dabbling notes relating to key words and moments. Then go straight into drafting, talking through your writing choices as you go.

DISCUSS

- *Has anyone in the class used this technique before?*
- *What do you think of this technique? Is it helpful?*
- *What are the advantages and disadvantages of drafting your material without structured planning?*

CREATE

Encourage children to begin using this technique in their own writing during this lesson.

How to be a planner

Explain to children that writing needs to be planned but that there are different kinds of planners. Some writers like to plan in great detail while others prefer to discover as they go along.

There are different ways to plan but one of the most useful and versatile ways to plan is to use a planning grid. Display a completed 'Planning grid' ITR and talk through the different sections. Use the ITR annotation tools to model expanding on your ideas as you go, emphasising the importance of thinking about every part of your writing piece, especially the ending. You could also annotate the planning grid using the ITR annotation tools, to model expanding on your ideas. When you have finished, 'tell' your piece of writing to the class using the completed plan and checking it to see whether it makes sense. Remind children that plans are only a guide and that they can be changed at any time.

DISCUSS

- *Has anyone in the class used this technique before?*
- *What do you think of this technique? Is it helpful?*
- *What are the advantages and disadvantages of planning before you write?*

CREATE

Encourage children to begin using this technique in their own writing from this point onwards.

How to be a paragraph piler

STUDY

Explain to children that you are going to demonstrate one method of drafting writing. Paragraph Pilers like to draft their writing paragraph by paragraph. They write down a paragraph, read it back to themselves and check it for editing, then move on to the next one.

Model writing a paragraph for the children, using the plan from the class writing project. Follow the 'Drafting rules' ITR, underlining any 'sticky' bits or 'yawny' bits, circling any spellings that children might be unsure of, as well as adding boxes for missing punctuation. When you have finished doing this, model reading the piece of writing back to yourself, fixing the bits that you have identified as needed extra work. Move on to the next paragraph and do the same thing. Explain to children that paragraph pilers will draft their whole piece in this way.

DISCUSS

- *Has anyone in the class used this technique before?*
- *What do you think of this technique? Is it helpful?*
- *What are the advantages and disadvantages of drafting in this way?*

CREATE

Encourage children to begin using this technique in their own writing during this lesson.

How to be a sentence stacker

STUDY

Explain to children that you are going to demonstrate one method of drafting writing to them. Explain that sentence stackers like to draft their writing sentence-by-sentence. They write down a sentence, read it back and check it for editing, then move on to the next one.

Model writing a sentence, using the plan from the class writing project. Follow the 'Drafting rules' ITR, underlining the 'sticky' or 'yawny' bits, circling any spellings they are unsure of, as well as adding any boxes for missing punctuation. Then, model reading it back to yourself, fixing the bits that you have identified as needing extra work. Move on to the next sentence and do the same thing. Explain to children that sentence stackers will draft their whole piece in this way.

DISCUSS

- *Has anyone in the class used this technique before?*
- *What do you think of this technique? Is it helpful?*
- *What are the advantages and disadvantages of drafting in this way?*

CREATE

Encourage children to begin using this technique in their own writing during the lesson.

First reread and improve

STUDY

Remind children that revising their writing involves looking at it with fresh eyes and finding the places where it could be improved. Explain that writers will often revise their writing hundreds of times! To make it easier, explain that the children should reread their pieces of writing three times, focusing on a different aspect of the writing each time. This lesson examines what children could focus on during their first reread: what they want their reader to feel as well as fixing any sticky or yawny bits.

Using your own or one of the children's drafts, model revising the piece for composition (but not transcription at this stage), referring to the 'First reread and improve' section of one of the revision checklists. There are six different revision checklists for narrative, non-fiction and poetry in lower and upper KS2. Remind children to use the right-hand page in their books for making their revisions.

DISCUSS

- *Has anyone in the class used this technique before?*
- *What do you think of this technique? Is it helpful?*
- *Can you think of any other ways to make revisions to your writing?*

CREATE

Encourage children to begin using this technique in their own writing from this point onwards.

Second reread and improve

STUDY

Remind children that revising their writing involves looking at it with fresh eyes and finding the places where it could be improved. Some published writers will revise their writing hundreds of times! To make it easier, explain that children should reread their writing three times, focusing on a different aspect each time. For example, children can focus on the opening and ending of their piece during the second reread. Use your own or another child's draft. Model revising the writing piece for composition (not transcription at this stage), looking at the 'Second reread and improve' section of one of the revision checklists. There are six different revision checklists for narrative, non-fiction and poetry in lower and upper KS2. Remind children to use the right-hand page in their books for revision purposes.

DISCUSS

· *Has anyone in the class used this technique before?*
· *What do you think of this technique? Is it helpful?*

CREATE

Encourage children to begin using this technique in their own writing from this point onwards.

Third reread and improve

STUDY

Remind children that revising their writing involves looking at it with fresh eyes and finding the places where it could be improved. Writers will often revise their writing hundreds of times! To make it easier, ask children to reread their work three times, focusing on a different aspect each time. This lesson looks at what children could focus on during their third reread: looking at particular language features.

Use your own writing draft or another child's draft as an example. Model revising the piece for composition (not transcription at this stage), looking at the 'Third reread and improve' section of the one of the revision checklists. There are six different revision checklists for narrative, non-fiction and poetry in lower and upper KS2. Remind children to use the right-hand page in their books for revising.

DISCUSS

· *Has anyone in the class used this technique before?*
· *What do you think of this technique? Is it helpful?*

CREATE

Encourage children to begin using this technique in their own writing during this lesson.

How to edit your writing for capitals

STUDY

Explain to children that editing is different to revising because it focuses on the transcriptional aspects of writing such as correcting spellings and punctuation. It is an important part of the process because after all the hard work that children have put into their writing, they will want to avoid putting off their readers because of a few spelling or punctuation errors.

Show children the 'Upper KS2 editing checklist' ITR. Explain that reading for proofing is different to reading for pleasure. Your only reason for reading at the editing stage is to spot and fix errors. Point out to children the four items on the editing checklist and explain that you will reread your own writing example four times, checking one element at a time. Explain that on this occasion you will be looking for missing capital letters. Using your own or a child's writing example, model reading each individual word slowly and carefully, pointing out where capitals are needed and marking corrections onto the piece of writing, using a different coloured pen.

DISCUSS

- *Has anyone in the class used this technique before?*
- *What do you think of this technique? Is it helpful?*

CREATE

Encourage children to begin using this technique in their own writing during the lesson today.

How to edit your writing for use of vocabulary

STUDY

Explain to children that editing is different to revising because it looks at the transcriptional aspects of writing such as correcting spellings and punctuation. It is an important part of the process because after all the hard work that children have put into their writing, they will want to avoid putting off their readers because of a few spelling or punctuation errors.

Show children the 'Upper KS2 editing checklist' ITR. Explain that reading for proofing is different to reading for pleasure. Your only reason for reading at the editing stage is to spot and fix errors. Point out to children the four items on the editing checklist and explain that you will reread your own writing example four times, checking one element at a time. Explain that on this occasion you will be looking for opportunities to change the most boring or repetitive words in the piece of writing.

Using your own or a child's writing example, model reading each individual word slowly and carefully, looking specifically at verbs and adjectives, underlining repeated words and boring words, and taking suggestions from the class about how the verbs and adjectives could be improved. Mark corrections with a different coloured pen.

DISCUSS

- *Has anyone in the class used this technique before?*
- *What do you think of this technique? Is it helpful?*

CREATE

Encourage children to begin using this technique in their own writing during the lesson today.

How to edit your writing for punctuation

STUDY

Explain to children that editing is different to revising because it focuses on the transcriptional aspects of writing such as correcting spellings and punctuation. It is an important part of the process because after all the hard work that children have put into their writing, they will want to avoid putting off their readers because of a few spelling or punctuation errors.

Show children the 'Upper KS2 editing checklist' ITR. Explain that reading for proofing is different to reading for pleasure. Your only reason for reading at the editing stage is to spot and fix errors. Point out to children the four items on the editing checklist and explain that you will reread your own writing example four times, checking one element at a time. Explain that on this occasion you will be looking for incorrect punctuation.

Using your own or a child's writing example, model reading each individual word slowly and carefully, pointing out where punctuation is needed and marking corrections with a different coloured pen. Remind children to refer to the Tips and Tricks cards for help with punctuation.

DISCUSS

- *Has anyone in the class used this technique before?*
- *What do you think of this technique? Is it helpful?*

CREATE

Encourage children to begin using this technique in their own writing during the lesson today.

How to check and correct your unsure spellings

STUDY

Explain to children that editing is different to revising because it focuses on the transcriptional aspects of writing such as correcting spellings and punctuation. It is an important part of the process because after all the hard work that children have put into their writing, they will want to avoid putting off their readers because of a few spelling or punctuation errors.

Show children the 'Upper KS2 editing checklist' ITR. Explain that reading for proofing is different to reading for pleasure. Your only reason for reading at the editing stage is to spot and fix errors. Point out to children the four items on the editing checklist and explain that you will reread your own writing example four times, checking one element at a time. Explain that on this occasion you will be looking for incorrect spellings.

Using your own or a child's writing example, model reading each individual word slowly and carefully, circling any spellings you are unsure of. Check spellings in a dictionary or look at the 1000 common spelling words on pages 295–297, then mark any corrections that you make in a different coloured pen.

DISCUSS

- *Has anyone in the class used this technique before?*
- *What do you think of this technique? Is it helpful?*

CREATE

Encourage children to begin using this technique in their own writing during the lesson today.

Ways of publishing

STUDY

Explain to children that the final part of the writing process is to publish their finished piece and, if they wish, place it into the class library.

Explain to children that there are lots of other ways that they can publish their writing, both within school and out in the wider community. Show children the 'Ways of publishing' ITR and talk through some of the ideas. Encourage children to choose the ideas that appeal most to them and think about how these different ways of publishing affect how they prepare their finished writing piece for publication?

DISCUSS

- *Has anyone in the class used this technique before?*
- *What do you think of this technique? Is it helpful?*

CREATE

As part of the class writing session, allow time for children to choose a different way of publishing and prepare their final piece.

Mini-lessons: Functional grammar

Sentences with different forms

Explain to children that statements are used in writing to give information to their reader which may or may not be true, such as: *A famous footballer lives in my street.* A command is used to tell, urge, persuade or instruct someone to do or not do something. Commands can be used in different kinds of text and for different purposes, for example:

- *Stop!*
- *Eat that apple – it will do you good.*
- *Do not write on this page.*
- *Let's all go to the park.*
- *Turn left by the postbox.*

Explain to children that they can often use questions as a way of persuading their readers to respond to their writing. For example, they can ask rhetorical questions, meaning questions that don't necessarily require an answer, but instead engage readers a little more and make them think about or consider their position on an issue. For example:

- *Have you ever wondered what it would be like to swim with mermaids?*
- *Is that a good reason for hitting your brother?*

Explain that a question can also be used to make an 'offer' to someone. For example:

- *Do you want to learn how to make money quickly?*

Explain to children that questions are often asked by charactes in stories if they are seeking the truth, need more information, want to offer a choice to another character or even convey a threat. For example:

- *Who are you looking at?*

Explain that question marks signal that a question is being asked and are placed at the end of a sentence. Questions also sometimes appear in factual writing as a way of involving their reader in the subject area. For example:

- *Have you ever wanted to build your own car? Follow this guide and you'll be hitting the road in no time.*

Explain that exclamation marks are placed at the end of a sentence. Their function is to allow the writer to give a sign of strong positive or negative feeling, such as surprise, delight, shock, horror, amusement and excitement. They are often used in advertisements in order to attract your reader's attention.

DISCUSS

- *Which different types of sentence forms can be found in the books that you are reading?*
- *Do you use these types of sentence forms in your own writing?*

CREATE

Encourage children to use these different types of sentences during their lesson today.

Apostrophes to show possession

STUDY

Discuss with children how writers are able to use apostrophes to show that something belongs to someone. Show the class your own example of a sentence containing the possessive apostrophe + s, and talk about why you have used it.

Ask children:

- *Why have I put an apostrophe there?*
- *Apostrophes like these are not only used to talk about objects, people or places. Have you ever noticed them being used to talk about other things that might belong to someone?*

Explain to children how it is not only objects or physical possessions that people have ownership of. They can own a feeling or a quality in their character.

DISCUSS

- *Has anyone in the class used apostrophes to show possession in their own writing before?*
- *Can you find any examples in your favourite reading books?*

CREATE

Invite children to start using apostrophes to show possession during the lesson today.

Paragraphs

STUDY AND DISCUSS

Explain to children that writers often begin a new paragraph to show that they are introducing a new idea, or a change in time or a change of scene. Show children the 'Paragraphs' ITR. Then show children an example of your own work, where you have started a new paragraph. Explain why you started the new paragraph where you did. Ask children:

- *Why is it helpful to chunk your text into paragraphs for your reading?*
- *When do you use paragraphs in your writing? Why?*

Explain to children that they can start a new paragraph to show when there is a change in time or place, something new is happening or you are talking about a new topic or idea.

CREATE

Next time children are writing a story, ask them to read the story out loud to themselves. Ask:

- *Does your story flow?*
- *Are you giving your reader your writing in little chunks?*

Encourage children to look in some of their favourite reading books to see how other writers have used paragraphs.

Fronted adverbials: moving between place and time

STUDY

Remind children that if they want their reader to pay special attention to an adverb or adverbial phrase, they can place it at the beginning of a sentence. This sets their reader up for the rest of the sentence. Explain to children that fronted adverbials relating to time or place are really useful if they want to change the location or place in the text. Explain that fronted adverbials can also be helpful if children want to move the text on, by fast forwarding the moment in time. Show children the examples in the 'Fronted adverbials: moving between place and time' ITR.

Using the books that children are currently reading (including your book as a reader-teacher) invite children to collect examples of where writers have used fronted adverbials.

DISCUSS

- *Has anyone in the class used fronted adverbials in their own writing?*
- *Was it helpful in moving between places or time in the text?*

CREATE

Encourage children to begin using fronted adverbials during the lesson today.

Using nouns and pronouns for cohesion

STUDY AND DISCUSS

Introduce the topic by reminding children that pronouns are words that are used in place of nouns. Using the same nouns over and over again would be very boring for the reader. Show children the 'Using nouns and pronouns for cohesion' ITR. Click to reveal the example. Then click again to change the highlighted words to pronouns. Include your own example of a passage containing a repeated noun and then show it again with pronouns.

Ask children:

- *How are the two passages different?*
- *As the reader, which one do you prefer?*
- *Look in your reading books. Where is the writer using pronouns?*

Note: be careful when using pronouns. At times, you may want to mention the noun again so your reader doesn't get confused.

CREATE

Encourage children to try using pronouns in their writing, during the lesson.

Noun phrases with adjectives and prepositional phrases

STUDY AND DISCUSS

Introduce the topic to children by reminding them that writers use noun phrases to give their readers more information about the noun, for example: 'a very large cheesy pizza'.

Explain that, when they use adjectives, writers can give a fuller description of the noun. Adding a prepositional phrase also allows them to give more detail about the place, direction or time of an event or whatever it is that they want to talk about. Writers often use both adjectives and prepositional phrases in the same sentence, to provide their readers with detailed amounts of information. Show children the 'Noun phrases with adjectives and prepositional phrases' ITR.

Point out to children that prepositional phrases use a preposition as the first word.

Ask children:

- *Can you see what the writer has done?*
- *As the reader, what do you think about this technique?*
- *Have you used this technique in your own writing?*

CREATE

Invite children to include a noun phrase with adjectives and / or prepositional phrases when drafting or revising their writing during the lesson. When they have written an adjective or prepositional phrase, ask them whether they think it gives the reader a clearer description of what they are writing about.

Speech punctuation

STUDY AND DISCUSS

Introduce children to the concept of inverted commas (speech marks) by explaining that writers use them to help their reader see what is being said by a person or character. Writers place inverted commas at the beginning and end of the words, phrases and sentences spoken by each person or character. Show children the first example in the 'Speech punctuation' ITR.

Explain to children that if they want to include a conversation between people in their writing, such as in a story or memoir, it is always a good idea to write what each person says on a new line so your reader can really keep track of who is speaking at any one time. Show children the second example in the 'Speech punctuation' ITR.

Ask children:

- *Can you tell how many people are speaking?*
- *As the reader, what do you think? Is it clear?*
- *Has anyone in the class used this technique before?*

Explain to children that it is sometimes good to write what people actually say in non-fiction writing, as though your reader is hearing a real voice. Show children the third example in the 'Speech punctuation' ITR as an example of what they could write.

Ask children:

- *Can you think of other non-fiction writing where you might do this?*

CREATE

Explain to children that looking in the books they are reading and finding how writers have used inverted commas is one of the best ways of learning how to use them.

Invite children to use inverted commas round speech in their writing in their lesson today, regardless of whether they are drafting or revising a piece of writing. Once children have written or revised a piece of writing, ask them to be the reader. As the reader, ask children whether it was clear who was talking in their writing?

Determiners

STUDY AND DISCUSS

Introduce the topic by explaining to children that writers use determiners to give their readers important information about a person, place or thing. Explain that these are things that readers need to know! Show children your own example of a sentence or paragraph that uses a determiner and explain why you used it.

Ask children:

* *What does my determiner tell you about its noun?*

Explain to children that one of the most common determiners is the word 'the' but there are many other types of determiners that they can use. Explain that the most important thing these determiners do is to make sure that readers know as much as possible about the thing the writer is telling them about: for example, who it belongs to, where it is or how many there are.

CREATE

Ask children to look at what they are writing today to see where they are using determiners. Do they think they have made it clear for their reader?

Standard English

STUDY AND DISCUSS

Standard English is a type of English that most of us understand, even if we don't always speak it. Explain that Standard English started out long ago as the type of English that people spoke in and around the London area. The kings and their courts were in London so that type of English began to be seen as very important.

Remind children that there are also lots of other types of English: these are called Non-Standard. Explain that they are spoken in different parts of the United Kingdom, as well as in other parts of the world, such as America, Australia, India and the Caribbean. Standard English isn't better than Non-Standard English.

Explain to children that most people understand Standard English, even if they don't always use it when speaking. That is why, when children are writing at school, and out in the real world, they will mostly be writing in Standard English. However, explain that they can write in Non-Standard English if they want to show how a particular person or character might actually speak in real life, and that is fine too. Show children the first example on the 'Standard English' (ITR).

Ask children:

* *Which bits of what Perks said are Non-Standard here?*
* *Have you ever use Non-Standard English like this in your own writing?*

Show children the second example on the 'Standard English' (ITR) to show more examples of Non-Standard English.

Ask children:

* *What can you see that's Non-Standard here?*
* *Do you know where the writer, John Agard, was born? (Guyana)*

CREATE

Encourage children to look for examples in their books where writers have used Non-Standard English. Remind children that they can also use this technique to make it clear to their readers how a character might speak in real life.

Simple and multiclause sentences

STUDY

Explain to children that it is usually a good idea to include a variety of sentences in their writing. Too many simple sentences used one after the other can be annoying for their reader. However, too many multi-clause sentences can be exhausting for their reader. It's about having a variety.

Explain that writers often join together ideas using either co-ordinating or subordinating conjunctions. Show children an example of this on the 'Simple and multiclause sentences' (ITR).

DISCUSS

Ask children:

- *What's the problem with each of the examples on the board?*
- *If you had to choose, which do you prefer?*
- *What changes would you make to these passages? What advice would we give this writer?*

CREATE

Using the books that children are currently reading, encourage children to look for examples of where writers have used simple and multi-clause sentences. Then, encourage children to do the same in their own writing.

Relative clauses and relative pronouns

STUDY AND DISCUSS

Introduce the topic of relative clauses to children by telling them that writers use them to provide the reader with more information about a noun. Explain that we can use a relative pronoun (*who, which, where, when, what, that*) to start the relative clause. We can use either commas (usually) or sometimes brackets or dashes around it to show that the information provided in the clause is additional, meaning just a little extra. Explain that it's like adding something in a whisper. Show children the 'Relative clauses and relative pronouns' ITR.

Ask children:

- *Can you see what the writers have done here?*
- *As the reader, what do you think of this technique?*
- *Have you done anything like this in your own writing?*

Explain to children that by adding in the relative clause *'who had been sitting quietly at their feet'*, the writer has provided the reader with a little bit of extra information. Without it, the sentence would still have made sense, and the reader knows the important information is that Sammy jumped up and started barking.

Point out to children that if the writer thinks *all* the information in a sentence is important, then they can go ahead and write the sentence without including commas, dashes or brackets.

CREATE

Explain to children that relative clauses are there to tell your reader a little bit more about a noun and, because nouns are everywhere, you can add these little bits of information into most types of writing! You could include them in fiction texts, biographies, memoirs, book reviews, match reports, news features and discussion texts. Invite children to try and include relative clauses and relative pronouns when drafting or revising their writing today. Ask children, as readers of the piece of writing, whether the relative clause adds a little extra information to the noun.

Parenthesis

STUDY AND DISCUSS

Explain to children that using parenthesis is a great way to add a little extra information about something in your writing. Explain to children that they can put this information between dashes, commas or brackets. Explain that a parenthesis is a kind of whisper or a an afterthought; it adds extra detail that may be interesting but isn't vital to your piece of writing. Ask children to look at the examples on the 'Parenthesis' ITR.

Ask children:

- *Can you see what each writer is doing in this example?*
- *Have you ever used this technique in your writing?*

Explain to children that writers use parenthesis a lot in their writing, for example, J.R.R. Tolkien in *The Hobbit*.

CREATE

Remind children to look for and notice examples of parenthesis in the books that they are reading at the moment, as well as trying to understand why the writer is using it. Invite children to use a parenthesis in their own writing today, marking it with brackets, dashes or commas.

Using modals

STUDY AND DISCUSS

Explain to children that they can't always be certain about the things in their lives and that is where modals come in to their writing.

Explain that people use modals when they are speaking and it isn't any different when they are writing. They will just make the meaning in their writing even clearer. Show children the main modals in the 'Using modals' ITR.

Explain to children that modals can tell the reader how likely it is that something will happen.

Ask children to take a look at the examples on the ITR screen.

Ask children:

- *What have the writers done to make the meaning in their writing clear?*
- *From these examples, can you tell in what kinds of writing these modals have been used?*

Explain to children that using modals can also enable them to tell the reader that it is a good idea to do something or that something is absolutely necessary. Show children the examples on the ITR screen.

Ask children:

- *Can you tell in what kinds of writing these modals have been used?*
- *Have you ever used modals in your writing?*

CREATE

Explain to children that they are probably using modals in their own writing without even realising it. Encourage children to try using modals in their own writing during the lesson.

Cohesion

STUDY AND DISCUSS

Explain to children that cohesion is when a writer refers to things they have already mentioned, but without repeating the same words over and over again, which would be very annoying for the reader – and for the writer too! Explain to children that pronouns and adverbials of time do this job very well. Explain that the thing that they have mentioned could be in a previous part of the paragraph, in a previous sentence, or even in the same sentence. Show children the 'Cohesion' ITR.

Ask children:

- *Can you see what the writers have done here?*
- *Why do you think that the writers have taken this approach?*
- *As the reader of this writing piece, does this technique make the writing easy for you to follow?*
- *Have you used this technique in your own writing?*

Show children some examples of annotations in writing in the ITR. Finally, tell the children that they can make a link in this way to something that they mentioned in a previous paragraph – as long as it is not too far back in the text!

CREATE

Ask children to look out for how the writer of the book they are currently reading (fiction or non-fiction) is using cohesion devices to link ideas in paragraphs. Explain that it is one of the best ways of learning how to do it themselves. Invite children to try out these ways of building cohesion within a paragraph in their writing during the lesson today, whether it is a piece of writing they are revising or even a new piece of writing. Once children have written or revised a piece of writing, ask them to put themselves in the place of the reader and ask themselves whether the writing was clear and easy to follow.

Replace *and* with ; for rhythm

STUDY AND DISCUSS

Introduce to children the idea that writers sometimes use semi-colons to join two ideas together in one sentence instead of writing two separate sentences, as long as the ideas are clearly connected. Show children the 'Replace *and* with ; for rhythm' ITR.

Ask children:

- *Can you see what the writers have done in these examples?*
- *Why have they used semi-colons in this way?*
- *As the reader, what do you think of this technique?*
- *Have you ever used semi-colons in your own writing?*

CREATE

Encourage children to try to find an example of a semi-colon used in one of the books that they are reading at the moment. Invite children to use a semi-colon in their own writing today, when drafting or revising a piece of writing. Explain to children that one point to remember is that a colon can also be used like this. Both types of punctuation are correct; it is up to the writer which one they would like to use in their writing.

Name: _____

Writing wheel

WRITING
POWER
ENGLISH

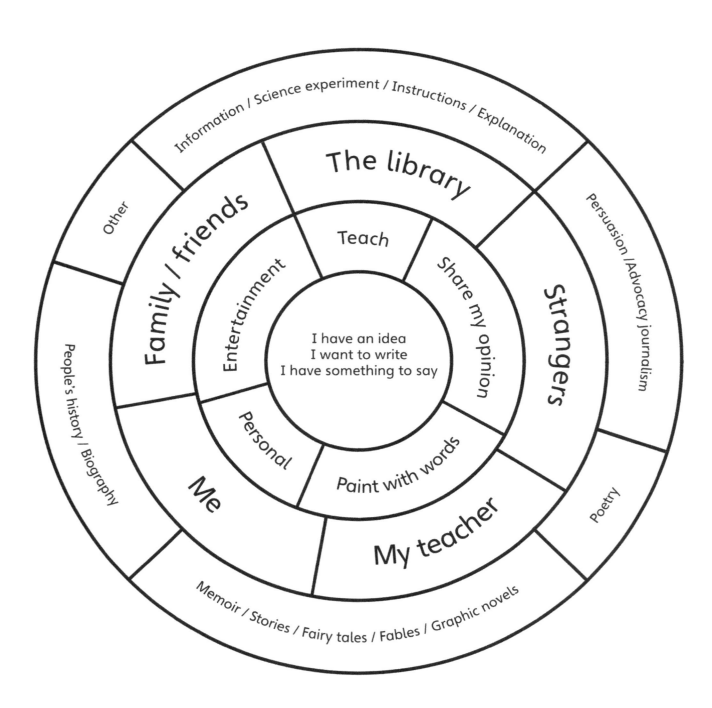

Information / Science experiment / Instructions / Explanation

The library

Other

Family / friends

Teach

Share my opinion

Persuasion /Advocacy journalism

Entertainment

I have an idea
I want to write
I have something to say

Strangers

People's history / Biography

Personal

Paint with words

Me

My teacher

Poetry

Memoir / Stories / Fairy tales / Fables / Graphic novels

© Ross Young and Felicity Ferguson 2019. Copying permitted for purchasing institution only. This material is not copyright free.

Name: _____

Editing checklist

C	**Capitals** Remember to use capitals: • to start all sentences • for all proper nouns (names of people, places, brand names, days, months) • to start speech • for titles.	
U	**Use of vocabulary** • Change your most boring or repetitive words. • Choose **verbs** and **nouns** carefully.	
P	**Punctuation** Remember to use commas for: • lists Eggs, bread, milk, flour and sugar *Then she opened the lid again, lifted the pig out, and held it against her cheek.* (Charlotte's Web, p4, E.B. White) • for **fronted adverbials** *Carefully, the class edited their work for commas.* • for **subordinate clauses** *If you start a sentence with a subordinate clause, it will need a comma.* • for **relative clauses** *Mr Young, who doesn't like commas, edited his work.* Remember to punctuate speech accurately. • Use **speech marks** for direct speech. • Use a **new line** for as new speaker. • End your speech with a **full stop**. *"Hey, watch it!" said an orange lump on a chair.* *"You watch it," muttered Stanley, too tired to care.* *"What'd you say?" the Lump demanded.* *"Nothin'," said Stanley.* (Holes, p44, Louis Sachar)	
S	**Spellings** • Read your writing and circle any unsure spellings. • Look up your unsure spellings using a common word list, spell checker, the internet or a dictionary.	

© Ross Young and Felicity Ferguson 2019. Copying permitted for purchasing institution only. This material is not copyright free.

Name: _____

Presentation tips

When you're publishing your work, don't forget to notice all your edits!
- Write the correct spellings you looked up.
- It's good to write your name and the date at the top.
- Don't forget your title!
- Make sure your handwriting can be read easily by others – particularly strangers.
- Be multi-modal. This means using diagrams, drawings, pictures, different fonts, chapter breaks, paragraph breaks, symbols, headings and colours.

Things to think about when displaying your work on the page:
- How do you want your work to look on the page?
- Should your work be laid out in a particular shape?
- Remember you can leave spaces between lines or groups of lines.
- You could emphasise a word using capital letters.
- You could draw or paint a picture to accompany your work.

Things to think about when reading your work out loud:
- Should it be read quickly or slowly, speeding up or slowing down?
- What style of speaking is best? An angry voice, a soft voice, a whisper?
- Remember, you can pause to be dramatic.
- You can even ask your audience to join in with some parts.

© Ross Young and Felicity Ferguson 2019. Copying permitted for purchasing institution only. This material is not copyright free.

Name: _____

Fill your ideas heart with anyone and anything that is important to you!

© Ross Young and Felicity Ferguson 2019. Copying permitted for purchasing institution only. This material is not copyright free.

Name: _____

Drafting rules

Got a sticky or yawny bit? - Put a line under the bit you are unsure about. - Carry on.	**Don't know how to spell a word?** - Invent the spelling. - Put a circle around it. - Carry on.
Don't know what to write next? - Read it to a partner. - Get your partner to ask you questions.	**Not sure of punctuation?** - Put a box where the punctuation might need to go. - Carry on.

Think you have finished?
Start or continue with a personal writing project!

© Ross Young and Felicity Ferguson 2019. Copying permitted for purchasing institution only. This material is not copyright free.

Narrative revision checklist

Name: _____

1st reread and improve	2nd reread and improve	3rd reread and improve	BONUS reread and improve – tips from published writers!
Think! What do you want your readers to feel?	Make your opening outstanding.	Try out the following things on your revision page. If you like them, add them to your piece:	Show don't tell. Can you replace words like *is, was, have, had, did?*
	Make your ending powerful and thoughtful.	**Fronted adverbials for:** - Time - Place - How	Put an exciting moment in your writing into slow motion.
Fix your 'sticky' bits.	Use: - shock! - question? - action - speech - description	**Subordinating clauses:** - when … - as … - although … - if … - after … - even … - because … - before … - now …	Personify a feeling or an object to give it personality. Write a simile or a metaphor that you could add to your writing.
Fix your 'yawny' bits.		**Relative clauses** For example: *That boy scored the winning goal* can become *That's the boy who scored the winning goal.*	Check: does your writing create a film in your readers' minds? Think about wide angles and zooming in.
		Brackets or dashes instead of commas For example: *My nan likes to go swimming* can become *My nan (who is 82) likes to go swimming.*	Check that you have a good variety of sentences. Have you used commands, statements, questions and exclamations? Are they a mix of short and long sentences? Some writers read their stories over 100 times!

© Ross Young and Felicity Ferguson 2019. Copying permitted for purchasing institution only. This material is not copyright free.

WRITING
POWER
ENGLISH

Name: _____

Non-fiction revision checklist

1st reread and improve	2nd reread and improve	3rd reread and improve	BONUS reread and improve – tips from published writers!
Think! What do you want your readers to feel?	Read your text to someone who knows little or nothing about your topic to see if they understand you.	Try out the following things on your revision page. If you like them, add them to your piece.	Try using a poetic voice.
Fix your 'sticky' bits.	Check if any special / technical vocabulary needs to be explained to your partner.	**Fronted adverbials for:** - Time - Place - How	Try using anecdotes. Ask yourself the following questions: - Can you entertain your reader?
Fix your 'yawny' bits.	Do you need to chunk your information into sections and use sub-headings?	**Subordinating clauses:** - when ... - as ... - although ... - if ... - after ... - even ... - because ... - before ... - now ...	- Can you shock your reader? - Can you upset your reader?
		Relative clauses For example: *That boy scored the winning goal* can become *That's the boy who scored the winning goal.* **Brackets or dashes instead of commas** For example: *My nan likes to go swimming* can become *My nan (who is 82) likes to go swimming.*	Some writers read their pieces over 100 times!

© Ross Young and Felicity Ferguson 2019. Copying permitted for purchasing institution only. This material is not copyright free.

POWER ENGLISH — WRITING

Name: _____

Poetry revision checklist

1st reread and improve	2nd reread and improve	3rd reread and improve	4th reread and improve
What do you want your readers to feel?	Think about **sounds and repetition**.	Think about seeing things differently.	Think about changing words.
Fix your 'sticky' bits.	Try out:	Try out:	Try out:
Fix your 'yawny' bits.	- alliteration	- metaphor	- cutting adjectives by choosing better nouns
	- onomatopoeia	- simile	- cutting adverbs by choosing better verbs
	- rhyme	- hyperbole	- cutting pronouns by replacing with nouns for cohesion
	- repeated lines	- personification	- cracking open the most important line or verb
	- rhythm	- showing not telling	
		- sensory detail	
		• action	
		• feeling	
		• noticing	
		• hearing	
		• tasting	
		• smelling	
		• thinking	
		- persona	
		- symbolism	
		- metonymy	

© Ross Young and Felicity Ferguson 2019. Copying permitted for purchasing institution only. This material is not copyright free.

WRITING
POWER
ENGLISH

Name: _____

Ask yourself ...

Use these prompts to help you come up with new ideas for your ideas heart.

Who are the most important people in my life?

What memories do I have about these people?

What stories have my family told me about their lives?

What am I most afraid of?

What hopes and dreams do I have for the future?

What do I want to change?

What do I like to daydream about or imagine?

What makes me and my friends laugh?

What are the things / people / foods / animals / hobbies that I love?

Where are my favourite places?

What hobbies / people / sports / animals do I know a lot about?

What are my earliest memories?

Can I remember a time I learned to do something, or did something for the first time?

Is there a time when I had a feeling that surprised me?

Is there an event that changed my life?

What have I seen that I cannot forget?

Are there things that particularly frustrate me?

Is there a time when I have felt ashamed?

What is my community like?

How do I feel about my community?

How do I feel about my school?

What keeps me awake at night?

What do I think about when I go for a walk?

© Ross Young and Felicity Ferguson 2019. Copying permitted for purchasing institution only. This material is not copyright free.

Name: _____

Explanation texts planning grid

	The purpose (why, how) of my explanation text is to ...
Use a **question** to hook your reader in.	*Do you ...?* *Have you thought about why ...?* *Need to know more about how ...?*
Step-by-step explanation Explain **how** the action or the process is achieved or **how** an idea develops.	*The first thing to understand ...* *This is done by ...*
Explain **why** it happens.	*This occurs because ...*
What you think Tell your reader why this is an important topic for you to write about.	

© Ross Young and Felicity Ferguson 2019. Copying permitted for purchasing institution only. This material is not copyright free.

POWER ENGLISH WRITING

Name: _____

Memoir planning grid

	The purpose of my memoir is to …
Introduce the **place** and **your event**: • who • what • where • why • when	
Write, in order, the most important moments. Include these fronted adverbials: • *Last week,* • *First,* • *When we finally got there,* • *After that,* • *Finally,*	
Write: 1. All the **thoughts** that went through your mind. 2. The **emotions** you felt.	1. I thought: 2. I felt:
Why was this event **important** to you? What did you **learn** from it?	

© Ross Young and Felicity Ferguson 2019. Copying permitted for purchasing institution only. This material is not copyright free.

WRITING
POWER
ENGLISH

Name: _____

Dabbling your character(s)

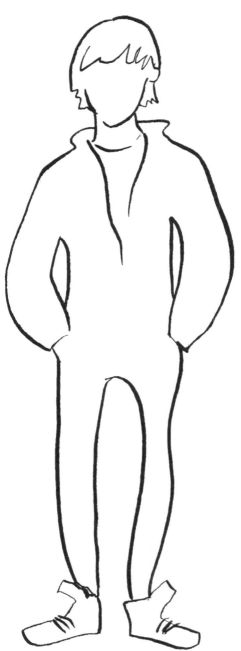

Knowing your character(s) really well is the best way to ensure that you write a really great story.

Published writers spend most of their time thinking about their character(s).

Sometimes it's worth drawing your character(s) to help you understand them in more detail.

It might help to label your character(s) with different notes and phrases.

Ask lots of *what*, *why* and *how* questions about your character(s). Write down your answers as dabbles.

How your character sees the world and how they feel will affect how you describe certain settings, objects or the things that they do. Think about this when dabbling, drawing or writing your actions or setting descriptions.

Use *imagism*. Don't say what your character thinks or feels; instead, *describe* it.

You don't have to use all of your notes in your writing but you should now know your character(s) really well.

Think about some of the things on the Developing characters sheet, and write your answers in and around your drawing.

© Ross Young and Felicity Ferguson 2019. Copying permitted for purchasing institution only. This material is not copyright free.

Name: _____

Developing your character(s)

What does your character look like?

Describe your character's face carefully.

Describe what your character's clothes look like.

Imagine you are looking at your character. Try to describe little details that other people might miss.

Use personification to describe parts of your character's face or body.

What or who could you compare your character to?

What is your character's name?

How old is your character?

Does their name match their personality?

How does your character talk?

Describe your character's typical emotions and behaviour. Use descriptive language rather than naming emotions.

Has something happened to them in the past to make them the way they are now?

What motivates your character to do the things they do?

What do other people think of your character? What do they think of themselves? What do they think of the world?

Does your character know the difference between right and wrong?

What is the most precious object in the world to your character? Why?

Who is the most important person in your character's life? Why?

What does your character believe in? What is important to them?

Are you are using your character to represent something? Are they a metaphor for something? Are you using your character to show human behaviours or emotions?

© Ross Young and Felicity Ferguson 2019. Copying permitted for purchasing institution only. This material is not copyright free.

Name: _____

Dabbling your setting(s)

Knowing your setting(s) really well is a great way to ensure you write a really effective story.

You do not have to use all of your notes in your writing but you will now know your setting(s) really well.

Published writers spend a lot of their time thinking about their setting(s).

Think about some of the things on the following page. Write your answers in and around your drawing.

Ask lots of *what*, *why* and *how* questions about your settings(s). Write down your answers as dabbles.

You might find it helps to label your setting(s) with different notes and phrases.

Sometimes it is worth drawing your settings(s) to help you understand them.

How your character sees the world and how they feel will affect how you describe certain settings. Think about this when dabbling, drawing or writing your setting descriptions.

© Ross Young and Felicity Ferguson 2019. Copying permitted for purchasing institution only. This material is not copyright free.

WRITING

POWER ENGLISH

Name: _____

Developing your setting(s)

Where is your setting? Think carefully about the location.

What does your setting look like?

Does the name of your setting match the way it looks?

What is the weather like?

What time of day is it?

Is your setting from a particular historical period?

What can your character(s) smell when they are in your setting?

What can your character(s) hear when they are in your setting?

Describe your setting as though you are looking through your character's eyes. What can they see? How does it make them feel?

Use powerful nouns and verbs to describe your setting.

Imagine you are looking at your setting. Try to describe little details that other people might miss.

Use personification to describe parts of your setting.

What could you compare your setting to?

Has something happened to your setting in the past to make it look the way it does now?

What do other people think of your setting?

Are you are using your setting to represent something? Is it a metaphor for something? Are you using your setting to show human behaviors or emotions?

If the setting was a person, what would they be like, how would they behave, what would their mood be and how would they feel?

How will you ensure your setting is vivid through your drawings?

© Ross Young and Felicity Ferguson 2019. Copying permitted for purchasing institution only. This material is not copyright free.

WRITING POWER ENGLISH

Name: _____

Graphic novel planning grid

	The purpose of my memoir is to …
Introduce your **setting** and your **character**. Try opening your story with the following and pick your favourite: • **a question** • **a description** • **an action** • **dialogue** • **shock / surprise**	
The **problem**	
How the character **feels** about the problem	
The ending - the **resolution** Write a list of potential endings and then pick your favourite. It could be: An ending that matches your opening sentence in some way. A short, sharp emotional line. A poetic line.	

© Ross Young and Felicity Ferguson 2019. Copying permitted for purchasing institution only. This material is not copyright free.

WRITING POWER ENGLISH

Name: _____

Persuasive writing planning grid

	The purpose of my persuasive article is to …
Headline	
In one or two sentences, introduce the **name**, **place** and **purpose** of the charity.	
Tell your reader **why** the charity has to exist.	
What does the organisation do to **help**?	
Explain who the **staff** are, what they are like and how they are **funded**.	
Give a **personal story** about something the charity has done for you or someone else.	
Use your **quote** from an expert.	
Persuade your reader to start supporting the charity.	
Give **contact details**. How do people get in touch?	
If you haven't already, tell your reader **why** you decided to write about this charity.	

© Ross Young and Felicity Ferguson 2019. Copying permitted for purchasing institution only. This material is not copyright free.

POWER ENGLISH

WRITING

Name: _____

Short stories planning grid

	The purpose of my short story is to ...
Opening Try opening your story with the following and pick your favourite: • a question • a description • an action • dialogue • shock / surprise	
The problem This could be: • between your character and nature • between your character and powerful people (for example, parents, police or teachers) • a problem within the character themselves.	
How the character **feels** about the problem.	
The ending – the resolution Write a list of potential endings and then pick your favourite: • message ending • feeling ending • action ending.	

© Ross Young and Felicity Ferguson 2019. Copying permitted for purchasing institution only. This material is not copyright free.

WRITING
POWER
ENGLISH

Name: _____

Character planning grid

	I want my reader to think all this about my character:
Name: What's their name and how old are they?	
Sight: What do they look like?	
Smell: What might they smell like?	
Touch: What is their mood like and what would they feel like to touch?	
Sound: What do they sound like and what might they say?	
Action: What might they do and how they might do it?	
Motives: Why do they do the things they do?	
Taste: If your character had a taste, what would they taste like?	
Monologue: What do they spend their time thinking about?	
Reputation: What do other people think of them? How do they live their life?	
Comparison: What would you compare them to?	
Disguise: What are you disguising your character as?	

© Ross Young and Felicity Ferguson 2019. Copying permitted for purchasing institution only. This material is not copyright free.

POWER ENGLISH

Name: _____

Biography planning grid

	The purpose of my historical biography is to ...
Title Have an eye-catching title. Include the person's name.	
Introduce **who**, **when**, **where**. Briefly mention what they achieved in their life. When finding out about your subject's greatest achievement, ask your interviewee to think about a diamond moment.	
What did they do in their early life?	
Their main achievement or strongest memory (use dates) What led up to this? Why do they remember it? Include an anecdote or a quote from the person or someone who knew them. You may want to use an artefact here (e.g. a photograph, letter, newspaper article, email, audio, video, postcard or object).	
What did they do after their main achievement or memory (use dates)?	
Why are they important to **you** and should be seen as **important** by others?	

© Ross Young and Felicity Ferguson 2019. Copying permitted for purchasing institution only. This material is not copyright free.

Name: _____

Homework letter

Dear parents, carers and children,

Our new writing topic is going to be on persuasive writing, specifically advocacy journalism. Journalists use this technique when they champion a cause, support it and try to stand up for it. When writing a persuasive article, children will learn how to take notes, do interviews and write an article that people will want to read. You will often see these kinds of reports in newspapers, magazines, leaflets, and on websites.

Over half term, we would like you to talk with your family and choose a local charity, organisation or cause that is worthwhile to you.

Your homework is to get information about your chosen topic. To do this you will have to get answers to the following questions:
• What is the aim of the organisation?
• What kinds of activities does the organisation do?
• Can children and schools help in any way?
• How is the organisation funded?
• Can you tell me about the staff who work for the organisation?
• Could you give me a few facts and figures which would interest my readers?
• Is there a particular little story I could tell about something which has happened as a result of your work?
• What do you like most about your work? Can I quote you directly?

It would be great if you could find out this information by conducting a real interview face-to-face or on the phone. To help you get an interview, explain that you are doing a school project on journalism and that we will send them a copy of your finished piece for them to use. If this seems too difficult, you can find the answers to these questions on the internet instead.

If you are unsure of what an advocacy journalism piece looks like, we have attached to this letter an example. This should give you an idea of what we are looking for.

<u>Don't write the article at home!</u> Just bring your notes into school.

If you have any questions, please do not hesitate to ask.

Thank you for your continued support,

© Ross Young and Felicity Ferguson 2019. Copying permitted for purchasing institution only. This material is not copyright free.

Name: _____

Homework letter

Dear parents / carers,

After half-term, our English topic will be Biography. This is a type of writing that celebrates the stories of people from our families or the local community. During the holidays, we would like the children to choose a significant person in their life to interview. They should then plan their interview notes, ready to write their drafts when they come back to school.

Attached, we have provided:

• an example of a biography text

• a blank planning grid.

There are some tips and suggested interview questions below. The examples are simply a guide for you and your child. We hope you will agree that this topic should be interesting and rewarding for all involved. Once finished, we will make sure that a published copy of your child's biography is sent home for your family to read and enjoy.

Thank you for your continued support,

***

Interview questions

When you interview someone, it is good to ask different types of questions. Some questions will be 'closed', and the answers will give you factual information. For example:

• Where / when were you born?

• How old were you when this event happened?

The most effective questions will be 'open'. These give your interviewee the opportunity to provide you with more detailed information. It may lead to them telling you stories about their life. For example:

• Can you tell me more about that?

• That sounds really interesting – why did that happen?

• How did you feel when …

The most important thing is to really listen to what your interviewee is telling you. You should respond to what they are saying. Do keep in mind what you think is most interesting and what your readers will want to hear. Try to draw out more detail with open questions.

Do not be afraid to ask the interviewee to repeat information. You must try to write what you were told as accurately as possible. If you cannot write quickly, you could draw what you are being told instead.

© Ross Young and Felicity Ferguson 2019. Copying permitted for purchasing institution only. This material is not copyright free.

Name: _____

Information text planning grid

	The purpose of my information text is to …
Classification Introduce your topic.	
Description Describe and give details and facts about your topic. Be multi-modal. Write down some headings.	
Effect Write about why this topic is important to you or the world.	

© Ross Young and Felicity Ferguson 2019. Copying permitted for purchasing institution only. This material is not copyright free.

The 1000 common spelling words (Years 5 and 6)

A
able
about
above
accident
accidentally
accommodate
accompany
according
achieve
across
act
action
actually
add
addition
address
adjective
afraid
Africa
after
again
against
age
aggressive
ago
agreed
ahead
air
all
allow
almost
alone
along
already
also
although
always
am
amateur
America
among
amount
an
ancient
and
angle
animal
another
answer
any
anything
apparent

appear
apple
appreciate
are
area
arms
army
around
arrived
art
as
ask
at
attached
available
average
awkward
away

B
baby
back
bad
ball
bank
bargain
base
bear
beat
beautiful
became
because
become
bed
been
before
began
begin
behind
being
believe
bell
belong
below
beside
best
better
between
bicycle
big
bill
birds
bit

black
block
blood
blow
blue
board
boat
body
bones
book
born
both
bottom
bought
box
boy
branches
break
breath
breathe
bright
bring
British
broken
brother
brought
brown
bruise
build
building
built
burning
business
busy
but
buy
by

C
calendar
called
came
can
cannot
can't
capital
captain
car
care
carefully
carry
case
cat

catch
category
cattle
caught
cause
cells
cemetery
centre
century
certain
chance
change
chart
check
chief
child
children
choose
church
circle
city
class
clean
clear
climbed
close
clothes
cloud
coast
cold
colour
column
come
committee
common
communicate
community
company
compare
competition
complete
compound
conditions
conscience
conscious
consider
consonant
contain
continued
control
controversy
convenience
cook

cool
copy
corn
corner
correct
correspond
cost
cotton
could
couldn't
count
country
course
covered
cows
create
cried
criticise
crops
cross
crowd
curiosity
current
cut

D
dance
dark
day
dead
deal
death
decided
decimal
deep
definite
describe
desert
design
desperate
details
determine
determined
develop
developed
dictionary
did
didn't
died
difference
different
difficult
direct

direction
disappear
disastrous
discovered
distance
divided
division
do
doctor
does
doesn't
dog
done
don't
door
down
draw
drawing
dress
drive
drop
dry
during

E
each
early
ears
earth
east
easy
eat
edge
effect
eggs
eight
eighth
either
electric
elements
else
embarrass
end
energy
engine
England
English
enjoy
enough
entered
entire
environment
equal

equation
equipment
especially
Europe
even
evening
ever
every
everyone
everything
exactly
exaggerate
example
excellent
except
exciting
exercise
existence
expect
experience
experiment
explain
explanation
express
extreme
eyes

F
face
fact
factories
factors
fair
fall
familiar
family
famous
Far
farm
farmers
fast
father
favourite
fear
February
feel
feeling
feet
fell
felt
Few
field
fight

figure
filled
finally
find
fine
fingers
finished
fire
first
fish
fit
five
flat
floor
flow
flowers
fly
follow
food
foot
for
force
foreign
forest
form
forty
forward
found
four
fraction
France
free
French
fresh
frequently
friends
from
front
fruit
full
fun

G
game
garden
gas
gave
general
get
girl
give
glass
go
God
gold
gone
good

got
government
grammar
grass
great
Greek
green
grew
ground
group
grow
guarantee
guard
guess
guide
gun

H
had
hair
half
hand
happened
happy
harass
hard
Has
hat
have
he
head
hear
heard
heart
heat
heavy
height
held
help
her
here
high
hill
him
himself
hindrance
his
history
hit
hold
hole
home
hope
horse
hot
hours
house

how
however
huge
human
hundred
hunting

I
ice
idea
identity
if
I'll
imagine
immediately
important
in
inches
include
increase
Indian
indicate
individual
industry
information
insects
inside
instead
instruments
interest
interesting
interfere
interrupt
into
iron
is
island
isn't
it
it's
itself

J
Japanese
job
joined
jumped
just

K
keep
kept
key
killed
kind
king
knew

know
knowledge
known

L
lady
lake
land
language
large
last
late
laughed
law
lay
lead
learn
least
leave
led
left
legs
leisure
length
less
let
let's
letter
level
library
lie
life
lifted
light
lightning
like
line
list
listen
little
live
located
long
look
lost
lot
loud
love
low

M
machine
made
main
major
make
mall

man
many
map
march
mark
marvellous
match
material
matter
may
maybe
me
means
measure
meat
medicine
meet
melody
members
men
mention
metal
method
middle
might
mile
milk
million
mind
mine
minute
miss
mischievous
modern
molecules
moment
money
months
moon
more
morning
most
mother
mountains
mouth
move
movement
much
muscle
music
must
my

N
name
nation
natural

naughty
near
necessary
need
neighbour
never
new
next
night
no
north
northern
nose
not
note
nothing
notice
noun
now
nuisance
number

O
object
observe
occasionally
occupy
occur
ocean
of
off
office
often
oh
oil
old
on
once
one
only
open
opportunity
opposite
or
order
ordinary
other
our
out
outside
over
own
oxygen

P
page
paint

pair
paper
paragraph
parliament
park
part
particular
party
passed
past
pattern
pay
peculiar
people
per
perhaps
period
person
persuade
phrase
physical
picked
picture
piece
place
plains
plan
plane
planets
plant
play
please
plural
poem
point
pole
poor
popular
position
possible
possession
potatoes
pounds
power
practise
prejudice
prepared
present
president
pressure
pretty
printed
privilege
probably
problem
process
produce

products
profession
programme
promise
pronunciation
property
provide
pulled
purpose
pushed
put

Q
quarter
questions
queue
quickly
quiet
quite

R
race
radio
rain
raised
ran
rather
reached
read
ready
real
reason
received
recent
recognise
recommend
record
red
region
regular
reign
relevant
remain
remember
repeated
report
represent
rest
restaurant
result
return
rhyme
rhythm
rich
ride
right
ring

rise
river
rolled
room
root
rope
rose
round
row
rule
run

S
sacrifice
safe
said
sail
same
sand
sat
save
saw
say
scale
school
science
scientists
score
sea
seat
second
secretary
section
see
seeds
seem
seen
sell
send
sense
sent
sentence
separate
serve
set
settled
seven
several
shall
shape
sharp
she
ship
shoes
shop
short
should

shoulder
shouted
show
shown
side
sight
sign
signature
silent
similar
simple
since
sincerely
sing
single
sir
simple
sister
sit
site
six
size
skin
sky
sleep
slowly
small
smell
smiled
snow
so
soft
soil
soldier
soldiers
solution
solve
some
someone
something
sometimes
son
song
soon
sound
south
southern
space
speak
special
speed
spell
spot
spread
spring
square
stand

stars
start
state
statement
stay
steel
step
stick
still
stomach
stone
stood
stop
store
story
straight
strange
stream
street
strength
stretched
string
strong
students
study
subject
substances
such
suddenly
sufficient
suffix
sugar
suggest
suggested
sum
summer
sun
supply
suppose
sure
surface
surprise
swim
syllables
symbol
symbols
system

T
table
take
talk
tall
teacher
team
tell
temperature

ten
terms
test
than
that
the
their
them
themselves
then
there
therefore
these
they
they're
thick
thin
things
think
third
this
thorough
those
though
thought
thousands
three
through
thus
tied
time
tiny
to
today
together
told
tone
too
took
tools
top
total
touch
toward
town
track
trade
train
travel
tree
triangle
trip
trouble
truck
true
try
tube

turn
twelfth
two
type

U
uncle
under
underline
understand
unit
until
up
upon
us
use
usually

V
valley
value
variety
various
vegetable
vehicle
verb
very
view
village
visit
voice
vowel

W
wait
walk
wall
want
war
warm
wasn't
watch
water
waves
way
we
wear
weather
week
weight
we'll
well
went
were
west
western
what

wheels
when
where
whether
which
while
white
who
whole
whose
why
wide
wife
wild
will
win
wind
window
wings
winter
wire
wish
with
within
without
woman
women
wonder
won't
wood
words

Y
yacht
yard
years
yellow
yes
yet
you
young
your
you're
yourself

Class writing projects: recommended texts

Poetry that hides in things	Memoir	Information	Short Stories	Flash fiction
All My Own Stuff by Adrian Mitchell	The Fib, The Swap, The Trick and other stories by George Layton	The Earth Book by Jonathan Litton	Tales from the Inner City by Shaun Tan	Rules of Summer by Shaun Tan
	Keeping Clear of Paradise Street by Brian Moses	Dragonology: The Complete Book of Dragons by Dugald Steer, Helen Ward and Douglas Carrel	Once Upon a Place by Eoin Colfer	Short! A Book of Very Short Stories by Kevin Crossley-Holland
	Michael Rosen's Sad Book by Michael Rosen	True or False by Andrea Mills	Of Lions and Unicorns: A Lifetime of Tales from the Master Storyteller by Michael Morpurgo	Short Too! by Kevin Crossley-Holland
	Home by Carson Ellis	Until I Met Dudley by Roger McGough	From Hereabout Hill by Michael Morpurgo	A Pocketful of Stories by Stuart Purcell
	Homecoming by Michael Morpurgo	Wallace & Gromit: The Complete Cracking Contraptions Manual by Derek Smith and Graham Bleathman	Shakespeare Stories by Leon Garfield	
	Boy by Roald Dahl	Flanimals by Ricky Gervais	Bambert's Book of Missing Stories by Reinhardt Jung	
	War Boy: A Wartime Childhood by Michael Foreman	The Emperor's Egg by Martin Jenkins	The Chronicles of Harris Burdick by Chris Van Allsburg	
		The Way Things Work by David Macaulay and Neil Ardley	Story Shop: Stories for Literacy by Nikki Gamble	
			What Would Happen? by Crispin Boyer and National Geographic Kids	
			Unreal! by Paul Jennings	
			Uncanny! by Paul Jennings	

Explanation	Graphic novel	Poetry (inspired by ...)	Biography	Advocacy journalism
How to Handle Grownups by Jim Eldridge	The Arrival by Shaun Tan	Love That Dog by Sharon Creech	Goodnight Stories for Rebel Girls by Elena Favilli and Francesca Cavallo	Amnesty International's website (www.amnesty.org.uk)
Why? Encyclopedia: Brilliant Answers to Baffling Questions by DK	Northern Lights by Philip Pullman	Poetry for a Change by Various	Stories for Boys Who Dare to Be Different by Ben Brooks	First News
How Dogs Really Work by Alan Snow	The Golden Compass by Philip Pullman	Rhythm and Poetry by Karl Nova	Women in Science: 50 Fearless Pioneers Who Changed the World by Rachel Ignotofsky	The Week
How Things Work by Tamara J.Resler	The Adventures of John Blake by Philip Pullman	Happy Poems by Roger McGough		Charity magazines
How Things Work Encyclopedia by DK	Bravo Mr William Shakespeare by Marcia Williams	Where the Sidewalk Ends by Shel Silverstein		
The Way Things Work by David Macaulay and Neil Ardley	The Iliad and the Odyssey by Marcia Williams	Poetry Jump-Up! By Grace Nichols		
How to Wash a Woolly Mammoth by Michelle Robinson	Chaucer's Canterbury Tales by Marcia Williams	You'll Love This Stuff by Morag Styles		
	Oliver Twist by Marcia Williams			
	Some Swell Pup or Are You Sure You Want a Dog by Maurice Sendak			

Discussion	Historical account	Advocacy journalism	Social / political poetry	Autobiography
Real-Life Mysteries by Susan Martineau	History's Mysteries by Kitson Jazynka and National Geographic Kids	This Book Is Not Rubbish by Isabel Thomas	If I Were in Charge of the World And Other Worries by Judith Viorst	How to Write Your Life Story by Ralph Fletcher
Thinkers' Games by Jason Buckley	Our Island Story by H.E. Marshall	First News	Dreams of Freedom: In Words and Pictures by Amnesty International	Boy by Roald Dahl
Politics for Beginners by Louie Stowell	What on Earth Happened? by Christopher Lloyd		Reaching for the Stars: Poems about Extraordinary Women and Girls by Liz Brownlee, Jan Dean and Michela Morgan	Going Solo by Roald Dahl
The If Machine: Philosophical Enquiry in the Classroom by Peter Worley	What Happened When in the World by DK			Looking Back: A Book of Memories by Lois Lowry
History's Mysteries by Kitson Jazynka and National Geographic Kids	100 Things to Know About History by Various			War Boy: A Wartime Childhood by Michael Foreman
What is right and wrong? Who decides? Where do values come from? And other big questions by Michael Rosen and Annemarie Young				
First News				

Poetry: anthology of life

What I'll Remember When I Am a Grownup by Gina Willner-Pardo

101 Poems about Childhood by Various

Grow your own Poems by Peter Dixon

Been to Yesterday: Poems of a Life by Lee Hopkins

Baseball, Snakes, and Summer Squash: Poems about Growing Up by Donald Graves

The Best of Children's Poetry (ed) Jennifer Curry

Heard It in the Playground by Allan Ahlberg

Please Mrs Butler by Allan Ahlberg

Overheard in a Tower Block by Joseph Coelho

Quick, Let's Get Out of Here by Michael Rosen

Neighborhood Odes by Gary Soto

A Fire in my Hands by Gary Soto

A Caribbean Dozen: Poems from 13 Caribbean Poets by Grace Nichols

Swings and Shadows: A Childhood in Poetry by Anne Harvey

The Nation's Favourite Poems of Childhood by Esther Rantzen

Books about writing

Before They were Authors: Famous Writers as Kids by Elizabeth Haidle

How to be a Young Writer by Oxford Dictionaries and Christopher Edge

The Best Story by Eileen Spinelli

You Have to Write by Janet S.Wong

Dear World, How Are You? by Toby Little

The Word Collector by Peter H. Reynolds

How a Book is Made by Aliki

How this Book was Made by Mac Barnett

My Worst Book Ever! by Allan Ahlberg

What Do You Do with an Idea by Kobi Yamada

The Pencil by Allan Ahlberg

The Story Machine by Tom McLaughlin

How to Write Your Best Story Ever! by Christopher Edge

How to Write Poems by Joseph Coelho

How to Write a Story by Simon Cheshire

Singing for Mrs Pettigrew: A Storymaker's Journey by Michael Morpurgo

What is Poetry? by Michael Rosen

Thirteen Secrets of Poetry by Adrian Mitchell

Such Stuff: A Story-Maker's Inspiration by Michael Morpurgo

Glossary

Advocacy journalism: *A journalistic article that intends to champion a cause, idea, movement or charity.*

Dabbling: *The process of playing around with drawings, words, phrases, thoughts and ideas on paper, to develop an early writing idea.*

Diamond moment: *The focus for a piece of writing. The vital part that requires the most focus and attention. The heart or spirit of a poem, story or memoir. The area of focus in non-fiction.*

Discoverer: *Someone who doesn't plan and is instead adventurous and dives straight in. They will see where their first draft takes them and will often use it as a plan for their second, more cohesive, draft.*

Distant goals: *Defining what the writing project's ultimate aim is. These goals are heavily related to authenticity, purpose and the audience for the writing. Where will the writing end up?*

Drafting: *Putting down on paper or screen, for the first time, the writer's intentions for their piece.*

Editing: *Attending to the transcriptional aspects of writing, including error hunting. This process includes checking capitalisation, use of vocabulary, punctuation and spelling, in preparation for formal publication of the writing piece.*

Fables: *A short story, usually involving animals or children, that conveys a moral message.*

Field: *The subject matter usually adopted by writers within a chosen genre.*

Flash fiction: *Sometimes called 'micro-fiction' or 'sudden fiction', flash-fiction isn't just a very short story. It is only a flash moment, part of a much larger, untold story. A story where a great deal is left unexplained. It is typically no longer than 1000 words, but can be as short as 100 words (known as a 'drabble'), or even 50 words (known as a 'dribble').*

Functional grammar: *An approach to the teaching of grammar that involves sharing and applying the functional purpose and use of certain grammar or linguistic devices. It usually involves the teaching structure of introducing an item and its functional purpose; sharing real-life authentic examples of the particular grammatical item in use; discussing its effect in a piece of writing; then inviting children to try using it in their own writing.*

Generating ideas: *The process of mining one's own mind for potential ideas / topics for writing and then considering the value of each topic or idea.*

Genre: *Types of writing that have particular intentions and usually follow certain conventions, styles or formats which, in turn, make them identifiable or effective in their purposes.*

Genre booklet: *A resource for teachers and children, that outlines the typical characteristics of purpose and audience: the relationship between the reader and the writer, as well as structures, semantics and linguistic features of certain forms of writing.*

Historical account: *An explanation text that aims to account for, or explain why, something has happened in the past, using evidence to support each explanation.*

Imagism: *The technique of not writing explicitly what you think or feel; only describing it.*

Memoir: *The sharing of personal narrative, anecdotes or vignettes that closely resemble the features of story-telling or story writing.*

Mode: *How a genre will typically look and the visual devices a writer will employ.*

Lexis: *Possible vocabulary that a writer may employ for their writing to be effective.*

Painting with words: *The artistic use of techniques such as noun phrases, showing not telling, personification, pathetic fallacy, comparison, alliteration, simile, metaphor, symbolism and / or imagism in fiction, poetry or non-fiction.*

Paragraph piler: *A writer who plans and then drafts, revises and edits their paragraphs before moving on to write the next one. The writer forms each paragraph perfectly before they move on to the next one.*

Pathetic fallacy: *The personification of the natural world.*

People's history: *A genre that brings to light the memoirs, anecdotes and vignettes of everyday people, based within our families or communities.*

Planners: *Writers who need to have a detailed and well thought-out plan before they begin drafting.*

Planning: *Preparing the structure and content of a piece of writing, in preparation for a draft. Alternatively, preparing or rehearsing what you might want to write about next.*

Planning grid: *A way of approaching the writing planning process, that utilises planning grids to share the typical cohesive structures that genres are built upon.*

Process goals: *Goals set by writers to finish a certain writing process by a certain deadline.*

Product goals: *Goals that, if achieved, will result in a writing product being effective and achieving its intended purpose.*

Process writing: *The theory that writing goes through a recursive process that involves generating ideas, dabbling, planning, drafting, revising, editing, publishing and / or performing. It is recursive because writers will move between these processes all the time and don't typically go through them in a linear way.*

Publishing: *The final process of sending writing out into the world, for others to read. The writing piece has now become a writing product for others to consume and enjoy.*

Pupil conferencing: *When writers (adult or peer) talk to each other about how their writing is going (see page 30 for more details).*

Register: *The formality, choice of vocabulary, linguistic features, communicative purpose, social context and relationship with the reader that a genre typically carries, applies or uses.*

Revision: *Rereading and improving a completed sentence, paragraph or whole draft. The focus is usually on purpose, audience and the effectiveness of the piece. This is not the same as editing.*

Roar of the waterfall: *Finding the roar of the waterfall is identifying where your writing should start. Often, apprentice writers will write a long, meandering opening to their writing that can be cut right back once they have identified where the 'roar of their waterfall' begins.*

Rumbling reading tummy: *The phenomenon of having a 'rumbling reading tummy' happens when a reader feels 'hungry' for more detail or information in certain parts of a writing piece. If readers have not been left feeling satisfied then changes may need to be considered.*

Self-regulation: *Independence from external intervention; the feeling of ownership over your writing craft or product. Self-regulation is closely linked to the concept of writing 'as' and 'for' pleasure.*

Semantics: *The language or linguistic features a writer may employ for their writing to be meaningful.*

Sentence stacker: *A writer who will make a plan and then draft, revise and edit their sentences before they write their next one. The writer forms each sentence perfectly before they move on to the next one.*

Show don't tell: *The writing technique of removing the moments where the writer simply 'tells' their reader what is happening. This is usually done when is, was, are, were, are used. These sentences can be reworked by removing these particular verbs and instead, showing readers what is occurring rather than simply telling them.*

Slam poetry: *The performance, sometimes competitively, of spoken word poetry. The poems are often (but not always) about political or social ideas and topics.*

Sticky bit: *Part of your writing that doesn't run smoothly or sounds strange. This is often due to a change of tense, verb agreement, use of a / an, pronoun and noun use, lack of punctuation, missing words or a lack of explanation.*

Tenor: *The formality and closeness of the relationship between a writer, the text and the reader(s).*

Teacher-writer: *A teacher who writes only when they need to.*

Writing *as* pleasure: *Wanting to practise and develop your writing craft. Feeling sufficiently confident and empowered to engage with the processes of writing, including talking about them as well as being part of a community of writers.*

Writing *for* pleasure: *Sharing a piece of writing to be proud of, as well as the discovery and establishment of your own writing voice.*

Writing product: *The finished piece. The product to be shared with the world as a published piece.*

Writing study: *A mini-lesson focusing on teaching a writing technique or strategy that will help children independently tackle a writing process. Alternatively, these are lessons that teach strategies or techniques to make writing more effective for the intended readers.*

Writer-teacher: *A writer who happens to teach, or a teacher who happens to write. These individuals write for pleasure in their personal lives and will use their writerly knowledge as the basis for planning their writing study lessons. They will share their knowledge, techniques, strategies and ways of navigating the various processes involved in writing, with their class. Where possible, they will write alongside the children in the classroom setting and take part in class writing projects. They will also publish their own writing into the class community and beyond.*

Writing workshop: *An approach to the teaching of writing that involves replicating the conditions of writing. This process takes place outside of school and involves creating a community of authentic writers. It involves enacting the following lesson structure: daily writing instruction (through mini-lessons), writing time and class sharing / author's chair.*

Yawny bit: *Part of the writing piece that labours the point so that it becomes potentially boring for the reader. Unnecessary or pedantic detail that could otherwise be removed.*